AUTO-BIOGRAPHY

This page enables you to compile a list of useful data on your car, so that whether you're ordering spares or just checking the tyre pressures, all the key information - the information that is 'personal' to your car - is easily within reach.

Registration number: ....

Model: ....

Body colour: ....

Paint code number: ....

Date of first registration: ....

Date of manufacture (if different): ....

Chassis or 'VIN' number: ....

Engine number: ....

Gearbox number: ....

Axle casing number: ....

Tyre size

    Front: ....Rear:................................

Tyre pressure (normally laden)

    Front: ....Rear:................................

Tyre pressure (fully laden)

    Front: ....Rear:................................

Ignition key number: ....

Door lock key/keys number: ....

Fuel locking cap key number: ....

Alarm remote code: ....

Alarm remote battery type: ....

Radio security code no.: ....

Insurance

    Name and address of insurer:...

    ....

    Policy number:...

Modifications

    Information that might be useful when you need to purchase parts:..

    ....

    ....

Suppliers

    Address and telephone number of your garage and parts suppliers:..

    ....

First published in 1995 by Porter Publishing Ltd.

Porter Publishing Ltd.
The Storehouse
Little Hereford Street
Bromyard
Hereford HR7 4DE
England

British Library Cataloguing in Publication Data.

A catalogue record for this book is available from the British Library.

ISBN 1-899238-07-7

Series Editor: Lindsay Porter
Design: Martin Driscoll, Lindsay Porter and Lyndsay Berryman
Layout and Typesetting: Pineapple Publishing, Worcester
Printed in England by The Trinity Press, Worcester.

Titles in this Series:

Absolute Beginners' Service Guide
Caravan Owner's Manual & Service Guide
Classic 'Bike Service Guide
Diesel Car Engines Service Guide
Ford Fiesta (All models to 1995) Service Guide
Ford Escort (Front Wheel Drive) & Orion Service Guide
Ford Sierra (All models) Service Guide
Land Rover Series I, II, IIA & III Service Guide
Land Rover Defender, 90 & 110 Service Guide

Metro (1980-1990) Service Guide
Mini (all models 1959-1994) Service Guide
MGB (including MGC, MGB GT V8 and MG RV8) Service Guide
Vauxhall Astra & Belmont (All models-1995) Service Guide
Vauxhall Cavalier Service Guide
VW Beetle Service Guide

- With more titles in production -

MG Midget & Austin-Healey Sprite

Step-by-Step Service Guide

by Lindsay Porter and Peter Wallage

FOREWORD

The MG Midget and Austin Healey Sprite are loved by their owners because they have a unique personality, they are inexpensive to own and maintain and yet they provide much more motoring enjoyment than everday, robot built hatchbacks and saloons. If that wasn't enough, our Midgets and Sprites are easy to service and repair and we don't need expensive diagnostic equipment and high hourly garage charges.

Indeed with some basic tools, a fair degree of common sense and this excellent book, any servicing requirements can be carried out safely and efficiently at home.

Lindsay Porter is already well known and highly respected for his books on purchase and restoration of MGs and their servicing and repair. When the MG Owners' Club attends shows and we are asked by prospective buyers what to look out for when choosing an MG we introduce them to these step by step guides. In every instance, the information gained from Lindsay helps the person looking for a particular MG to examine a potential purchase with far more knowledge than before of the potential horrors lurking under what might seem to be a perfect exterior.

But you and I already own our MG Midget or Austin Healey Sprite, we are keen to do our own servicing but we lack the knowledge of the "tricks of the trade". Now our problem is solved. Thanks to Lindsay Porter and

his co-author of this volume, his friend and colleague Peter Wallage, we can learn how to do our own servicing, step by step, with good sense.

Owning and maintaining any MG is about teamwork and friendship. True we could manage alone but isn't it easier to enlist the help of others? After all how much time can we save if we don't make all the mistakes ourselves but learn from others and share in their knowledge too?

Teamwork involves everyone from the supplier of the parts to service our cars through to the club's free technical help line which can assist when we are stuck. But we now welcome two more very useful members of the team, Lindsay Porter and Peter Wallage. Their knowledge, experience and easy to understand step by step service guide is bound to improve our knowledge, help us to own and service our cars for longer and at reasonable cost.

We congratulate Lindsay and Peter for their dedication and we thank Porter Publishing and their sponsors Castrol for producing, once again, just what we need.

Roche Bentley
Club Secretary
MG Owners' Club
Swavesey, Cambridgeshire

CONTENTS

	Auto-Biography	*1*
	Foreword	*4*
	Introduction and Acknowledgements	*6*
	Using This Book	*7*
CHAPTER 1:	*Safety First!*	*8*
CHAPTER 2:	*Buying Spares*	*12*
CHAPTER 3:	*Service Intervals, Step-by-Step*	
	Using the Service Schedules	*15*
	500 Miles, Weekly or Before a Long Journey	*18*
	1,500 Miles - or Every Month	*29*
	3,000 Miles - or Every Three Months	*31*
	6,000 Miles - or Every Six Months	*51*
	Spark Plug Conditions	*65*
	12,000 Miles - or Every Twelve Months	*66*
	24,000 Miles - or Every Twenty Four Months	*73*
	36,000 Miles - or Every Thirty Six Months	*76*
CHAPTER 4:	*Repairing Bodywork Blemishes*	*77*
CHAPTER 5:	*Rustproofing*	*81*
CHAPTER 6:	*Fault Finding*	*85*
CHAPTER 7:	*Getting Through the MOT*	*89*
CHAPTER 8:	*Facts & Figures*	*99*
CHAPTER 9:	*Tools & Equipment*	*103*
APPENDIX 1:	*Lubrication Chart*	*108*
APPENDIX 2:	*American & British Terms*	*109*
APPENDIX 3:	*Specialists & Suppliers*	*110*
APPENDIX 4:	*Service History*	*111*

Introduction

Though most of my MG motoring has been in MGBs and a pre-war TA - called a Midget in those days but considerably bigger than the cars in this book - I have always had a soft spot for the post-war Sprite and Midget. I remember, with considerable nostalgia, trips in my cousin's Frogeye Sprite. It was nippy, very manoeuvrable, sat low down near the road and, with a crackle from the exhaust and the wind in our hair, this was the very essence of cheap sports-car motoring.

It reintroduced the original concept of MGs, cars built mainly from existing production parts to provide exciting, fast and safe motoring for the impecunious young enthusiast. You could pretend you were Stirling Moss, even at 60 mph.

I say reintroduced because, at that time, the MG alternatives were the saloon Y Series and the later T-series, admirable cars but tending towards the sybaritic comforts of the more moneyed buyer and, of course, to the demands of export markets.

The Sprite and Midget brought fun back into motoring, and they are fun to maintain. Long may they continue. And continue they will so long as there is a dedicated band of enthusiasts for them. It is for those enthusiasts that this book is written because no car can survive for very long without planned, preventative maintenance. Follow the steps given here and your Midget will survive most of today's electronically controlled offerings which demand a sophisticated computer to find out what's gone wrong.

Porter Publishing's Service Guides are the first books to give you all the servicing information you need, with step-by-step instructions, along with a complete Service History section for you to fill in as you carry out regular maintenance on your car month by month. Use the information in this book and you will be able to:

◆ See for yourself how to carry out the jobs at every Service Interval from weekly and monthly checks right up to long-term maintenance items.
◆ Carry out regular body maintenance and rustproofing, saving yourself a fortune on body repairs over the years to come.
◆ Enhance the value of your car by completing a full Service History of every maintenance job you carry out.

We wish you a bright future of reliable, safe motoring in the knowledge that every job is a job that YOU know had been done - with a considerable cash saving as a bonus.

Happy Midget Motoring!

Peter Wallage

Acknowledgements

No book like this could possibly be a solo effort and my thanks are due to numerous people who have helped to make its final production possible. First to Lindsay Porter for the work in this book that is 'his', for asking me to produce this manuscript and for the long hours he spent in laying down the basic format for the series which arranges the myriad of jobs necessary in a logical, straightforward, sequence. It is all designed to take the mystique out of maintenance and make it easy to follow even for the as-yet inexperienced enthusiast who is tackling the daunting task of maintenance for the first time as well as providing the more experienced mechanic with the most complete service information available anywhere.

However much you think you know about car maintenance it isn't until you talk with a marque specialist that you appreciate all the finer details of a particular model. My thanks are due to Andrew Marsh, who runs MG specialists Maidstone Sports Cars for sparing two long days out of his busy working week to demonstrate all the finer points of Midget maintenance, as well as the big ones. Together, they make the distinction between a car that runs and one that is a pleasure to own and drive.

My thanks, too, to Stuart Payne at LMG Kent in Bexleyheath, another MG specialist and enthusiast, for going over a Midget to point out all the areas that are vulnerable to rust and how to apply rustproofing to arrest it and kill its insidious work.

More assistance came from Dunlop SP Tyres, from Sykes-Pickavant who kindly supplied almost all the high-quality tools used here, from Halfords in the loan of other equipment and to David's Isopon who supplied expertise on body repair and finishing which is second to none. And, of course, my thanks to Richard Price at Castrol whose advice and extensive knowledge of lubrication we value and whose products we can unhesitatingly recommend.

Lastly, my thanks to my wife Valerie for taking most of the photographs in this book and for the hours she spent at the computer putting order and coherence into my masses of notes, and to anyone else who I might inadvertently have left out.

Peter Wallage

OIL AND WATER DON'T MIX

It is important to remember that even a small quantity of oil is harmful to water and wildlife. And tipping oil down the drain is as good as tipping it into a river. Many drains are connected directly to a river or stream and pollution will occur.

Each year the National Rivers Authority deals with over 6,000 oil related water pollution incidents. Many of these are caused by the careless disposal of used oil.

The used oil from the sump of just one car an cover an area of water the size of two football pitches, cutting off the oxygen supply and harming swans, ducks, fish and other river life.

OIL POLLUTES WATER
USE YOUR BRAIN-
NOT THE DRAIN!

Follow the Oil Care Code

◆ *When you drain your engine oil - don't oil the drain!* Pouring oil down the drain will cause pollution. It is also an offence.

◆ Don't mix used oil with other materials, such as paint or solvents, because this makes recycling very difficult.

◆ Take used oil to an oil recycling bank. Telephone FREE on 0800 663366 to find the location of your nearest oil bank, or contact your local authority recycling officer.

OIL CARE
FOLLOW THE CODE

This book is produced in association with Castrol (U.K.) Ltd.

"Cars have become more and more sophisticated. But changing the oil and brake fluid, and similar jobs are as simple as they ever were. Castrol are pleased to be associated with this book because it gives us the opportunity to make life simpler for those who wish to service their own cars. Castrol have succeeded in making oil friendlier and kinder to the environment by removing harmful chlorine from our range of engine lubricants which in turn prolong the life of the catalytic converter (when fitted), by noticeably maintaining the engine at peak efficiency. In return, we ask you to be kinder to the environment too... by taking your used oil to your Local Authority Amenity Oil Bank. It can then be used as a heating fuel. Please do not poison it with thinners, paint, creosote or brake fluid because these render it useless and costly to dispose of."

Castrol (U.K.) Ltd.

CHAPTER 1 - SAFETY FIRST!

It is vitally important that you always take time to ensure that safety is the first consideration in any job you do. A slight lack of concentration, or a rush to finish the job quickly can often result in an accident, as can failure to follow a few simple precautions. Whereas skilled motor mechanics are trained in safe working practices you, the home mechanic, must find them out for yourself and act upon them.

Remember, accidents don't just happen, they are caused, and some of those causes are contained in the following list. Above all, ensure that whenever you work on your car you adopt a safety-minded approach at all times, and remain aware of the dangers that might be encountered.

Be sure to consult the suppliers of any materials and equipment you may use, and to obtain and read carefully any operating and health and safety instructions that may be available on packaging or from manufacturers and suppliers.

Important Points

ALWAYS ensure that the vehicle is properly supported when raised off the ground. Don't work on, around, or underneath a raised vehicle unless axle stands are positioned under secure, load bearing underbody areas, or the vehicle is driven onto ramps.

DON'T suddenly remove the radiator or expansion tank filler cap when the cooling system is hot, or you may get scalded by escaping coolant or steam. Let the system cool down first and even then, if the engine is not completely cold, cover the cap with a cloth and gradually release the pressure.

NEVER start the engine unless the gearbox is in neutral (or 'Park' in the case of automatic transmission) and the hand brake is fully applied.

NEVER drain oil, coolant or automatic transmission fluid when the engine is hot. Allow time for it to cool sufficiently to avoid scalding you.

NEVER attempt to loosen or tighten nuts that require a lot of force to turn (e.g. a tight oil drain plug) with the vehicle raised, unless it is properly supported and in a safe condition. Wherever possible, initially slacken tight fastenings before raising the car off the ground.

TAKE CARE when parking vehicles fitted with catalytic converters. The 'cat' reaches extremely high temperatures and any combustible materials under the car, such as long dry grass, could ignite.

NEVER run catalytic converter equipped vehicles without the exhaust system heat shields in place.

TAKE CARE to avoid touching any engine or exhaust system component unless it is cool enough so as not to burn you.

ALWAYS keep antifreeze, brake and clutch fluid away from

vehicle paintwork. Wash off any spills immediately.

NEVER siphon fuel, antifreeze, brake fluid or other such toxic liquids by mouth, or allow prolonged contact with your skin. There is an increasing awareness that they can damage your health. Best of all, use a suitable hand pump and wear gloves.

ALWAYS work in a well ventilated area and don't inhale dust - it may contain asbestos or other poisonous substances.

WIPE UP any spilt oil, grease or water off the floor immediately, before there is an accident.

MAKE SURE that spanners and all other tools are the right size for the job and are not likely to slip. Never try to 'double-up' spanners to gain more leverage.
SEEK HELP if you need to lift something heavy which may be beyond your capability. Don't forget that whenever you are lifting, keep your back straight and bend your knees!

ALWAYS ensure that the safe working load rating of any jacks, hoists or lifting gear used is sufficient for the job, and is used only as recommended by the manufacturer.

NEVER take risky short-cuts or rush to finish a job. Plan ahead and allow plenty of time.

BE meticulous and keep the work

area tidy - you'll avoid frustration, work better and lose less.

KEEP children and animals right-away from the work area and from unattended vehicles.

ALWAYS wear eye protection when working under the vehicle or using any power tools.

BEFORE undertaking dirty jobs, use a barrier cream on your hands as a protection against infection. Preferably, wear thin gloves, available from DIY outlets.

DON'T lean over, or work on, a running engine unless strictly necessary, and keep long hair and loose clothing well out of the way of moving mechanical parts. Note that it is theoretically possible for fluorescent striplighting to make an engine fan appear to be stationary - check! This is the sort of error that happens when you're really tired and not thinking straight. So don't work on your car when you're overtired.

REMOVE your wrist watch, rings and all other jewellery before doing any work on the vehicle - especially the electrical system.

ALWAYS tell someone what you're doing and have them regularly check that all is well, especially when working alone on, or under, the vehicle.

ALWAYS seek specialist advice if you're in doubt about any job. The safety of your vehicle affects you, your passengers and other road users.

Fire

Petrol (gasoline) is a dangerous and highly flammable liquid requiring special precautions. When working on the fuel system, disconnect the vehicle battery earth (ground) terminal whenever possible and always work outside, or in a very well ventilated area. Any form of spark, such as that caused by an electrical fault, by two metal surfaces striking against each other, by a central heating boiler in the garage 'firing up', or even by static electricity built up in your clothing can, in a confined space, ignite petrol vapour causing an explosion. Take great care not to spill petrol on to the engine or exhaust system, never allow any naked flame anywhere near the work area and, above all, don't smoke.

1. Invest in a workshop-sized fire extinguisher. Choose the carbon dioxide type or preferably, dry powder but never a water type extinguisher for workshop use. Water conducts electricity and can make worse an oil or petrol-based fire, in certain circumstances. Have it overhauled by a fire extinguisher specialist every year.

Fumes

In addition to the fire dangers described previously, petrol (gasoline) vapour and the vapour from many solvents, thinners, and adhesives is highly toxic and under certain conditions can lead to unconsciousness or even death, if inhaled. The risks are increased if such fluids are used in a confined space so always ensure adequate ventilation when handling materials of this nature. Treat all such substances with care, always read the instructions and follow them implicitly.

Always ensure that the car is outside the work place in open air if the engine is running. Exhaust fumes contain poisonous

carbon monoxide even if the car is fitted with a catalytic converter, since 'cats' sometimes fail and don't function with the engine cold. Never have the engine running with the car in the garage or in any enclosed space.

Inspection pits are another source of danger from the build-up of fumes. Never drain petrol (gasoline) or use solvents, thinners adhesives or other toxic substances in an inspection pit as the extremely confined space allows the highly toxic fumes to concentrate. Running the engine with the vehicle over the pit can have the same results. It is also dangerous to park a vehicle for any length of time over an inspection pit. The fumes from even a slight fuel leak can cause an explosion when the engine is started.

Mains Electricity

2. Best of all, use rechargeable tools and a DC inspection lamp, powered from a remote 12V battery - both are much safer. However, if you do use a mains-powered inspection lamp, power tool etc, ensure that the appliance is wired correctly to its plug, that where necessary it is properly earthed (grounded), and that the fuse is of the correct rating for the appliance concerned. Do not use any mains powered equipment in damp conditions or in the vicinity of fuel, fuel vapour or the vehicle battery.

Also, before using any mains powered electrical equipment, take one more simple precaution - use an RCD (Residual Current Device) circuit, breaker. Then, if there is a short, the RCD circuit breaker minimises the risk of electrocution by instantly cutting the power supply. Buy one from any electrical store or DIY centre. RCDs fit simply into your electrical socket before plugging in your electrical equipment.

The Ignition System

Extreme care must be taken when working on the ignition system with the ignition switched on or with the engine cranking or running.

Touching certain parts of the ignition system, such as the HT leads, distributor cap, ignition coil etc, can result in a severe electric shock. This is especially likely where the insulation on any of these components is weak, or if the components are dirty or damp. Note also that voltages produced by electronic ignition systems are much higher than conventional systems and could prove fatal, particularly to persons with cardiac pacemaker implants. Consult your handbook or main dealer if in any doubt. An additional risk of injury can arise while working on running engines, if the operator touches a high voltage lead and pulls his hand away on to a conductive or revolving part.

The Battery

Never cause a spark, smoke, or allow a naked light near the vehicle's battery, even in a well ventilated area. A certain amount of highly explosive hydrogen gas will be given off as part of the normal charging process. Care should be taken to avoid sparking by switching off the power supply before charger leads are connected or disconnected. Battery terminals should be shielded, since a battery contains energy and a spark can be caused by any conductor which touches its terminals or exposed connecting straps.

Before working on the fuel or electrical systems, always disconnect the battery earth (ground) terminal.

When charging the battery from an external source, disconnect both battery leads before connecting the charger. If the battery is not of the 'sealed-for-life' type, loosen the filler plugs or remove the cover before charging. For best results the battery should be given a low rate trickle charge overnight. Do not charge at an excessive rate or the battery may burst.

3. Always wear gloves and goggles when carrying or when topping up the battery. Even in diluted form (as it is in the battery) the acid electrolyte is extremely corrosive and must not be allowed to contact the eyes, skin or clothes.

Brakes and Asbestos

Whenever you work on the braking system mechanical components, or remove front or rear brake pads or shoes: i) wear an efficient particle mask, ii) wipe off all brake dust from the work area (never blow it off with compressed air), iii) dispose of brake dust and discarded shoes or pads in a sealed plastic bag, iv) wash hands thoroughly after you have finished working on the brakes and certainly before you eat or smoke, v) replace shoes and pads only with asbestos-free shoes or pads. Note that asbestos brake dust can cause cancer if inhaled.

Obviously, a car's brakes are among its most important safety related items. Do not dismantle your car's brakes unless you are fully competent to do so. If you have not been trained in this work, but wish to carry out the jobs described in this book, it is strongly recommend that you have a garage or qualified mechanic check your work before using the car on the road.

Brake Fluid

Brake fluid absorbs moisture rapidly from the air and can become dangerous resulting in brake failure. Castrol (U.K.) Ltd. recommend that you should have your brake fluid tested at least once a year by a properly equipped garage with test equipment and you should change the fluid in accordance with your vehicle manufacturer's recommendations or as advised in this book if we recommend a shorter interval than the manufacturers. Always buy no more brake fluid than you need. Never store an opened pack. Dispose of the remainder at your Local Authority Waste Disposal Site, in the designated disposal unit, not with general waste or with waste oil.

Engine Oils

Take care and observe the following precautions when working with used engine oil. Apart from the obvious risk of scalding when draining the oil from a hot engine, there is the danger from contaminates that are contained in all used oil.

Always wear disposable plastic or rubber gloves when draining the oil from your engine. i) Note that the drain plug and the oil are often hotter than you expect. Wear gloves if the plug is too hot to touch and keep your hand to one side so that you are not scalded by the spurt of oil as the plug comes away. ii) There are very real health hazards associated with used engine oil. In the words of one manufacturer's handbook "Prolonged and repeated contact may cause serious skin disorders, including dermatitis and cancer." Use a barrier cream on your hands and try not to get oil on them. Where practicable, wear gloves and wash your hands with hand cleaner soon after carrying out the work. Keep oil out of the reach of children. iii) NEVER, EVER dispose of old engine oil into the ground or down a drain. In the UK, and in most EC countries, every local authority must provide a safe means of oil disposal. In the UK, try your local Environmental Health Department for advice on waste disposal facilities.

Plastic Materials

Work with plastic materials brings additional hazards into workshops. Many of the materials used (polymers, resins, adhesives and materials acting as catalysts and accelerators) readily produce very dangerous situations in the form of poisonous fumes, skin irritants, risk of fire and explosions. Do not allow resin or 2-pack adhesive hardener, or that supplied with filler or 2-pack stopper, to come into contact with skin or eyes. Read carefully the safety notes supplied on the can, tube or packaging.

Jack and Axle Stands

Throughout this book you will see many references to the correct use of jacks, axle stands and similar equipment - and we make no apologies for being repetitive. This is one area where safety cannot be overstressed - your life could be at stake.

Special care must be taken when any type of lifting equipment is used. Jacks are made for lifting the vehicle only, not for supporting it. Never work under the car using only a jack to support the weight. Jacks must be supplemented by adequate additional means of support, positioned under secure load-bearing parts of the frame or underbody. Axle stands are available from many discount stores, and all auto parts stores. Drive-on ramps are limiting because of their design and size but they are simple to use, reliable and the most stable type of support, by far. We strongly recommend their use.

Full details on jacking and supporting the vehicle will be found in *Raising a car - Safely!* near the beginning of *Chapter 3*.

Fluoroelastomers

MOST IMPORTANT! PLEASE READ THIS SECTION!

If you service your car in the normal way, none of the following may be relevant to you. Unless, for example, you encounter a car which has been on fire (even in a localised area), subject to heat in, say, a crash-damage repairer's shop or vehicle breaker's yard, or if any second-hand parts have been heated in any of these ways.

Many synthetic rubber-like materials used in motor cars contain a substance called fluorine. These materials are known as fluoroelastomers and are commonly used for oil seals, wiring and cabling, bearing surfaces, gaskets, diaphragms, hoses and 'O' rings. If they are subjected to temperatures greater than 315 degrees C, they will decompose and can be potentially hazardous. Fluoroelastomer materials will show physical signs of decomposition under such conditions in the form of charring of black sticky masses. Some decomposition may occur at temperatures above 200 degrees C, and it is obvious that when a car has been in a fire or has been dismantled with the assistance of a cutting torch or blow torch, the fluoroelastomers can decompose in the manner indicated above.

In the presence of any water or humidity, including atmospheric moisture, the by-products caused by the fluoroelastomers being heated can be extremely dangerous. According to the Health and Safety Executive, "Skin contact with this liquid or decomposition residues can cause painful and penetrating burns. Permanent irreversible skin and tissue damage can occur". Damage can also be caused to eyes or by the inhalation of fumes created as fluoroelastomers are burned or heated.

After fires or exposure to high temperatures observe the following precautions:
1. Do not touch blackened or charred seals or equipment

2. Allow all burnt or decomposed fluoroelastomer materials to cool down before inspection, investigations, tear-down or removal.

3. Preferably, don't handle parts containing decomposed fluoroelastomers, but if you must, wear goggles and PVC (polyvinyl chloride) or neoprene protective gloves whilst doing so. Never handle such parts unless they are completely cool.

4. Contaminated parts, residues, materials and clothing, including protective clothing and gloves, should be disposed of by an approved contractor to landfill or by incineration according to national or local regulations. Oil seals, gaskets and 'O'

rings, along with contaminated material, must not be burned locally.

Workshop Safety - General

1. **Always have a fire extinguisher of the correct type at arm's length when working on the fuel system - under the car, or under the bonnet.**

   If you do have a fire, DON'T PANIC. Use the extinguisher effectively by directing it at the base of the fire.

2. **NEVER use a naked flame near petrol or anywhere in the workplace.**

3. **NEVER use petrol (gasoline) to clean parts. Use paraffin (kerosene) or white spirits.**

4. **KEEP your inspection lamp well away from any source of petrol (gasoline) such as when disconnecting a carburettor float bowl or fuel line.**

5. **NO SMOKING. There's a risk of fire or transferring dangerous substances to your mouth and, in any case, ash falling into mechanical components is to be avoided.**

6. **BE METHODICAL in everything you do, use common sense, and think of safety at all times.**

CHAPTER 2 - BUYING SPARES

Reliable though Sprites and Midgets undoubtedly are, there are, of course, occasions when you need to buy spares in order to service them and keep them running. There are a number of sources of supply of the components necessary when servicing your car, the price and quality varying between suppliers. As with most things in life, cheapest is not necessarily best. Generally, our advice is to put quality before price - this policy usually works out less expensive in the long run. But how can you identify quality? It's sometimes difficult, so stick with parts from suppliers with a reputation, those recommended to you by others and parts produced by well-established brand names. But don't just pay through the nose. The same parts are often available at wildly different prices so, if you want to save money, invest your time in shopping around.

In any event, when buying spares, take with you details of the date of registration of your car, also its chassis (or VIN) number, found on the 'chassis' rail in the engine bay, as shown below (ill.1), and the engine number, as shown on page 13 (ill.2). These can be helpful where parts changed during production, and can be the key to a more helpful approach by some parts salespeople. You may, by now, have entered this key information on the *Auto-Biography* pages at the front of this book, for ease of reference.

Rover Dealers

Always consider your local Rover dealership as a source of supply of spares. One benefit is that the spares obtained will be genuine items.

In addition, if the parts counter staff are enthusiastic about the vehicles, they may be only too pleased to help fellow-enthusiasts locate the spares required. Sometimes they will go to the trouble of contacting other dealers, on your behalf, in search of an elusive part, and this can usually be delivered within a day or so, if located at another dealer within the same group of companies, for example. Prices are occasionally reduced from the usual retail level - watch for special offers which are often listed at the parts counter. Try to avoid Saturday and Sunday mornings when buying. Weekends are often very busy for parts counters, and you may find the staff have more time to help you if you visit in the evening, while on your way from work. At these times you are also less likely to have to queue for a long time. The biggest disadvantage - and it is a big one - is that there are an awful lot of Midget parts that either won't be in stock or that just aren't stocked by your Rover dealer.

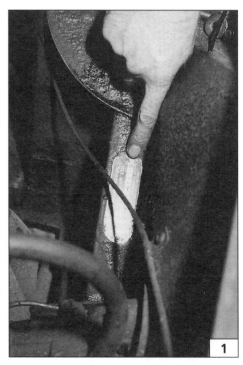

Parts Factors/Motor Accessory Shops

Local parts factors and motor accessory shops can be extremely useful for obtaining servicing parts at short notice - many accessory outlets open late in the evening, and on both days at weekends. Most servicing parts for the Midget are readily available so, for example, requests for routine items such as brake pads and shoes, spark plugs, contact breaker points, rocker cover gaskets, oil and air filters, are unlikely to draw a blank look from the sales assistant.

Some outlets supply original-equipment spares but, in many cases, the components are pattern parts. In this case, if there is a choice, opt for well-known, respected names, even if the prices are a little higher than those required for possibly dubious cheap import items. This is especially important when shopping for safety-related items such as brake pads. In this example, experience has shown that cheap pads can be subject to excessive brake fade under enthusiastic driving and, in any case, such pads often wear rapidly.

Don't overlook the trade motor factors outlets in the UK. A number of them have branches all over the country - find them in Yellow Pages. Don't be put off by the apparent emphasis on 'the trade'! If they've got it and you want to pay for it, they'll sell it to you!

Specialist Suppliers

There are a multitude of spares suppliers catering for the needs of Austin-Healey and MG owners, including among them, of course, those who run their own Sprites and Midgets. They are particularly useful when buying components needed for restorations, but of course will also be pleased to help you with regard to servicing components. Most of the major suppliers run mail order services, and next-day deliveries are usually available. The spares supplied are often original specification items (this is not always the case, though, so enquire when buying), and prices are competitive. The only drawback is that you will have to pay postage and packing charges, in addition to the cost of the spares.

Many MG and Austin-Healey specialists advertise regularly in the many classic car magazines. Many include lists of the parts they have on offer, and the prices they are asking. Again, watch out for special offers which can save you money. If you plan ahead. Often you can buy spares now at a preferential rate, and keep them in stock until needed.

The overwhelming advantage of buying from a specialist (also, see Clubs, below) is that a good specialist will have the best stock of parts and the most useful fund of specialised knowledge to be found anywhere.

Clubs

Members of the Austin-Healey Club, MG Car Club and the MG Owners' Club benefit from general spares information provided by those organisations, while their Club magazines often contain helpful pointers with regard to spares availability. The MG Owners' Club provides members with a handbook, on joining the Club, and this gives details of the various specialists. In addition, the Club runs its own spares service, and many special offers on components are made available to members.

Buying Secondhand

We would strongly advise against buying secondhand brake, suspension, and steering components, unless you know the source of the parts, and really are sure that they are in first class condition. Even then, be sure that you see the vehicle they have been taken from, and avoid any such parts from accident-damaged cars. On the other hand, it might make sense to buy, say, a distributor, or carburettors which you know to be low-mileage units, to replace your worn out components. Such moves can help your car run more sweetly and less expensively. In every case, ensure that the components you are buying are compatible with your particular vehicle, and carry out basic checks to ensure that they too are not badly worn. In particular, in the case of distributors, ensure that the main spindle cannot be moved from side to side more than just perceptibly (if it can, the bearings are worn and setting the points gap/dwell angle and ignition timing accurately will be impossible). With regard to carburettors, similarly check to make sure that there is minimal sideways play between the throttle spindle and the body of the unit. If there is excessive movement, the carburettor is worn, the result being air leaks and erratic slow running.

Checks on Running Gear Components

Although many outlets sell reconditioned components on an exchange basis, the quality of workmanship and the extent of the work carried out on such units can vary greatly.

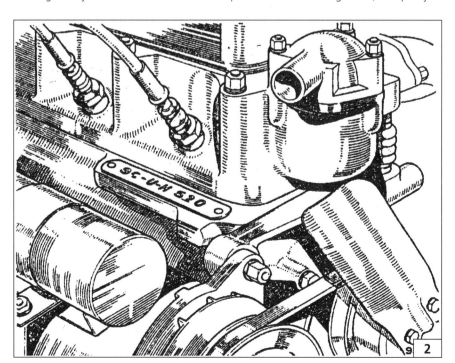

Therefore, if buying a rebuilt unit, always check particularly carefully when buying. It has to be said that, wherever possible, reconditioned units are best obtained from main agents, or from reputable specialist suppliers. Always talk to fellow owners before buying they may be able to direct you to a supplier offering sound parts at reasonable prices. When buying, always enquire about the terms of the guarantee (if any).

In any event, the following notes should help you make basic checks on some of the commonly required components:

BRAKES (NEW parts ONLY!): Look for boxes bearing genuine AP Lockheed or BMC, British Leyland, Austin Rover, or Rover labels. If buying at an autojumble, inspect the contents of the box and reject any obviously rusty stock.

STEERING: Ball joints, king pins - buy new, again rejecting any moisture-damaged stock. Stub axles are available from almost all specialist suppliers on an exchange basis. Ensure that the inner surfaces of the king pin bushes appear to have been properly reamed, and have uniform, smooth surfaces. With a new king pin inserted, the stub axle should rotate about the pin smoothly, without any undue slack or free play evident.

Steering racks are available as exchange units. Ensure that you rotate the operating shaft fully from lock to lock, feeling for any undue free play, roughness, stiffness, or notchiness as you do so. Reject any units showing signs of any of these problems or, of course, oil leaks or split gaiters.

SUSPENSION: Lever arm shock absorbers, such as those used on the 'Spridget', have relatively short working lives, and many have now been rebuilt several times during their lifetime. In some cases, reconditioning by less than scrupulous organisations can simply mean a quick clean-up and a new coat of paint. Therefore, it pays to buy from a reputable supplier. When buying, take a close look around the joints between the operating arm(s) and the body of the unit. If fluid seepage is evident, reject the shock absorber. In addition, with the shocker upright, work the operating arm(s) up and down several times by hand, throughout the full length of the stroke. After two or three strokes the arm should move with a uniform, firm resistance throughout the length of the operating stroke. If resistance is patchy, or if the arm moves with little pressure needed, the unit is faulty. Again, look elsewhere. Indeed some owners prefer to pay more (usually, quite a lot more) to purchase new, unused shock absorbers, about which there are fewer doubts.

TYRES: For the ultimate in long life, roadholding and wet grip, brand new radial tyres from a reputable manufacturer offer the best solution, especially where the car is used all year round, on an everyday basis. Remoulds are available at lower initial cost, but life expectancy is not as long as with new tyres. Cross-plies are still available, but apart from originality considerations, they are less efficient in terms of handling qualities and life expectancy. They are also, these days, becoming expensive.

It is true that secondhand tyres can offer an inexpensive short-term solution to keeping a car on the road, but beware. Such tyres may have serious, hidden faults. If you purchase such covers, you are taking a risk in that you have no knowledge of the history of the tyres or what has happened to them, how they have been repaired, and so on. Our advice - very strongly given - is to stick to top quality, unused tyres from a reputable manufacturer. They may cost a little more, but at least you will have peace of mind, and should be able to rely on their performance in all road and weather situations. After all, your life - and those of other road users - could depend on it.

Saving Money

Finally, if you want to buy quality and save money, you must be prepared to shop around. Ring each of your chosen suppliers with a shopping list to hand and your car's personal data from the *Auto-Biography* at the front of this book in front of you. Keep a written note of prices, whether the parts are proper brand name parts or not and - most importantly - whether or not the parts you want are in stock. Parts expected 'soon' have been known never to materialise. A swivel pin in the hand is worth two in the bush. (Bad pun!)

Please read the whole of the Introduction to this Chapter before carrying out any work on your car.

SERVICE INTERVALS, STEP-BY-STEP

CHAPTER 3
SERVICE INTERVALS STEP-BY-STEP

Everyone wants to own a car that starts first time, runs reliably and lasts longer than average. There's no magic about how to put your car in this category, it's all a question of thorough maintenance. If you follow the Service Jobs listed here - or have a garage or mechanic do the jobs for you - you can almost guarantee that your car will still be going strong when others have fallen by the wayside ... or the hard shoulder! This Service Schedule is just about as thorough as you can get. It's an amalgam of all the maker's recommended service items plus all the 'Inside Information' from the experts that we could find. If you want your car to be as well looked after as possible, follow the Jobs shown here but, if you don't want to go all the way, you can pick and choose the most essential items from the lists. But do bear in mind that the Jobs we recommend are done for very good reasons:

♦ *body maintenance* is rarely included in most service schedules. We believe it to be essential.

♦ *preventative maintenance* features high in our list of priorities. That's why so many of our Service Jobs start with the word 'Check'. Checking means more than just glancing at an item; it means physically checking that things are in good condition, that nuts and bolts are tight and that pressures and levels are correct.

♦ *older cars* need more jobs doing on them than new cars because things deteriorate - it's as simple as that - so we list all the jobs you need to carry out to ensure that your car, old or new, is kept in fine fettle.

USING THE SERVICE SCHEDULES

At the start of each Service Job you'll see a heading in bold type like this:

☐ **Job 14. Check rear sidelamps.**

Following the heading will be all the information you need to carry out that job. Please note that different models of car may have different settings, so please check in *Chapter 8, Facts and Figures.* Exactly the same number and heading will be found in *Appendix 4, Service History,* at the back of the book where you will want to keep a full record of all the work you have carried out. After you have finished servicing your car you will be able to tick off all the jobs and thus, service by service, build up a complete Service History of the work carried out on your car.

You will also find other key information immediately after each job title and, in most cases, there will be reference to an illus-

tration, - a photograph or line drawing, whichever is easiest for you to follow - usually on the same page.

If the Job shown applies only to certain vehicles, the Job title will be followed by a description of the type of vehicle to which the Job applies. For example, *Job 7, Check breather hoses,* applies only to cars with 1,500 cc engines. Other special headings are also used. One reads **OPTIONAL,** which means that you may wish to use your own discretion as to whether to carry out this particular Job or whether to leave it until it crops up again in a later service. Another is **INSIDE INFORMATION.** This tells you that here is a special tip that you wouldn't normally get to hear about other than through the inside knowledge and experience of the experts at Maidstone Sports Cars who helped in compiling this Service Guide. The third is **SPECIALIST SERVICE,** which means that we recommend you to have this work carried out by a specialist. Some jobs, such as checking front wheel alignment, or setting headlamp aim, need accurate measuring equipment while oth-

---

We are grateful to MG specialists Maidstone Sports Cars for their kind assistance with this chapter.
Almost all of the work carried out was photographed there.

ers, such as checking emissions, need specialist equipment such as an exhaust gas analyser. Where we think that you are better off having the work done for you, we say so.

> **SAFETY FIRST!**
> *The other special heading could be the most important one of all SAFETY FIRST! This information must always be read with care and taken seriously. In addition, please read* **Chapter 1, Safety First!** *at the beginning of this book before carrying out any work on your car. There are many hazards associated with working on a car but all of them can be avoided by adhering strictly to the safety rules. Don't skimp on safety!*

Throughout the Service Schedule, the work in each 'shorter' service interval is meant to be an important part of the next 'longer' service interval. For example, under *1,500 mile Service, Mechanical and Electrical - Around the Car,* Job 18, you are instructed to check the tyres for wear or damage. This job also has to be carried out at 3,000 miles, 6,000 miles, 9,000 miles and so on. It is therefore shown in the list of extra jobs to be carried out at each of these longer service intervals, but only as a job number, without the detailed instructions that were given first time round.

The Catch-up Service

When you first buy a used car you can never be certain how well it has been looked after. Even one with a 'full service history' is unlikely to have been looked after as well as one with a

Porter Publishing Service Guide History! So, if you want to catch up on all the servicing that may have been neglected on your car, just work through the entire list of Service Jobs listed for the *36,000 miles - or Every Thirty Six Months service,* and your car will be bang up to date and serviced as well as you could hope for. Do allow several days for all of this work, not least because it will almost certainly throw up a number of extra jobs - potential faults that have been lurking beneath the surface - all of which will need putting right before you can 'sign off' your car as being in tip-top condition.

The Service History

Those people fortunate enough to own a new car, or one that has been well maintained from new, will have the opportunity to keep a service record, or 'Service History', of their car, usually filled in by a main dealer. Until now it hasn't been possible for the owner of an older car to keep a formal record of servicing. But now you can, by using the tick-list in *Appendix 4, Service History.* Indeed, you can go one better than the owners of new cars because your car's Service History will be more complete and more detailed than any manufacturer's service record, (which often just lists the service interval), with the extra bonus that there is space for you to keep a record of all those extra items that crop up from time to time such as new tyres, replacement exhaust, new parts or extra accessories. So, for example, if your battery goes down only 11 months after buying it, you'll be able to look up where and when you bought it. All you have to do is to remember to fill in your Service History in the first place.

> **RAISING A CAR - SAFELY**
> *You will often need to raise your car of the ground in order to carry out the Service Jobs shown here. To start off with, here's what you must never do: NEVER work beneath a car held only on a jack, not even a trolley jack. Quite a number of deaths have been caused by a car slipping off a jack while someone has been working underneath. The safest way is by raising the car on a proprietary brand of ramps. Sometimes, though, there is no alternative but to use axle stands. Please read the following information, and act on it!*

When using car ramps:

(I) Make absolutely certain that the ramps are parallel to the wheels of the car and that the wheels are exactly central on each ramp.

(II) Always have an assistant to watch both sides of the car as you drive up. Drive up to the end 'stops' on the ramps but never over them! Apply the handbrake firmly, put the car in first or reverse gear.

III

IV

(III) Chock both wheels remaining on the ground, both in front and behind, so that the car can't move in either direction. This also applies when the car is supported on axle stands.

INSIDE INFORMATION: Ramps tend to move as you drive on to them. To prevent this, wrap a strip of old carpet round the first 'rung', double it back and drive over the doubled piece of carpet as you approach the ramps. This will prevent them from skidding.

On other occasions, you might need to work on the car while it is supported on an axle stand or pair of axle stands. These are inherently less stable than ramps, so you must take much greater care when working beneath them. In particular:

• ensure that the axle stand is on flat, stable ground, never on ground where any of the legs can sink in.

• ensure that the car is on level ground, that the handbrake is off and that the transmission is in neutral.

• raise the car with a trolley jack - invest in one if you don't already own one; the car's wheel changing jack is often too unstable. Place a piece of cloth over the head of the jack if your car is nicely finished on the underside. Ensure that the floor is sufficiently clear and smooth for the trolley jack wheels to roll as the car is raised and lowered, otherwise it could slip off the jack.

(IV) Place the head of the jack beneath the front cross-member when raising the front of the car.

V

VI

(V) At the front, place the axle stands with their heads inside the inner part of the front bottom wishbones making sure that when the car is lowered the wishbone sits firmly in the head of the axle stand where it cannot slip.

(VI) At the rear of the car, place the head of the jack securely under the bottom of the differential casing.

(VII) Place the axle stands each side of the jack, close to the spring seats, and manoeuvre them until the axle tube casing sits firmly in the head of the stands.

If, for any reason, you can't use the location points recommended here, take care to locate the head of the axle stand on a strong, level, stable part of the car's underside. A chassis member is sometimes suitable provided it is not sloping but, at Maidstone Sports Cars, they do not recommend using the chassis rails at the front because they are too near the centre and the car would be unstable. With the exception of the inner part of the front bottom wishbone, never locate the axle stand's head on a moving part of the suspension nor on a rear leaf spring. The car could move which would cause the axle stand to slip. Never use the floor of the car. It is just too weak.

Just as when using ramps - only even more importantly - apply the handbrake firmly, put the car in first or reverse gear and chock both wheels remaining on the ground, both in front and behind.

Be especially careful when applying force to a spanner or when pulling hard on anything when the car is supported off the ground. It is all too easy to move the car so far that it topples off the axle stand or stands. And remember that if a car falls on you, YOU COULD BE KILLED!

VII

CHAPTER THREE

Whenever working beneath a car on your own, have someone primed to keep an eye on you! If someone pops out to see how you are getting on every quarter of an hour or so, it could be enough to save your life! Do remember that, in general, a car will be more stable when only one wheel is removed and one axle stand used than if two wheels are removed in conjunction with two axle stands. You are strongly advised not to work on the car with all four wheels off the ground, on four axle stands. The car could be very unstable and dangerous to work beneath.

When lowering the car to the ground, remember to remove the chocks, release the handbrake and place the transmission in neutral.

INSIDE INFORMATION: When you have to pull hard on a spanner or socket bar, pull with one hand and use the other to push against the car as a reaction point. That way you are less likely to move the car than when just pulling.

500 Miles, Weekly, or Before a Long Journey

These are the regular service checks that you need to carry out to help keep your car safe and reliable. They don't include the major Service Jobs but they should be carried out as an integral part of every 'proper' service.

500 mile Mechanical and Electrical - The Engine Bay

☐ **Job 1. Engine oil level.**

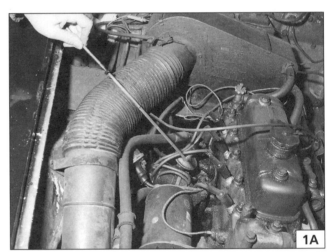

Check the engine's oil level with the car on level ground.

1A. Lift the dipstick out, wipe it with a clean cloth, push it back in and lift it out again. Take a look at the level of the oil on the dipstick. You may have to do this three or four times before you get a clear reading as the oil sometimes smears as the stick is pulled out.

1B. The oil level should be somewhere between the MAX and MIN levels. Make sure the dipstick is pushed right home when replacing it.

1C. The oil filler cap is on the top of the rocker cover. On 948cc, 1098cc and 1275cc engines it is black plastic (except on the very earliest cars, when it should be metal) and at the front. On the 1493 cc engine it is metal and at the back. The caps just twist and lift off.

INSIDE INFORMATION: i) While you are dipping the oil look over the engine for signs of oil leaks. If you find any, wipe the engine clean and check again after a few miles. What starts as a minor weeping could soon develop into a major leak. ii) If you have to top up the oil, wait a few moments after adding new oil for it to flow down into the sump. If you dip again too quickly you can get a false reading. iii) When topping up engine oil it often helps to stop dribbles if you twist the container slightly as you stop pouring.

☐ Job 2. Clutch fluid level.

2. Check/top up clutch fluid reservoir. The level should be just at the bottom of the filler neck. Make sure that the breather hole in the reservoir cap is clear. Note: on early models the clutch and brake hydraulic circuits shared a single hydraulic reservoir, so Job 2 and Job 3 are taken care of in one operation.

INSIDE INFORMATION: i) Check the ground on which the car has been parked, especially beneath the engine bay and inside each road wheel, for evidence of clutch or brake fluid leaks. If any are found, investigate further before driving the car. ii) Clutch fluid will damage painted surfaces if it is allowed to come into contact. Take care not to spill any but, if there is an accident, refit the reservoir filler cap and wash off any accidental spillage immediately with hot, soapy water.

☐ Job 3. Brake fluid level.

SAFETY FIRST!
i) If brake or clutch fluid should come into contact with the skin or eyes, rinse immediately with plenty of water. Particularly with eyes, if irritation, soreness or loss of vision persists, see a doctor as soon as possible. ii) The brake fluid level will fall slightly during normal use but, if it falls significantly below the bottom of the filler neck, stop using the car and seek specialist advice. iii) If you get dirt into the brake or clutch hydraulic system it can cause failure. Wipe the reservoir filler cap clean before removing it. iv) Use only new brake fluid from an air-tight container. Old fluid will have absorbed moisture and this could cause the brakes to fail when carrying out an emergency stop or other heavy use of the brakes - just when you need them most and are least able to do anything about it!

Check/top up the brake fluid reservoir. The level should be just at the bottom of the filler neck. Make sure that the breather hole in the reservoir cap is clear.

INSIDE INFORMATION: i) Check the ground on which the car has been parked, especially beneath the engine bay and inside each road wheel, for evidence of clutch or brake fluid leaks. If any are found, investigate further before driving the car. ii) Brake fluid will damage painted surfaces if it is allowed to come into contact. Take care not to spill any but, if there is an accident, refit the reservoir filler cap and wash off any accidental spillage immediately with hot, soapy water.

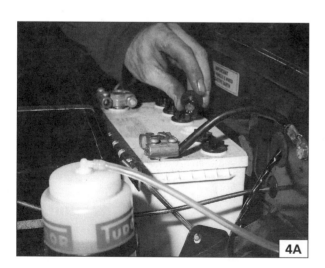

☐ Job 4. Battery electrolyte.

SAFETY FIRST!
i) The gas given off by a battery is highly explosive. Never smoke, use a naked flame or allow a spark to occur in the battery compartment. Never disconnect the battery (it can cause sparking) with the battery caps removed. ii) Batteries contain sulphuric acid. If the acid comes into contact with the skin or eyes, wash immediately with copious amounts of cold water and seek medical advice. iii) Do not check the battery levels within half an hour of the battery being charged with a battery charger. The addition of fresh water could then cause the highly acid and corrosive electrolyte to flood out of the battery.

4A. Unless the battery is 'maintenance free' and 'sealed for life', remove the battery caps or cover and, with the car on level ground, check the level of the electrolyte - the fluid inside each battery cell. Sometimes it is difficult to see the level, so use a lead lamp or torch and tap the side of the battery casing to produce ripples on the top of the electrolyte. The plates inside the battery should be just covered with electrolyte. If the level has fallen, top up with distilled water. NEVER use tap water, it can ruin your battery! Dry off the top of the battery after topping up.

4B. If you are suffering from a persistently flat battery, it may be that one or more of the cells is past its useful life. The easiest way to check this is to check the specific gravity of the electrolyte in each cell. (Note: you cannot carry out this check on a 'sealed for life' battery. These have to be checked for heavy discharge by a battery

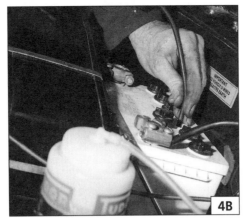

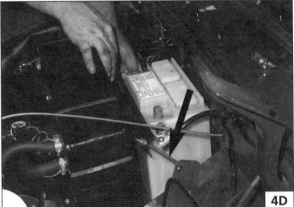

specialist). The specific gravity is checked with a hydrometer. To use this, squeeze the rubber bulb and insert the rubber tube in a battery cell. Release pressure on the bulb and some of the electrolyte will be drawn into the transparent tube. Hold the hydrometer vertically and check the float inside the transparent tube. The float is marked, often with coloured bands, to show full charge, medium charge and flat. If all the cells are low on charge, particularly after the car has been standing for some time, you may have a fault somewhere in the electrical system which is allowing current to drain away. If only one, or some, of the cells show a low charge and the rest are well up, it is almost certain that you need a new battery.

4C. Check that the battery terminals are tight and not corroded, and that they are covered with a smear of Vaseline (petroleum jelly) or copper-impregnated grease.

4D. Check also that the battery clamp (arrowed) is correctly located and tight. A loose battery will suffer from a reduced life-span.

4E. INSIDE INFORMATION: If the battery terminals are badly corroded with white 'furr', wash off with hot water, taking care that none gets into the battery cells and that all of this corrosive stuff is washed off the car's bodywork.

INSIDE INFORMATION: It is well worth investing in a hydrometer. They are cheap and, as well as checking the state of charge of your battery, you will find it is ideal to use as a syringe when topping up the battery with distilled water. Once water is mixed with acid inside the battery, it won't freeze. So, in extremely cold weather, run the car (out of doors) after topping up so that you put a charge into the battery. This will mix the fresh water with the rest of the electrolyte, cutting out the risk of freezing and a cracked battery case.

☐ **Job 5. Windscreen washer reservoir.**

5. Check and top up the level of fluid inside the windscreen washer reservoir. Remember that, in cold weather, a stronger concentration of washing fluid will help to prevent the washer from freezing up. Check the recommended dilution on the package.

Job 6. Cooling system.

6A

6A. Carry out a visual check for leaks on all cooling system hoses in and around the engine bay.

6B. Check that none of the hoses is chafing on any part of the bodywork or radiator air deflector plates.

6C. Check the level of the coolant in the expansion tank, or in the top of the radiator on early cars without an expansion tank. If necessary, top up with a 50% mixture of antifreeze and water. On early cars which have a filler cap in the radiator, top up to within half an inch of the filler cap neck.

6B

6D. On later cars fitted with an expansion tank there is a filler plug on the sloping part of the radiator at the top on the right hand side. On cars with 1500 cc engines, the filler cap is a black plastic cap in the top of the thermostat housing. Top up with a 50% mixture of antifreeze and water until the coolant reaches the indicated level in the expansion tank.

6C

Job 7. Inspect pressure cap.

7. Whenever you remove the pressure cap on a radiator or expansion tank make it a force of habit to inspect the condition of the pressure seal. If it is worn, fit a new cap complete making sure that you have the correct pressure poundage for your engine.

6D

7

500 mile Mechanical and Electrical - Around the Car

☐ **Job 8. Check horns.**

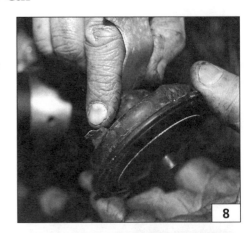

8. Try the horn push and, if the horns fail to work, check the wiring to the horns or the connections on the horns themselves.

SPECIALIST SERVICE. Horn wiring and connections can be more complex than they appear at first. For instance, on some models, both terminals at the horn should be 'live'! If there is no obvious problem with wiring connections, have the horn, the circuitry and the switches checked over by a specialist.

☐ **Job 9. Windscreen washer.**

9. Check the operation of the screen washers. If they fail to work, check that the pump is operating and, if not, check the electrical connections. If the pump is working but either or both jets are not operating, check the piping to them for blockages or poor connections and then check with a pin that the jets are clear. Some jets are adjustable for angle by inserting a pin and twisting the jet. Others are adjustable with a screwdriver as shown.

☐ **Job 10. Windscreen wipers.**

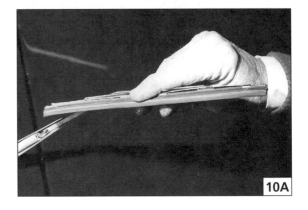

10A. Check the wiper blade rubbers for cuts or other damage and clean them with methylated spirit (industrial alcohol) to remove traffic film.

10B. One type of wiper blade is held to the arm by a spring loaded peg. To remove the blade, depress the spring with a small screwdriver and slide the sleeve of the wiper blade off the arm.

10C. Later type blades are held in a hook on the arm. To remove these, hold the arm away from the screen, depress and hold in the button (10C.1) and slide the wiper blade towards the screen (10C.2). Then move it sideways (10C.3) to disengage it from the hook. (Illustration, courtesy Rover Cars)

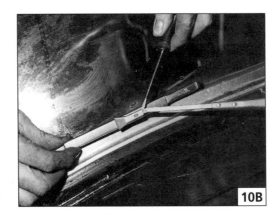

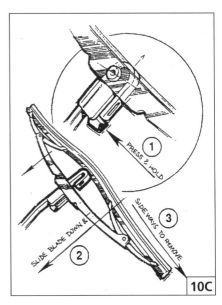

Job 11. Tyre pressures.

11. Use a reliable pressure gauge to check the tyre pressures and check them cold, not after a run as the tyres will then be warm and the gauge will show an increased pressure.

Job 12. Check headlamps.

SPECIALIST SERVICE: It is not possible to set the headlamp aim accurately at home. In *Chapter 7, Getting Through the MoT*, we show you how to trial-set your headlamps before going to an MoT Testing Station (in the UK). This method is suitable only if you are going to have the settings re-checked by a garage with beam aligning equipment.

12A. Some headlamp rims are held on by a small screw at the bottom but others are a push fit over small lugs on the headlamp shell. The safest way to remove these is to insert a broad-bladed screwdriver between the bottom of the rim and the rubber seal and twist gently. As a safety precaution should the screwdriver slip, put a piece of cardboard or a cloth against the paintwork under the lamp.

12B. When the rim is off, the headlamp aim is altered by turning two adjustment screws round the chromium plated bezel - *not* the three fixing screws (12C.2)!

12C. The components for a sealed beam set-up are the simplest to deal with. The beam is set by turning in and out screws shown at numbers 12C.6 and 12C.7. Headlamp rims were never meant to be removed, it sometimes seems! Do so by carefully levering between lamp and rim, taking enormous care not to crack the glass. You could lever at a similar point, between body and rim, with a piece of card to stop the screwdriver from damaging the body. Either method can go wrong, but the first is more straightforward. (Illustration, courtesy Rover Cars)

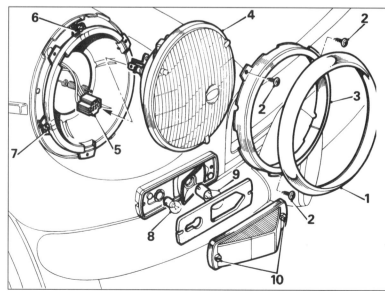

1. Headlamp rim
2. Inner rim retaining screws
3. Inner rim
4. Headlamp unit
5. Wiring socket
6. Vertical beam adjustment screw
7. Horizontal beam adjustment screw
8. Sidelamp bulb
9. Direction indicator bulb
10. Lens retaining screws

12D. After removing the three screws (12C.2) holding the inner rim (12C.3), the unit inside will slip to the floor and break, if you're not careful! Sealed beam units just plug straight out and in again (12C.5).

12E. Latest, 'rubber bumper' Midgets have headlamps with integral sidelamps. When replacing a bulb, NEVER touch the bulb with your fingers. If you do so, wipe it clean with methylated spirit (industrial alcohol). Make sure that the spring holding the bulb in place fits over the bulb spigots and under the retaining spigots on the lamp unit (12E.10). Also, make sure that the seal (12E.6) is properly fitted before refitting the lamp unit to the car's body. (Illustration, courtesy Rover Cars)

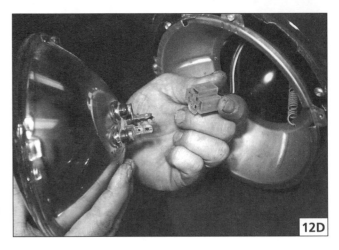

12D

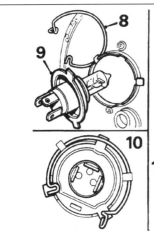
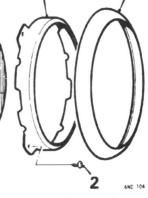

1. Headlamp rim	6. Rubber seal	11. Vertical beam adjustment screw
2. Inner rim retaining screws	7. Sidelamp bulb holder	12. Horizontal beam adjustment screw
3. Inner rim	8. Headlamp bulb retaining spring	13. Sidelamp bulb
4. Headlamp rim	9. Headlamp bulb	
5. Wiring socket	10. Bulb and spring correctly fitted	

12E

12F. 'Frogeye' headlamp units also had an integral sidelamp. Although many have been converted to sealed beam units, many still have headlamp bulbs. (Illustration, courtesy Rover Cars)

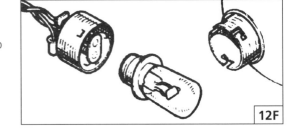

12F

☐ **Job 13. Check front sidelamps and indicators.**

Check the operation of both front sidelamps and indicators and, if necessary, replace any bulbs which have blown.

POST-FROGEYE AND CHROME BUMPER CARS ONLY

13A. Sidelamp lenses are removed by undoing two small screws. Under the lens, the indicator bulb has a lift-off amber cover.

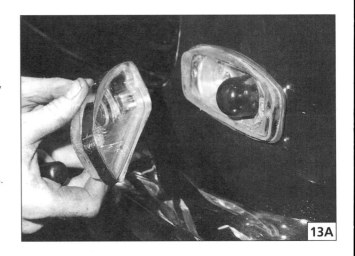

13A

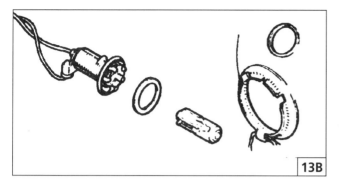

13B

FROGEYE AND RUBBER BUMPER CARS ONLY

13B. Rubber bumper cars' sidelights are part of the headlamp assembly (see 12E) and so were Frogeyes', the sidelamps fitting the headlamp bowl as shown here. (Illustration, courtesy Rover Cars)

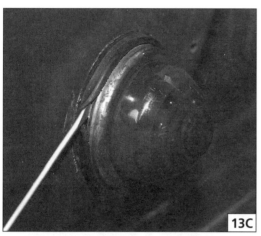

13C

13C. On early models, prise out the chrome retaining bezel...

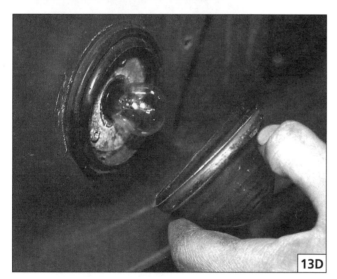

13D

13D. ...and pull the indicator lens away from the rubber base.

INSIDE INFORMATION: Bulbs are removed in the normal way by pressing in and twisting anticlockwise, but sometimes they refuse to budge. A piece of cloth will sometimes give you a better grip and help to protect your fingers should the glass break. If it does break, or if the glass comes free from the brass ferrule, bend one side of the ferrule down, squirt some releasing fluid behind it and, after five minutes or so, grip the bent part of the ferrule with a pair of pliers.

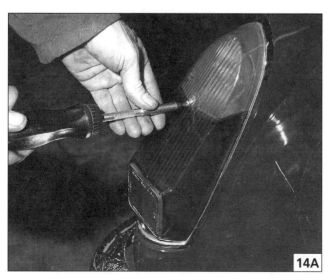

14A

☐ **Job 14. Check rear sidelamps.**

Check operation of rear sidelamps, stop lamps and rear indicator lamps. Check condition of reflectors and clean the lenses.

14A. The rear lamp lenses, including the rear reflectors, are held by two self-tapping screws, one at the base of the lens and one halfway up.

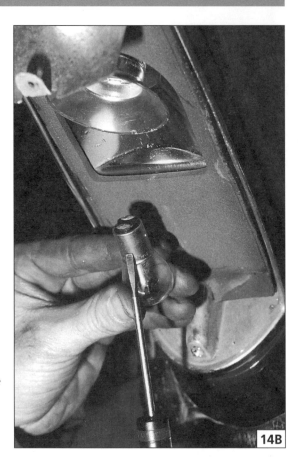

14B. Note that the rear lamp/stop lamp bulbs have two offset pegs so they cannot be fitted the wrong way round. Unlike the front sidelamps, corrosion is seldom a problem inside the rear lamps.

LATE US MIDGETS ONLY

14C. Certain models are fitted with direction indicator side repeater lamps in the front wings. To change the bulb in these, slide the unit to the right and ease it away. Twist out the bulb holder and remove the bulb. (Illustration, courtesy Rover Cars)

□ **Job 15. Check number plate lamps.**

POST-FROGEYE CHROME BUMPER CARS ONLY

15A. There are two number plate lamps, set in the inner ends of the bumpers, one each side of the number plate. The lenses are held by two screws. Check their operation, clean the lenses and replace bulbs if necessary.

15B. These small nuts and washers can be pigs to get at!

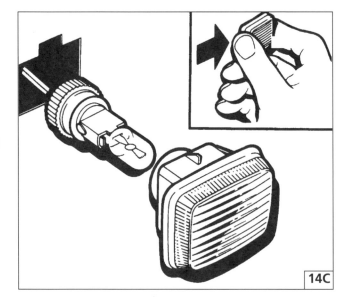

15C

FROGEYE AND RUBBER BUMPER CARS ONLY

15C. These cars have a pair of bulbs each side of the number plate. A single screw - sometimes straight, sometimes cross-head holds each cover in place.

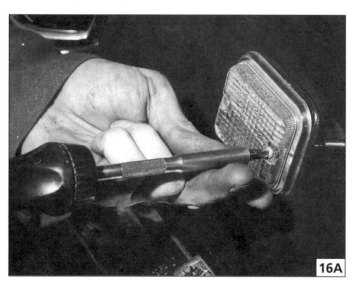

16A

☐ **Job 16. Check reversing lamps.**

WHEN FITTED

The reversing lamps operate automatically when reverse gear is engaged with the ignition on. Check operation, clean the lenses and replace bulbs if necessary.

16A. Reversing lamp lenses are held by two screws.

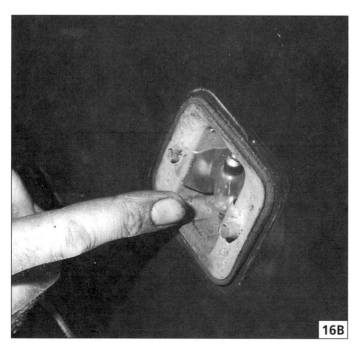

16B

16B. The bulbs in the reversing lamps are tubular festoon type which are sometimes difficult to grip with the fingers. An easy way to remove them is with a small screwdriver under one of the metal end caps.

☐ **Job 17. Check wheel spinners.**

WIRE WHEELED CARS ONLY

17A. Check the tightness of the centre nuts holding the wheels. In some cases these nuts may be the type with 'ears' so use the correct hide faced mallet to avoid damaging the chromium plated surface.

17B. In other cases, as here, they will be 'safety' hexagon nuts which need a special 'flogging' spanner.

INSIDE INFORMATION: The tightness should be checked with the weight of the car off the wheel otherwise there is a danger that the nut will feel tight when it isn't. Remember that the nuts on each side of the car have different hand threads. Check on the nut itself for an arrow giving the tightening or undoing direction.

500 mile Bodywork and Interior - Around The Car

☐ **Job 18. Valet bodywork.**

Before washing the soft top use a soft brush to remove dust and loose dirt, then wash the bodywork with water and a suitable car body detergent. Take care not to get 'wash-wax' on the glass as it can cause smeared wipers for miles. If you use a wand wash at a service station, choose the wash programme that does not contain a wax. Wash the wheels and tyre walls last. Leather the paintwork dry and use a separate leather on the glass to avoid transferring wax to the glass. After the body is dry, polish the paintwork and chromium with any reputable car polish.

INSIDE INFORMATION: In very wet or muddy weather, road dirt can collect under the leading edge of the soft top where it meets the top of the screen. Open the soft top and wash this area clean. If you have been using the car in icy weather when salt has been spread on the roads, use the power jet wand wash at a service station to wash out under the wheel arches and the general underside of the car. Careful attention to this can avoid many corrosion problems later.

1,500 Miles - or Every Month, Whichever Comes First

1,500 mile Mechanical and Electrical - Around the Car

☐ **Job 19. Check tyres.**

19. Check tyres for tread depth, using a tread depth gauge, not judging by eye. Remember that, at the time of writing, the minimum legal tread depth in the UK is 1.6 mm. However, tyres are past their best roadholding by the time the tread has worn this shallow so you may like to replace them earlier. Also check both sides of the tyres for uneven wear, bulges, scuffs or other damage to the sidewalls.

INSIDE INFORMATION: If you find any damage, however slight, to the sidewalls, or deep cuts in the tread, and are in doubt, check with a tyre expert whether or not it is safe to carry on using the tyre on the road. There are legitimate repairs which can be carried out on a tyre to prolong its useful life - but only by a qualified tyre expert. Ignoring damage could cost you your life and that of others, too. Raise each wheel up off the ground, using an axle stand, when checking the tyres or you will not be able to check the inner wall properly, nor the part of the tread which is in contact with the ground.

☐ **Job 20. Check spare tyre.**

Check the tread depth, check for damage, check for wear and the pressure on the spare tyre, too. You should inflate the spare tyre to the maximum pressure recommended for high speed or high load running. Then, if you have a puncture, it is easier to carry a pressure gauge and let some air out rather than have to put some in!

SAFETY FIRST!
*Tyres which show uneven wear can tell their own story - if you know how to speak the language. If you find that a tyre is starting to wear more on one side then the other, or that the wear is uneven round the tyre, consult your specialist MG dealer or a tyre specialist. It probably means that something on the suspension or steering is out of alignment. Putting it right is probably just a matter of adjusting the front wheel alignment, but it could possibly mean worn or damaged suspension. Having it checked and put right now could save you heavier repair bills - including the cost of new tyres - later. Also see **Chapter 7, Getting Through the MoT.***

1,500 mile Bodywork and Interior - Around the Car

☐ **Job 21. Touch-up paintwork.**

21. Treat stone chips and scratches to prevent or eliminate rust. If rust is already evident, treat with a rust killer before applying touch-up colour paint. Allow the paint to harden thoroughly before using a polish.

☐ **Job 22. Aerial/antenna.**

22. Clean the sections of an extending chromium plated or stainless steel aerial mast. Wipe a little releasing fluid (not oil, which attracts dirt) on to the aerial and work the sections in and out a few times.

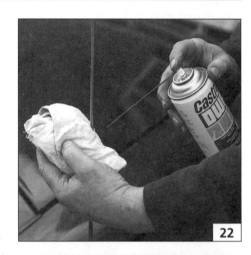

☐ **Job 23. Valet interior.**

23. Use a vacuum cleaner to remove dust and grit from the interior and carpets. Grit which has worked its way under the carpets can, in time, cut through them from the underside. Unless the carpets are stuck down, lift them and vacuum underneath. The small 12-volt vacuum cleaners which run off your car battery are not very efficient so, if you cannot use a domestic vacuum cleaner for this job, use the cleaner at a service station with a valeting facility. Proprietary upholstery cleaners are very efficient and well worth using if the upholstery or trim has become very grubby. Do not use domestic detergents or washing up liquid as some of them contain salt as a bleaching agent and this can attack the colour of the upholstery and also tends to rot stitching. Deep stains, such as oil, in a carpet will sometimes yield to white spirit or methylated spirit, and a solution of domestic washing soda in hot water is surprisingly efficient on oil and grease stains. Take deep stains out before cleaning the rest of the upholstery and always try any cleaner on an inconspicuous part of the upholstery first to make sure it does not remove the colour.

Do not use a detergent on seat belts. They should be washed with warm water and a non-detergent soap. Allow them to dry naturally and do not let inertia type belts retract until they are perfectly dry.

☐ **Job 24. Improve visibility.**

Traffic grime and diesel fumes can build up on the outside of the windscreen and resist the washing fluid in your car's screen washer. Give the glass a thorough clean with a proprietary glass cleaner and wipe the edges of the wiper blades with methylated spirit (industrial alcohol) to remove any grease.

1,500 mile Bodywork - Under the Car

SAFETY FIRST!
Always wear goggles when cleaning the underside of the car.
Read carefully the information at the start of this chapter on lifting and supporting the car.

☐ **Job 25. Clean mud traps.**

25A. The area up round the headlamp bowls under the front wings is a favourite place for rust to get a hold because of caked and often wet mud. Using the power jet hose at a service station will shift much of it but, when the car has dried, check underneath to make sure none has been missed.

25B. Another mud trap on Midgets is the lip of the front wing at the bottom of the wheel arch. There are no drain holes here, so hosing does not always clean it. The accumulated dirt has to be scraped and brushed out.

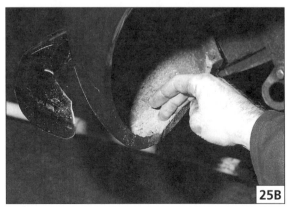

3,000 Miles - Every Three Months, Whichever Comes First

3,000 mile Mechanical and Electrical - The Engine Bay

First carry out Jobs 2 to 7

26A

☐ **Job 26. Adjust sparking plugs.**

26A. Remove the high tension leads from the plugs after numbering them to make sure you get them back in the right firing order. Use a socket set with a proper plug spanner which has a rubber insert to avoid damage to the plug insulators. Some special plug sockets also have an internal circlip to hold the plug when you lift the socket away. You can also get special 'wobble' extensions for your socket set which have a curve on the squared end so that the extension can rock slightly in the socket to avoid putting side pressure on the plug if you don't hold the extension quite straight.

26B. Check the sparking plugs to make sure they are in acceptable condition (see the colour illustrations on page 65) and then clean the electrodes with a brass brush - not a steel one - applied vigorously.

26B

26C. After cleaning, check that i) the round terminal for the HT leads is tight - check it with a pair of pliers - and ii) that the gap is correct. - see *Chapter 8, Facts and Figures.* In most cases, the gap will need closing and the best way to do this is to tap the earth electrode lightly with a pair of pliers or similar tool, checking the gap after each tap. If the gap is too small, open it by levering the earth electrode away from the centre electrode taking great care not to damage the centre electrode nor its insulation. When the gap is correct, the appropriate feeler gauge should slide in easily without being loose. If in doubt, renew the plugs. Running with old worn plugs is false economy but, having said that, don't change them just for the sake of it. Look for evidence of burning, bad staining or the earth electrode wearing so thin that it is in danger of breaking off.

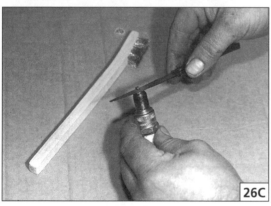

26C

26D. Finally, make sure the threads are clean, screw the plugs in the cylinder head by hand and tighten to the recommended torque. See *Chapter 8, Facts and Figures.* Carry out the next job before replacing the HT leads.

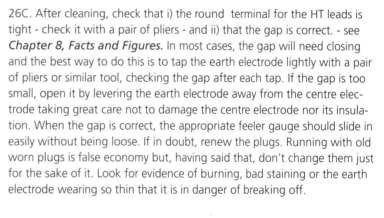

Spark Plugs Tightening
Ensure that the plug threads in the head are clear. Use a thread chaser if necessary. Screw plug in by hand until it is seated. New plugs with flat seats are turned a further 90 degrees with a spark plug wrench. Already used flat-seat plugs are turned by a further 15 degrees with the wrench.

INSIDE INFORMATION: An easy way of numbering the HT leads is to use dabs of typewriter correction fluid, marking the leads with one dab, two dabs and so on, with number one at the front. You need only mark the leads 1 to 3, the unmarked one must be 4. Alternatively, number them with strips of masking tape with the figures written on. Never assume that the gap on new plugs is correct. They are set to an average gap at the factory, but that may or may not be the right one for your engine.

26D

☐ **Job 27. Remove air trunking to the heater.**

948 cc, 1098 cc AND 1275 cc ENGINE ONLY

27. This is not strictly a service job but it makes access to the distributor so much easier. It also allows you to check that the trunking is free from damage and that it fits properly at each end. Leaks in the trunking, or at its ends, can let fumes into the inside of the car so, when you replace it after attention to the distributor, make sure it fits and is supported properly.

☐ **Job 28. Check HT circuit.**

28A. Clean the HT leads and check for signs of surface cracking, and loose connection where the lead fits on to the plug connector and into the distributor cap.

28B. These clips are not so easy to get at with the distributor fitted! Clean the distributor cap inside and out and check for any signs of 'tracking', burnt lines where carbon has lodged in a faint crack to provide a short circuit for the HT current. Any signs of tracking means that the cap could let you down with poor starting and bad running at any time as well as increasing your fuel consumption.

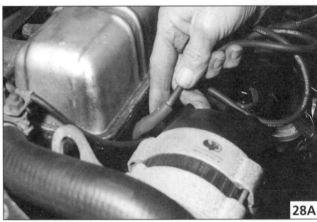

28C. Check also that the centre carbon brush still has plenty of length and that it is springy enough to bear on the centre of the rotor arm. Check the studs in the distributor cap for burning. Light burning can be cleaned up with fine glasspaper (better than emery paper because it does not leave any conducting dust behind).

28D. Check that the rotor arm fits firmly and not loosely on the centre cam of the distributor and check the end of it for burning. Again, light burning can be cleaned up but severe burning of either the cap studs or the rotor arm means renewal. Clean and check the insulated top of the coil. Again, tracking here can cause poor starting and misfiring.

INSIDE INFORMATION: If you have to renew either the HT leads or the distributor cap, mark the turrets of your existing cap with Tippex to match the markings on the HT leads. With a new cap, compare the positions of the markings with the old cap, using the depression where it locates on the body of the distributor as a reference point. On early cars you may still come across the older type of plug lead with a centre copper wire and split copper washers to hold the wire inside the terminals. The terminals that fit in the distributor cap and coil may also be the screw-in type and there may be radio suppressors either at the plug terminals or inserted in the HT leads. Modern resistive leads are much more efficient, as well as giving better suppression of radio interference, than the older type of wire-cored leads, the end terminals are usually moulded on to the leads and those at the distributor cap end are usually push-in. If you have the older type then, unless you are a stickler for originality for concours or other reasons, renew the leads, the cap and the coil, replacing them with modern components - the old ones will probably be well past their best. But make absolutely certain that the modern cap fits your old distributor perfectly and that the modern coil is the correct polarity.

Job 29. Check ignition LT circuit.

29. Check that the connections of the low-tension circuit at the coil and the distributor are firm.

Job 30. Distributor vacuum advance and retard pipe.

30. Check that the vacuum advance and retard pipe from the distributor to the carburettors is in good condition and fits tightly to its connectors.

Job 31. Distributor.

CARS WITH CONTACT BREAKER POINTS IGNITION ONLY

31. The distributor on a 948cc, 1098cc and 1275cc engine is tucked away down the right hand side of the engine where it is difficult to get at for anything other than checking the points gap and the points condition. On the 1493cc engine it is much easier to get at, higher up on the left hand side. You are not changing the points at this stage, that comes in a later service schedule. For now, unless they are burnt, you will just be examining them and setting the gap. With the ignition turned off, open the points with a small screwdriver. If they look burnt, it is a sign that they need renewing. You will probably need a new capacitor as well, as burnt points can be a sign of a faulty capacitor. We show you how to fit these in Job 72.

NOTE: on the later cars fitted with Lucas electronic ignition there are no points inside the distributor and no adjustment nor maintenance is necessary other than checking the timing if the distributor has been moved.

You should also take this opportunity to lubricate the distributor taking great care not to get grease or oil on the faces of the points. Smear just a trace of high melting point grease on the faces of the centre cam and allow a few drops of general lubricating oil to run down inside the points base plate to lubricate the mechanical advance and retard mechanism. If the car has been badly neglected from a service point of view, it does no harm to squirt a small amount of releasing fluid down under the baseplate before oiling to free the advance and retard mechanism should it have been sticking. An advance and retard mechanism which sticks or is jerky in operation can cause your engine to lose power. Should you get any oil or grease on the faces of the points, clean it off with methylated spirit but make sure this has absolutely evaporated before attempting to start the engine. All contact breaker distributors spark slightly at the points and, should this happen with methylated spirit vapour trapped inside, it could explode like a small bomb!

To set the points gap, turn the distributor shaft until the heel of the moving point is on one of the lobes of the centre cam. Slacken the adjusting screw and insert a feeler gauge of the appropriate thickness *(see Chapter 8, Facts and Figures)*. Adjust the moving point and tighten the screw when the feeler gauge is a sliding fit between the points (see Job 72). This will give you a points gap which is accurate enough for starting the engine but, to get the gap absolutely accurate, you need to use a dwell meter, see Job 33.

Job 32. Ignition timing.
You can time the ignition sufficiently accurately to get the engine running by turning the engine until the rotor arm is pointing towards the stud in the cap for number 1 cylinder and the timing mark on the crankshaft pulley is at the appropriate mark. In this position, slacken the clamp holding the body of the distributor, rotate it until the points are just about to open, and tighten the clamp. Static timing, however, cannot be as accurate as dynamic timing with a strobe lamp. Either have this done at an MG specialist or buy yourself a strobe lamp and follow the instructions that come with it.

☐ Job 33. Setting ignition dwell.

33A. Setting the points gap with feeler gauges is accurate enough for general running but, for spot-on accuracy and best fuel consumption, the gap should be set by using a dwell meter. Once again, this is a job that your MG specialist will do for you, or you can buy a dwell meter - DIY versions are not expensive - and learn to use it by following the instructions.

33A

33B. Once the distributor cap has been removed, first remove the rotor arm (33B.1) by pulling it off the centre rotor shaft. You're not changing the points at this stage, that comes later in the service schedule but with the ignition turned off, use a screwdriver to open the points up (33B.2) and see if they are badly pitted or burned. If there is any evidence of such marks, replace the points as shown earlier and replace the condenser as well because a faulty condenser will cause the points to burn. Since the heel on the points can wear down, you'll have to adjust the points gap. Turn the engine over by pressing on the fan belt and turning the fan, which will rotate the distributor shaft cam (33B.6). Stop turning when the heel on the points (33B.14) is at the top of the cam lobe (33B.3). Now slacken the screw (33B.8).

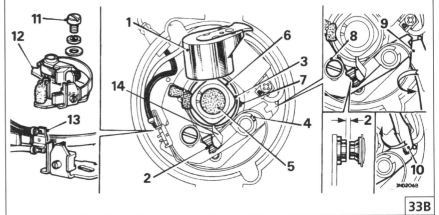

33B

33C. By inserting a screwdriver between the 'V'-shape in the base plate and the 'V' in the points (33B.9 and 33B.10) you will be able to open and close the points gap. Here you can see a feeler gauge inserted into the points gap. Adjust the gap until the feeler gauge makes contact with both sides of the points at once a tricky business it's easy to close the points up too far so that they snap shut as you pull out the feeler gauge and it's equally easy to leave them too far apart because it's difficult to discern when the feeler gauge is actually in contact. Still, you have to persevere!

☐ Job 34. Generator/alternator belt.

34A. There are two methods of checking the tension on the drive belt for the dynamo (alternator on later models). The first is to twist it as shown here. On the top run it should twist through about 90 degrees with moderate pressure. As a second check, there should be about 1/2 inch (12 mm) movement on the longest run when deflected with moderate thumb pressure. The deflection you are looking for is towards the pulley, pushing the belt into the grooves, not backwards and forwards.

34B. If the belt shows any signs of fraying or cracking it should be replaced. The modern type of belt with teeth on the inside can be checked properly only by taking it off. Look for signs of cracking between the teeth or polishing on the edges.

33C

INSIDE INFORMATION: Because it is difficult to check the modern type of belt without taking it off, it is wise to carry a spare as your car will not be driveable should the belt break (the sign is the ignition warning light coming on). Make sure, too, that you carry the right size spanners to be able to change the belt, and a piece of wood to tension it. With a new belt but no tools, you are still stranded!

34A

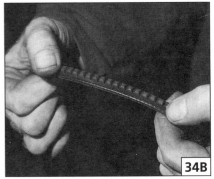

34B

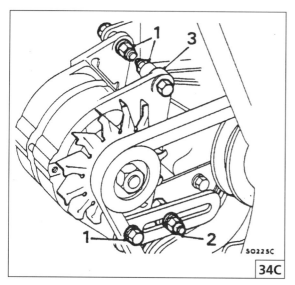

34C

34C. You will find slight differences in the method of mounting the dynamo or alternator depending on the model, but the principle is the same for all. First slacken off the mounting bolts and the adjustment bolts. If you are fitting a new belt, push the alternator or dynamo towards the engine and feed the belt over the pulleys. Then use a piece of wood between the engine and the dynamo or alternator to lever it out until you get the correct tension on the belt. Hold this tension while you tighten the adjusting nuts. With an alternator, lever against the end bracket rather than the body to avoid any risk of damage. Dynamos, with their heavy steel casings, are less susceptible to damage.

INSIDE INFORMATION: To make adjustment easier, slacken the bolts until the generator can be moved with moderate leverage on the piece of wood but not so slack that it flops down. Then, put a socket spanner on the adjustment bolts that goes through the long groove, lever the generator out and check the tension. Tighten the adjustment bolt and the generator will stay in that position while you tighten the other bolts. Don't overtighten a drive belt, it shortens its life and puts unnecessary strain on the end bearing of the generator.

☐ Job 35. SU carburettors.

OPTIONAL: SU carburettors can go out of tune quite often, especially when they are past their first flush of youth. If you wish to adjust them at this service, refer to Job 78 in the 6,000 mile service.

36A

☐ Job 36. Check air filters.

36A. On 948cc, 1098cc and 1275cc engines the air filter elements are in twin metal casings held by long through bolts with tubular spacers on the inside.

36B

36B. If the elements show just a slight soiling give them a light tap to remove any loose dust, and replace them with the soiled part turned to a different position. If, however, they are dirty, replace them.

36C

36C. On 1493cc engines, the filter elements are inside a single casing. The fuel pipe runs along the outside of the casing and this has to be unclipped before the casing can be removed.

INSIDE INFORMATION: Always clean the inside of the filter casings before fitting new elements and make sure that all fibre washers and gaskets are in good condition and seating properly when you tighten the casing bolts.

☐ **Job 37. Pipes and hoses.**

37A. Check all pipes and hoses in and around the engine bay for security and leaks.

37B. Particularly leak-prone is the oil cooler pipe. IMPORTANT NOTE: *Always* lock the hexagon on top of the oil cooler (it's 'built-in' and doesn't turn) before tightening the nut (arrowed). The radiator grille must first be removed. If the oil cooler top leaks because it has been twisted, renewal is the only answer.

3,000 mile Mechanical and Electrical - Around the Car

First, carry out Jobs 8 to 17, then 19 and 20.

☐ **Job 38. Hand brake travel.**

INSIDE THE CAR: Check the hand brake lever. It must be mounted securely and must stay firmly in the 'on' position when the button is released. Sometimes, if a hand brake slips off when pushed downwards, the ratchet and pawl mechanism is sticking and a squirt or two of releasing fluid will free them. However, it is more likely that the ratchet and pawl are worn and need replacing. Seek **SPECIALIST SERVICE** if you are in any doubt.

38. Pull the hand brake up. It should put the brakes on fully after three or four clicks of the ratchet. If the travel is excessive it can be adjusted, but don't adjust the hand brake cable until you have checked the adjustment of the rear brake shoes, see Job 125. The cable adjuster is a brass nut on the cable under the car. With the hand brake released, turn the adjusting nut half a turn at a time until the brakes are binding at three clicks and hard on at four. Check that, when the hand brake lever is released, the wheels are free to turn without binding.

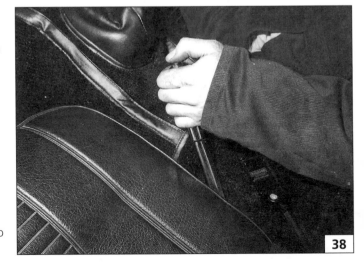

INSIDE INFORMATION: On cars which have been neglected, wheel binding when the hand brake is released is caused by the hand brake cable sticking because it has not been lubricated for years! If this is the case, and lubrication does not free it, seek specialist advice as there is a possibility that the inner cable has started to 'shred' inside the outer casing.

SAFETY FIRST!
Don't work under a car supported on axle stands while someone else is sitting in the car trying the hand brake. There is a risk that when they pull hard on the brake their movement could cause the car to slip on the axle stands. Make sure you are well clear of a raised car when someone is inside it. Read carefully the information at the start of this chapter on lifting and supporting the car.

3,000 mile Electrical and Mechanical - Under the Car

SAFETY FIRST!
Raise the front of the car after reading carefully the information at the start of this chapter on lifting and supporting the car.

☐ **Job 39. Steering rack.**

39A. Check that the steering rack is securely mounted to the body. Seen here without the radiator, for clarity; two bolts at each end of the rack hold it to aluminium brackets, which are in turn bolted to the crossmember. Also, check the pinchbolt holding the bottom end of the steering column to the rack. Tighten if necessary.

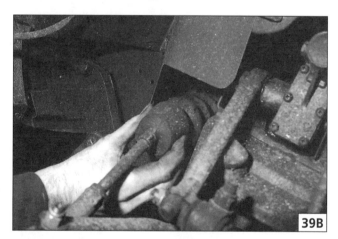

39B. Also, check the condition of the gaiter at each end. To check the right hand gaiter, turn the steering on to full left lock, and vice-versa. Squeeze and pull at the gaiters to check that there are no splits and that there is no cracking between the corrugations. If you find a gaiter that is in poor condition, particularly if it is split, don't wait until the next MoT, renew it now. If one gaiter needs renewing it is a fair bet that the other one is well past its prime, so renew both of them. As well as the safety aspect, it is false economy to wait. Gaiters are cheap, but steering racks are expensive.

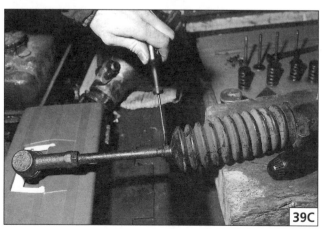

39C. Before you can renew the gaiter you will have to remove the track rod end ball joint, see Job 40. To remove the gaiter, undo the clips at each end. Sometimes these are both metal clips held by small nuts and bolts but, sometimes, the larger inner clip is a plastic pull-through ratchet type which has to be cut off. When you get the new gaiters you should get new clips with them. Our pictures show a rack off the car to make things clearer, but normally the job can be done quite easily with the rack in position.

3,000 MILE SERVICE

39D. When you remove the old gaiter you will lose any oil remaining in the rack, so this has to be replaced. Before you fit the smaller clip, use an oil can to inject the correct amount of oil into the gaiter. The capacity of the rack and the correct oil to use are given in *Appendix 1* and *Chapter 8, Facts and Figures.* If oil starts to dribble out before you have the full amount in, turn the steering to work the rack back and forth to distribute the oil. Add a little more to allow for that which dribbled out.

☐ Job 40. Track rod ends.

40A. Examine the rubber boots at each track rod end to check that they are not split or cracking. If they are, the track rod end will need renewing. In theory you can change the rubber boot without changing the track rod end but this is false economy as, if the boot has split, there is a good chance that the track rod end ball joint will be worn, or will soon wear, because water and road dirt has got in. In any case you will have to free the ball joint taper, which is the most awkward part of renewing the joint so, while you are about it, fit a new joint complete. They are not expensive. Even if the boot appears perfect, the joint may be worn. Test this by holding the wheel at 3 o'clock and 9 o'clock and turning it sharply one way and the other. If there is any looseness in the ball joint you will see and hear it.

40B. There are two types of tool you can use to free the taper and remove the track rod end, once the nut has been removed. One is like a pair of jaws with a large bolt to force them apart and the other is a large forked wedge which you drive in with a heavy hammer. Of the two, the forked wedge is probably the easier to use, and will deal with the most stubborn of tapers, but it ruins the rubber boot so, if you are removing the joint for another reason - say, to renew the steering rack gaiters - you will have to fit a new track rod end.

A third, time-honoured, method is to use two large hammers to 'spring' the taper. The hammers are brought together with a sharp blow simultaneously on each side of the taper housing in the steering lever. You may have to hit several times before you get the two hammers synchronised and the taper jumps free.

40C. Slacken the lock nut (arrowed) half a turn before you free the taper and, if you are just renewing the ball joint without renewing a steering gaiter, you can screw the new joint to within half a turn of the lock nut and then lock it. If you have to remove the locknut to replace a gaiter, unscrew the track rod end and either count the threads or measure the length of thread from the locknut to the end of the rod as a guide to fitting the new track rod end. Sometimes it's possible to see the mark on the thread where the locknut sat originally and to use this as a check marker. Don't forget to tighten the lock nut after you have fitted the new track rod end.

INSIDE INFORMATION: When you undo the self-locking nut on the old ball pin replace it with half a turn of thread to prevent the track rod jumping up into the air when the taper flies free. If, however, you put the nut back more than half a turn, you may have difficulty getting it off again as the ball pin will turn in its housing and there is nothing to grip to stop it. You might find the same problem when you fit the new track rod end. If the ball pin turns in its housing when you try to tighten the self-locking nut, use a long bar hooked under the chassis rail to force the track rod end downwards so that the taper of the ball pin is gripped in the end of the steering arm. Once the nut has gone tight it will pull the taper in and you can finish tightening it without fear of the ball pin turning.

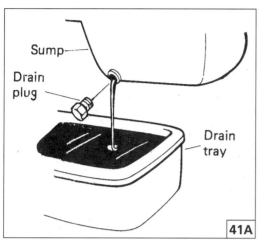

41A
Sump
Drain plug
Drain tray

Job 41. Drain engine oil.

If you are not draining the engine oil at this service don't forget to carry out Job 1, but wait until the car is lowered to an even keel so that you do not get a false reading on the dipstick.

> *SAFETY FIRST!*
> *Refer to the section on ENGINE OILS in **Chapter 1** before carrying out the following work.*

41A. Warm the engine a little before draining the oil so that the oil flows out more easily, but don't warm it so much that the oil becomes scalding hot. Running the engine until it will idle without using the choke should be sufficient.

Place a container under the drain plug with several sheets of old newspaper under the container to protect the garage floor from drips and spillage. Draining the oil can be a messy business!

41B. Remember to replace the drain plug once the oil has drained, and use a new copper washer which you can buy from the accessory shop or garage where you bought your oil. Buy it at the same time, then you don't forget it.

41B

> *SAFETY FIRST!*
> *Always wear gloves when draining old oil - see Chapter 1, ENGINE OILS. You may find that the sump drain plug is very tight. For some reason people feel compelled to overtighten drain plugs. Use a ring spanner rather than an open-ended spanner, which is more likely to slip or, if the plug is really tight, a socket with a long handle. Try to pull downwards to free the plug rather than sideways as there is less danger of jerking the car off the axle stands.*

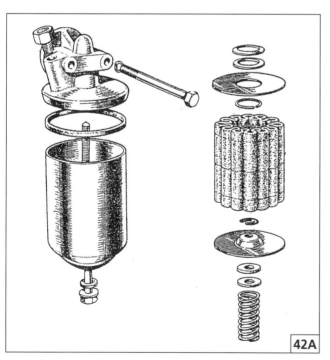

42A

INSIDE INFORMATION: The best container to use is a proper drain pan with a built-in funnel to pour the old oil away but, failing that, any container with enough capacity will do. The sump on 948cc, 1098cc and 1275cc engines holds 3.7 litres, so an old 5 litre oil container with one side cut away is large enough. On the 1,493cc engine the capacity is 4.5 litres which could make a 5 litre container on its side a little too full to lift out safely. Always dispose of old oil safely - never try to bury it or throw it down the drain. Your local council will have arrangements to take it off you.

Job 42. Remove oil filter.

Filters on 948cc, 1098cc and 1275cc engines come in two types, the early type which is a renewable element inside a steel canister with a fastening bolt at the bottom and the later type which is a thin metal disposable cartridge which screws into the filter housing. The filters sit on the right hand side of the engine at the front where they are none too easy to get at. You may find it easier to turn the front wheels on hard left lock and work through the triangular access hole as well as from underneath. The 1493cc engine uses only a disposable cartridge type filter and it is much easier to reach on the left hand side of the engine.

42A. This is the type of filter with a renewable element fitted to early 948cc, 1098cc and 1275cc engines. To remove it, first position your container under the filter, then loosen the centre bolt and allow the oil to drain out before finally undoing it and lifting the filter bowl away. Even allowing the oil to drain, it is still a messy job so have plenty of old newspaper around the floor of the garage.

42B. Inside the bowl the element may or may not be held by a spring clip, depending on the type.

42C. Almost certainly stuck to the bottom of the old filter will be a large washer.

42D. Beneath the washer is the spring referred to earlier. These sit on the inside of the container.

42E. On the outside, and towards the head of the bolt is a rubber seal and a washer. If you're extremely lucky, the rubber sealing ring between the container and the filter housing will have come away with the container but don't bank on it.

42F. In the majority of cases, the sealing ring will remain in the filter housing and will need to be prised out. A point from an old school drawing compass is ideal, as is a sharpened dart point. Scrape out any hardened or glued-in sealing ring that may remain.

42G. Disposable oil filters rarely come off by hand so a number of tools are available on the market to assist. Shown here (again an engine removed from the car for clarity) is a belt wrench but they come in other forms such as chain or three pronged finger. Most fit a 1/2 inch socket drive. It only needs a jolt to free the seal and then the filter will spin off.

☐ Job 43. Fit new oil filter.

43A. Thoroughly clean all components in the renewable element type container and make sure that all parts go back in the way they were removed. Apply a little grease or engine oil to the sealing ring and place in the lip of the housing. Grease should help the ring with the battle against gravity. Push the container against the spring and make sure that the lip sits squarely against the ring before finally tightening the long centre bolt.

INSIDE INFORMATION: On the early type filter with the loose element inside a bowl, replace the retaining bolt and washers, fit a new element and then, while holding the retaining bolt tight against the bowl, fill it with clean engine oil. This is to give the oil pump a supply of oil during the first critical few seconds when you restart the engine. Offer the bowl up carefully to the filter housing, engage the retaining bolt while holding it against the bottom of the bowl to minimise oil loss. You are bound to lose some, but try to keep the bowl as full as possible. Before finally tightening the bolt, turn the bowl back and forth to make sure it is seated home properly against the seal.

43B. Fitting a disposable cartridge filter is much simpler. Start by running a bead of clean oil round the rubber sealing ring.

43C. Offer the new cartridge up to the filter housing on the engine and screw it home. Don't force it, the cartridge casing is quite thin and easily distorted. Firm hand tightness is all that is needed. As you can see, access on the 948cc, 1098cc and 1275cc engines is rather restricted so you may have to work from the side as well as from underneath.

43D. On the 1493cc engine the filter is on the left hand side, higher up and sloping, where it is much easier to get at. This engine takes only a disposable cartridge filter.

☐ Job 44. Pour in fresh oil.

44. Lower the car to the ground and pour in fresh oil gradually so you do not get a sudden air lock in the rocker cover which can make the oil spurt out over the top. Dip the level occasionally, allowing time for the oil to drain down into the sump. After filling, run the engine for a few minutes to allow the oil to circulate and, in the case of a cartridge, to fill the filter. Switch off and dip the level again, finally topping up if necessary.

After running the engine, check underneath the car, especially in the areas of the sump plug and filter, making sure that there are no oil leaks.

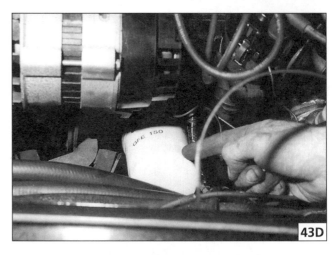

43D

> **SAFETY FIRST!**
> **Raise the front of the car off the ground once again, after reading carefully the information at the start of this chapter on lifting and supporting the car.**

☐ Job 45. Check front discs.

CARS WITH DISC BRAKES ONLY

45. Remove the wheels and check both sides of the front discs. Unless the discs are almost new, there are bound to be slight signs of ridging on the disc surface but it must not be excessive. New pads should not be fitted to a badly ridged disc. They will give very poor braking for quite a time until the friction surface beds into the ridges and, what's more, they will not last very long. As the disc wears it develops a slight ridge or rim on the circumference because the friction surfaces of the pads do not quite reach the outside of the disc. **SPECIALIST SERVICE.** The manufacturer lays down a minimum thickness for the disc but this is probably of academic interest to you as you need either double ended measuring callipers or a micrometer to measure it. Take the general condition of the disc - ridging and thickness of lip - into account and, if you have any doubts, seek the advice of a brake specialist.

44

☐ Job 46. Check front brake pads.

CARS WITH DISC BRAKES ONLY

45

46. You can check the wear on the front brake pads without carrying out any dismantling other than removing the wheels which makes it easier to see things. In this picture the Maidstone Sports Cars mechanic is holding a brand new pad alongside the calliper. The light coloured part is the friction material which goes in contact with the disc. Check the thickness of this friction material which you can do by looking end-on at the rear part of the calliper. The maker's recommendation is that the minimum thickness for the friction material is 1/16 inch (1.6 mm) but you have to bear in mind that you will not be checking the thickness again for another 3,000 miles or so, if the pads are approaching this condition, renew them early rather than late. It is normal for one pad to wear slightly more than the other but, if it appears that only one pad is doing the work and the other has hardly worn at all, it is a sign that the calliper is sticking. This means **SPECIALIST SERVICE.** Have the callipers checked by a garage.

46

Job 47. Renew front brake pads.

CARS WITH DISC BRAKES ONLY

> *SAFETY FIRST! and SPECIALIST SERVICE*
> *A car's brakes are among its most important safety features. Do not attempt any dismantling on your brakes unless you feel fully competent to do so. If you have not been trained in this work, but wish to carry out the jobs described here, we strongly recommend that you have your work checked by a qualified mechanic before taking the car on the road. See the section on BRAKES AND ASBESTOS in Chapter 1 for further important information.*

47A. First step in removing the old brake pads, should they need it, is to pull out the two split pins that hold the two spring clips in place. Note that the ends of the split pins will have been opened out and that you need to squeeze them flat with your pliers...

47B. ...before the split pin can be pulled out.

47C. With the split pin removed, lift away the retaining spring plate.

> *SAFETY FIRST!*
> *If the ends of the split pins shown any signs of breaking off, which will happen after the split pins have been closed and re-opened a number of times - fit new split pins. These are special items made specifically for your car so purchase them from your specialist.*

47D. It will be difficult to pull out the brake pads because the action of using the brakes will have kept them in close proximity to the brake discs. Use a pair of grips between the metal backing plate and the outside of the calliper to ease the pad away from the brake disc.

47E. You can now pull out the pads quite easily, together with the anti-rattle shim, if fitted. If you are fitting new pads, you'll probably have to push the pistons right the way back into the calliper, bearing in mind the following information about brake fluid being expelled from the top of the master cylinder.

You should also clean out the inside of the calliper in which the friction pad assemblies lie and scrape off any traces of dirt or rust from each piston.

INSIDE INFORMATION: Inside the brake callipers, as you will see when you pull out the pads, there is a piston on each side of the disc which pushes against the brake pads when you apply the brakes. The piston is itself pushed out by the hydraulic fluid which is forced down the brake pipe from the master cylinder. As you push the brake pads back against the piston, brake fluid will be pushed back up the pipe and into the master cylinder. Because you will need to push the pistons even further back into the calliper before fitting new pads the master cylinder will overflow. See below. Take a thin piece of lint-free cloth, moistened with brake cleaner or fluid and clean all around the piston (clean around the back like using dental floss).

47F

SAFETY FIRST!
DO NOT use any other cleaning fluid or abrasive.

If the pistons are rusty or damaged, **SPECIALIST SERVICE:** *have you garage fit replacement callipers. When pushing the pistons back in TAKE CARE NOT TO MARK OR DAMAGE THEM. Chances are that brake fluid will now overflow the master cylinder and make a terrible mess inside the engine bay - and do remember that brake fluid acts as a slow but efficient paint stripper. You could either siphon out some of the brake fluid from the master cylinder before pushing back the brake pads or take off the master cylinder cap and wrap large amounts of soft absorbent rags around the master cylinder so that any expelled fluid is quickly mopped up. You'll have to keep an eye on things to ensure that you don't have more fluid than the rags can cope with.*

47F. Slide each new pad into the calliper just to make sure that each one moves freely, scraping dirt out of the inside of the callipers if necessary. If you are refitting previously fitted pads, it is permissible to use a file - lightly! - to remove any rust that may have built up on the edge of each steel backing pad.

47G

You'll probably find a small sachet of this grease supplied with the new brake pads or you should be able to buy it from your parts supplier.

47G. Now smear a little more of that brake grease - but only a very small amount - on to the back of the pad, in other words on the back of the metal backing plate NOT on the friction surface of the pad, which is the part that pushes against the brake disc. Now the new pads can be fitted into place, together with the anti-rattle shim, where applicable, and the spring plate seen in 47C held down against the pads...

47H. ...while new split pins are slid back into place. (Don't re-use the old ones!) Use a screwdriver to open up the ends of the 'legs' on the split pins so that they cannot slip back out again.

Note that when the brakes are applied for the first time, the pedal will travel much further than normal until the pads reach their operating position. Only then will the brake pedal distance normalise. This will only take two or three applications of the pedal.

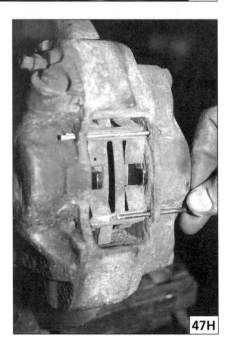

47H

SAFETY FIRST!
New brake pads will not work at their full efficiency until they have bedded in to the discs. Moreover, their surface can become glazed if they are applied very hard within the first few hundred miles. AP Lockheed advise that, for the first 150-200 miles (250-300 km), you should avoid braking hard unless you have to such as in an emergency, and that you allow extra braking distance until the new pads bed in to give their full efficiency.

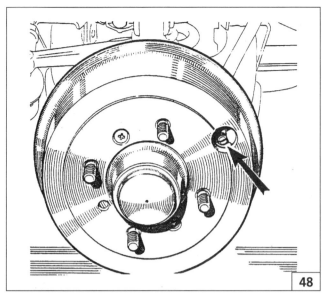

☐ Job 48. Adjust front brakes.

EARLY CARS WITH DRUM BRAKES ONLY

Early cars had drum front brakes and you can adjust these without taking the wheels off, though you have to lift the wheels free of the ground.

48. Remove the chromium plated hub cap and you will find a rubber dust plug covering a hole in the brake drum. Remove this and turn the wheel until, looking through the hole, you can see the head of a screw. You may need a torch or lead light to see it. This is the brake adjuster screw and there are two of them, one for each brake shoe. Turn each adjuster clockwise with a screwdriver to push the shoes out towards the drum until it goes hard and the wheel is locked. Apply the footbrake hard to centralise the shoes, then back each adjuster off until the wheel is just free to turn without binding. A light rubbing noise - more of a scuffing then a rubbing - can be ignored provided the wheel spins freely. Remember to replace the dust cover after adjustment.

☐ Job 49. Check front brake hoses.

49. Check the condition of the front brake hoses. Bend them quite sharply between your finger and thumb to look for cracking of the rubber. If you find any, or if the rubber looks deteriorated in any way, seek **SPECIALIST SERVICE** to have them replaced.

☐ Job 50. Lubricate front suspension.

50A. Lubrication of the front suspension and steering swivels is often neglected, but neglect here can be very costly as it is a prime cause of premature wear and MoT failure. There are three grease nipples on each side which need attention, one at the outer end of the bottom wishbone and two on the stub axle assembly. One of these feeds grease to the lower king pin bush and the other to the top bush. The lower one is on the inside of the stub axle but position of the top one varies depending on the age of the car. On earlier cars it is on the outside of the stub axle and on later cars it is on the front.

50B. INSIDE INFORMATION: If you find that you cannot get grease through any of the nipples it may be that the nipple itself is blocked. First, try placing a little rag over the nipple before pushing on the grease gun. If that doesn't work, unscrew it and hold it in the vice - or a self-gripping wrench if you haven't a vice - and try pumping grease through it by itself. Hold the nipple by the hexagon flats, not the thread. If you still cannot get grease through, the nipple needs replacing. Make certain you get a new grease nipple with the correct thread as accessory shops often stock them in both metric and Imperial sizes and sometimes Unified threads as well. Forcing in a grease nipple with the wrong thread will damage the stub axle and make it very difficult to fit a nipple with the correct thread.

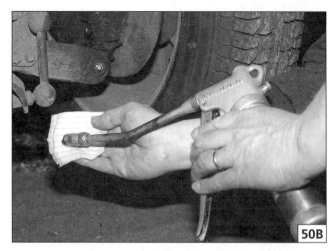

☐ Job 51. Refit front wheels.

51. Refit the front wheels and, on wire-wheeled cars, tighten the spinners. With bolt-on wheels, tighten the wheel nuts reasonably tight with the wheels off the ground and tighten them fully when the wheels are back on the ground with the weight of the car on them. We strongly recommend the use of a torque wrench to check the tightness of nuts on bolt-on wheels. If you do not have a suitable torque wrench, tighten the nuts fully and have the torques checked by a garage at the first opportunity. Wheel nut torques are important. Overtightened nuts can damage the threads, as well as possibly leaving you stranded by the roadside should you get a puncture and your car's wheel brace will not shift them! Nuts which are not tight enough can lead to loose wheels and very dangerous consequences.

INSIDE INFORMATION: When checking wheel nuts with a torque wrench, always slacken them slightly first and then torque to the correct figure. Otherwise an over-tightened nut will not show up. On cars with wire wheels, make it a habit every time you take the wheel off to grease the splines and the cone seating lightly. This will prevent the often encountered problem of a seized wire wheel which refuses to come off the splines after the spinner is undone.

SAFETY FIRST! and SPECIALIST SERVICE
A car's brakes are among its most important safety features. Do not attempt any dismantling on your brakes unless you feel fully competent to do so. If you have not been trained in this work, but wish to carry out the jobs described here, we strongly recommend that you have your work checked by a qualified mechanic before taking the car on the road. See the section on BRAKES AND ASBESTOS in Chapter 1 for further important information.

☐ Job 52. Adjust rear brakes.

52A. The rear brakes on early cars had a similar system of adjustment to the drum front brakes - see Job 48 - but had only one adjuster for each drum. Remove the dust cover from the adjustment hole in the brake drum and turn the drum until the hole is opposite the adjuster screw. Turn the adjuster clockwise with a screwdriver until it goes hard and the drum will not turn. Apply the footbrake hard to centralise the shoes, then back the adjuster off just enough to let the drum turn freely.

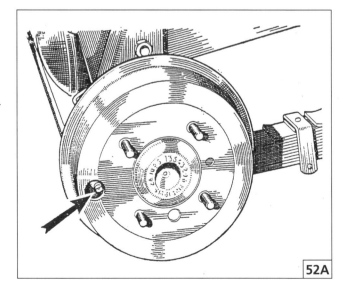

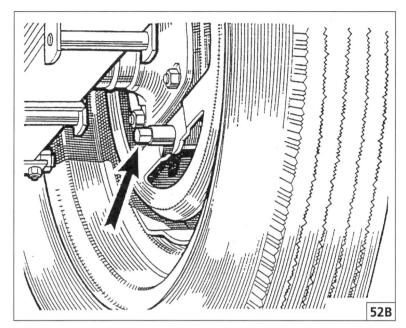

52B

52B. On later cars the rear brake shoe adjuster is on the inside of the backplate and has a small squared end to take the adjuster tool. Turn the adjuster clockwise (screwing it in to the backplate) until it goes hard and the drum is locked. Apply the foot-brake hard to centralise the shoes, then back the adjuster off just enough to let the drum turn freely

INSIDE INFORMATION: The later adjusters on Midget rear brakes, the ones with the small squared ends, are notorious for seizing and for the squared ends rounding off where people have tried to use an ill-fitting spanner to turn them instead of the proper tool. You can buy a brake adjusting tool at most accessory shops. It looks like a spanner but it is much thicker and has an open jaw at one end and a square hole at the other. Always use the square hole if you can, to get a better grip. If the squared end has rounded so much that you cannot get a grip, the adjuster needs replacing. This means strip-ping the brake shoes and, if you do not feel competent to do this yourself, it's SPECIALIST SERVICE time. If the adjuster is working OK, clean the threads with a wire brush and smear a layer of grease over them at the inner side of the back-plate, not the brake side. This will prevent the adjuster seizing before the next 3,000 mile service.

53

☐ Job 53. Rear check straps and bump stops.

53. Check that the large rubber bump stops, mounted on a platform on the rear axle just behind the wheel, are secure and in good condition. Attached to the same platform is the check strap for stopping the axle dropping too low on full rebound. Check that it is in good condi-tion and firmly attached at each end.

☐ Job 54. Lubricate hand brake linkage.

54A. Give three or four strokes of the grease gun to the nipple on the hand brake flexible cable. This is not the easiest of nipples to get grease through as it is not securely held. The cable waves about when you try to grease it. The nipple needs to be in good condition, and you need a lever type gun. The 'pump' type gun is almost useless for this job.

54A

54B. The swivel tree, just behind the rear axle, which equalises the hand brake pull to each rear wheel, has a grease nipple on the top. Be liberal with the grease here, it is a notorious wear point.

54C. Lubricate all the clevises at the ends of the hand brake rods using either engine oil or, as here, an all-purpose oil. IMPORTANT NOTE: Do NOT oil the brake components!

3,000 mile Bodywork and Interior - Around the Car

First carry out Jobs 18 and 21 to 25

☐ **Job 55. Wiper blades and arms.**

55. Run a few drops of oil on to the spindles of the wipers and check the operation and the 'sweep' of the arms. NOTE! Always wet the screen before running the wiper blades over it. Even a small amount of dust or grit can scratch the glass. If the sweep is wrong it can be altered by moving the wiper arms on the spindle splines. The method of fixing the arms varies. Sometimes there is a small screw to undo and on others there is a small catch, which you lift with a screwdriver after folding the arm back away from the screen. Make sure that the catch is engaged properly, or the fixing screw is tight, after adjustment.

☐ **Job 56. Check windscreen.**

Check the windscreen for scratches, cracks, chips or other damage. See *Chapter 7, Getting Through the MoT,* for what is and what isn't acceptable under UK regulations.

INSIDE INFORMATION: Small stone chips, cracks and scratches on a windscreen can often be repaired nowadays by windscreen specialists. If you find any damage, seek **SPECIALIST SERVICE** *as soon as possible. The longer you delay the more likely it is that weather will get in the crack or chip and make the repair more difficult. Early treatment could save you the cost of an expensive screen.*

57

Job 57. Rear view mirrors.

57. Check the rear view mirrors, inside and out, for condition, cracks and chips and make sure that they are securely mounted. A mirror which keeps going out of adjustment can let you down just when you need it most, and one that shakes and vibrates takes your eyes off the road ahead for too long - which could have nasty consequences!

Job 58. Check floors.

Lift the carpets and check for signs of wet on the floor underneath before any leaks are left for so long that you face the problem of rusted metal as well. Things are very cramped inside a Midget so, if you find any wetness, you will probably have to take the seats and the carpets right out to find the leak. Tracing leaks isn't the easiest of jobs, and sometimes the only way is to dry everything out and then get someone play a hose on the underside of the car, and over the bonnet while you look inside.

INSIDE INFORMATION: An effective, though slightly messy, way of tracing the source of a leak is to dry everything thoroughly and then sprinkle flour over suspect seams and joins while someone plays a hose on the outside. Small patches of wet show up immediately before the water has had a chance to run and confuse you. Leaks through spot-welded seams may be just an indication of the original sealant having dried out and crumbled, in which case a new dose of mastic sealant will cure the problem. But it might just be the first sign of something more serious, like rusting. If you are in any doubt about the soundness of any part of the floor pan structure, seek SPECIALIST SERVICE at once. An early professional repair will save you pounds later on as well as ensuring that your car is structurally sound and safe. After any repair or re-sealing, give the inside of the floor pan a coating of mastic such as body underseal. This doesn't normally dry right out but, when it is touch-dry, you can cover it with sheets of polythene to stop the carpets sticking to it.

59

Job 59. Chrome trim and badges.

59. Chromium plated trim strips and badges are a favourite place for body surface rust to start. Dribble some water dispersant or light oil behind them to stop the rust getting a start. If you find signs of rust or flaking paint round the trim, take it off and treat the area with rust killer and touch-up paint before it has a chance to develop into a large patch.

> **SAFETY FIRST!**
> **Raise the car off the ground only after reading carefully the information at the start of this chapter on lifting and supporting the car. Wear goggles when carrying out any cleaning, painting or undersealing underneath the car.**

3,000 mile Mechanical and Electrical - Under the Car

First carry out Job 25

Job 60. Inspect underside.

When the underside of the car is dry, inspect it for rust and damage to the underbody sealant. Look particularly for loose, flaking sealant and, if necessary, scrape it off with a flat bladed paint scraper. If you expose the metal, treat the area with rust killer, then a good quality paint and finally a new coat of sealant. While you are doing this you may also find small jobs to do like renewing clips for wiring, pipe runs and so on, and check particularly the brake pipes for corrosion. If the surface of the pipes look pitted and rough, seek SPECIALIST SERVICE and have the corroded pipes replaced with copper or cupro-nickel non-corroding pipes.

3,000 mile Mechanical and Electrical - Road Test

Job 61. Clean controls.

The door handles, steering wheel, switches and gear lever knob may well have become greasy from handling while you were carrying out the service. Clean them with a rag moistened with detergent upholstery cleaner in hot water.

Job 62. Check instruments and controls.

62. Switch on the ignition while sitting in the driving seat and check that all the warning lights which should come on, do come on. Warning lights which do not work are useless as warnings! Non-functioning may be just a case of a blown bulb, but it may be a symptom of deeper electrical trouble. If changing a bulb does not cure the problem, or if the warning lights fail to go out when they should, seek **SPECIALIST SERVICE** from an auto electrician. Check that all the switches are secure and working.

62

Job 63. Throttle pedal.

63A. Operate the throttle pedal several times to check that it is smooth over its complete travel. A throttle pedal which is stiff or, worse still, which sticks, can be dangerous as well as making driving a misery. If it is not as smooth as it should be, check the route of the throttle cable to make sure there are no sharp bends or kinks and check that the inner cable is not fraying where it comes out of the outer casing. Later throttle cables with a nylon inner sleeve are much smoother in operation that the older steel sleeve sort.

63B. If the fault for a jerky or stiff throttle pedal is not the cable, check the linkage at the carburettors for stiffness and lubricate if necessary.

63A

Job 64. Road test of brakes and steering.

> **SAFETY FIRST!**
> *Carry out the following tests only in daylight, in clear, dry conditions. Choose a quiet road when there are no other road users or pedestrians about. Use your mirrors to make sure there are no other vehicles following you before carrying out brake tests.*

63B

Only a proper brake tester at an MoT testing station can check the operation of the brakes accurately enough for the MoT test, but you can rule out some of the most obvious braking problems on a short road test in the following way. Always check the brakes at low speed first, before attempting to brake from higher speeds. Drive at about 20 mph, dip the clutch and, with your hands only lightly gripping the wheel, try braking first gently, then harder, though there is no need to do an 'emergency' stop.

Ideally, the car should pull up in a perfectly straight line. If the steering wheel kicks in your fingers, if there are any 'clonks' or other noises from underneath, if the car drifts heavily to one side as you brake, or if the brake pedal does not feel firm in operation, drive home very slowly and carefully to investigate further.

If all seems well, repeat the braking tests from a higher speed, say about 40 mph. Again, the car should, ideally, pull up in a straight line. If it drifts just gently to the left when you are on the nearside of the road, this may be due to road camber. Try to repeat the test on a non-cambered stretch of road or find a one-way street where you can try on the other side of the road to see if opposite camber has the same effect.

Check that the steering feels positive, does not kick back unduly over rough surfaces and that the car runs in a straight line when you are holding the steering wheel only lightly. Again, slight drifting may be due to road camber, but more persistent drifting needs investigating. Check that the steering self-centres when accelerating out of both left and right hand turns and, if you can find a suitably deserted stretch of road, pull the car from side to side to see that it straightens itself up. This check can be carried out at quite low speed, 15 to 20 mph is sufficient to show up any faults.

Braking and steering are a vital part of a car's safety. If you find any faults, or even if you are uneasy about anything, seek SPECIAL-IST SERVICE before you carry on using the car.

6,000 Miles - or Every Six Months, Whichever Comes First

6,000 mile Mechanical and Electrical - The Engine Bay

First carry out Jobs 2 to 6 then 27, 28, 34, 36 and 37

The first part of this section is carried out with the engine cold, partly for safety reasons - the risks involved in possible fuel spillage when changing the fuel filter near hot components - and partly for comfort and ease of working.

65A

☐ **Job 65. Cooling system.**

SAFETY FIRST!
Work on the cooling system only when the engine, and thus the coolant - is cold. When it is hot, the system is under pressure and you could get a nasty scald if you remove any caps or undo any hoses.

65A. Before starting any work on the cooling system, remove the pressure cap - and remove it slowly just in case there is any residual pressure in the system.

65B. Check the cooling system for leaks and all hoses for tightness and condition. Squeeze the large radiator hoses. If they go soft and soggy under your fingers the walls have started to collapse. Listen also for any cracking sounds which indicate that the hose is so old it has hardened and could give way. A hose which bursts always bursts in the most awkward possible place, so change any suspect ones now.

Pay particular attention to the heater hoses - they are often neglected. When heater hoses are tight up against the heater like this, the clip may not be gripping the end properly but it is not always easy to spot slight leaks. If you see any signs of coolant staining down the outside of the heater, undo the hose and reposition it slightly away from the heater casing.

948cc, 1098cc AND 1275cc ENGINES ONLY

65C. Not easily seen is this by-pass hose (between the cylinder head and water pump) shown here for clarity on an engine removed from the car. The best way to check this hose is to grope around and feel for any leaks. If one is apparent, the job is a little outside the scope of the home repairer, unless you feel capable of the cylinder head removal/replacement required, and help from a Sprite/Midget specialist should be sought. Concertina replacement hoses are available but their life span is suspect.

65B

65C

INSIDE INFORMATION: The heater matrix inside the casing is sometimes damaged when people exert a lot of force on a recalcitrant hose clip or pull and twist too hard on a hose which has stuck to the pipe. If an old heater hose does not come free easily, cut it through with a hacksaw and, if necessary, cut through the hose clip at an angle - but take great care not to cut into the heater pipe. Much the same applies to renewing one of the larger hoses. When you buy a new hose you may find it very tight to get on to the radiator or engine connection. Sometimes even the correct size hose seems too small. A useful tip is to smear the inside lightly with waterproof grease and then use a tapered glass bottle - like an orange squash bottle - as a mandrel to open the end of the hose slightly before fitting it.

☐ Job 66. Check coolant.

66A. An easy way to check the strength of the antifreeze in your coolant is to use a hydrometer, similar to the one used to check a battery but with a different scale. The float inside will indicate the strength of the antifreeze and, if it is too low, top up with neat antifreeze, replace the cap and run the engine for just a moment or two to circulate it but not enough for the coolant to get hot, then check the reading again. Don't take chances and guess that the antifreeze is strong enough, a ruined radiator - or even engine - is a high price to pay for not taking a little extra trouble.

66B. On 1493cc engines you check the coolant, and fill the system, through a plug on the top of the thermostat housing.

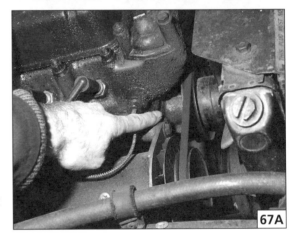

INSIDE INFORMATION: Be very careful about spilling antifreeze; it will strip your paintwork as effectively as any paint stripper even though it takes longer. Should you spill any, even diluted in the coolant, wash it off with plenty of cold water at once.

☐ Job 67. Check water pump.

67A. Check the water pump for leaks. It isn't always easy to spot leaks here, but look for tell-tale signs of coolant staining on the timing chain cover at the front of the engine and behind the pump where the leaking coolant may have been blown back by the fan.

67B. Water pumps on early engines had a lubricating plug in them arrowed in our line drawing. Unscrew the plug, screw in a grease nipple and give just one stroke of the grease gun. Overgreasing under pressure will force grease past the internal seals and may even start the pump leaking.

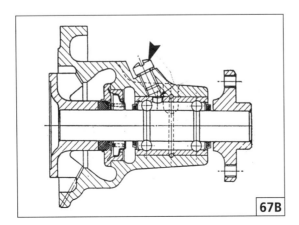

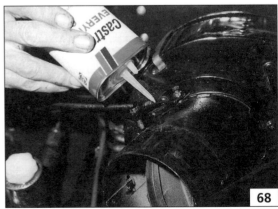

☐ Job 68. Lubricate heater controls.

68. Lubricate both heater controls, the fresh air valve shown here and the coolant valve on the engine. Dribble a few drops of oil on both the spindle and the inner cable control.

69.

☐ Job 69. Check fuse box.

69. Check that all the connections to the outside of the fuse box are tight, lift the cover and check that all the fuses are tight and have clean connections. This is particularly important if you have just bought the car as it isn't unknown for fuses to have been 'repaired' with pieces of wire and even bunched-up aluminium foil! If you find this, and the new fuse blows when you fit it, seek **SPECIALIST SERVICE**.

☐ Job 70. Lubricate dynamo.

EARLY CARS ONLY

70A. On early cars which have a dynamo instead of an alternator there will be a lubrication point for the rear bearing (arrowed). In most cases it will be a spring-loaded ball in the centre of the rear end plate as shown here. Push the end of an oil can in and squirt just a few drops inside. Don't over-oil - Lucas say that three drops each service is sufficient.

70B. It's just possible that you may have a very early dynamo on which the lubrication point is a tubular brass cap coming out of the rear end plate, at an angle. When you unscrew it you will find a spring and a felt wick inside. Take the spring and wick out of the brass cap, half-fill the cap with high melting point grease, replace the spring and wick and screw the cap back. Lubricate the tachometer drive on Frogeye models.

70A.

☐ Job 71. Fit new sparking plugs.

OPTIONAL: Fit new sparking plugs after checking that the gaps are correct. Some owners feel it is unnecessary to change a sparking plug that seems in good condition and working perfectly, but plugs fall off gradually in performance with age so you may not notice the deterioration in engine performance and economy. In any case, don't run plugs longer than 12,000 miles.

☐ Job 72. Renew contact breaker points and capacitor.

Like plugs, the efficiency of contact breaker points falls off gradually in normal use so that you get a fluffy rather than a sharp break in the low tension current. This means that the coil cannot deliver its full voltage to the plugs so you get a fall off in engine performance. You can't see any fall off in performance of a capacitor by examining it but, like other electrical components, the efficiency does deteriorate, shortening the life of the points. Both points and capacitors are so cheap that it is false economy to try to extend their life.

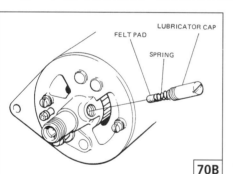

LUBRICATOR CAP
FELT PAD
SPRING

70B.

The distributor on 948cc, 1098cc and 1275cc engines is low down on the right hand side which makes replacement of the points and capacitor a very awkward job. We strongly recommend that you remove the distributor and take it to the bench for this job. To make things easier to get at, first remove the air trunking to the heater (Job 27). Then remove the distributor cap, disconnect the vacuum advance and retard pipe from the distributor, slacken the clamp bolt holding the distributor to the engine and lift the distributor out. It is driven by an offset dog which means that it can go back only one way so, provided you do not turn the engine over while the distributor is out, you will not upset the ignition timing.

Early cars were fitted with an older design of distributor which used separate fixed and moving points. This older design distributor can be easily identified as the connection for the low tension lead from the coil is a plastic block which is a sliding fit in the distributor body and which lifts out when you remove the distributor cap. The distributor on later cars uses a 'quick-fit' points design where the fixed and moving point are removed and replaced as an assembly. There are two types of 'quick-fit' points, one of which can be fitted to most of the older type of distributors as a direct replacement. The latest type, for the Lucas 45D distributor, needs a simple wiring alteration to change the terminal at the end of one of the wires inside some older distributors. If you have any doubts which type of points are fitted to your distributor then, before you buy a new set, drop into an MG Specialist or, indeed, any Rover main dealer, and ask if the person in the parts department would look under the bonnet to check which type you have.

The older type of separate fixed and moving points are no longer stocked by many accessory shops but they are available from some and at autojumbles from some dealers in 'new old stock' components. We would advise that, if possible, your older distributor is converted to take the later type of points but, in case it cannot be or you want to retain the older type for originality, we will run through the procedure for changing the early type points.

72A. This is the older design of points where (72A.1) is the plastic terminal block to take the low tension lead from the coil, (72A.2) is the fixed points held by a screw (not shown), (72A.3) is the moving points, (72A.4) is the fixing nut, (72A.5), (72A.6) and (72A.7) are an insulating sleeve and washers, (72A.8) is the capacitor also held by its own screw and (72A.9) is the wire which has to have its terminal changed to suit the latest type of 'quick-fit' points assembly. The wire from the capacitor also has a different end terminal for these points but, if you buy a new capacitor, it will come with this later terminal.

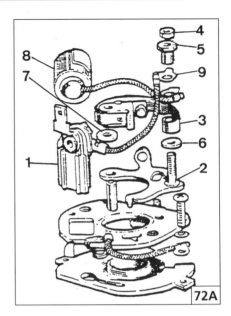

To remove the points, undo the small fixing nut (72A.4), lift out the insulating sleeve (72A.5), lift off the wires from the low-tension connector and the capacitor and then lift off the moving point. Under the moving point are two insulating washers, (72A.6) and (72A.7). Lift these off and keep them carefully, sometimes you get new ones with a points set, sometimes not. Then undo the screw which holds the fixed point (72A.2), and lift it off its post. Then undo the screw which hold the capacitor and lift it out.

Fitting the new points is an exact reversal of taking out the old ones. First fit the new capacitor, then fit the new fixed point but do not fully tighten its fixing screw. Replace the insulating washers (72A.6) and (72A.7), then the moving point, the two wires from the capacitor and the low tension terminal, and make sure that the insulating sleeve (72A.5) is correctly in position before tightening nut (72A.4) so that the spring of the moving points is completely insulated from the fixed point.

Contact breaker points renewal

1. Points gap
2. Pivot post
3. Distributor shaft cam
4. Baseplate lubrication point
5. Distributor shaft retaining screw
6. Fixing screw
7. Adjustment "V" slot
8. Wiring connections retaining nut
9. Insulating bush

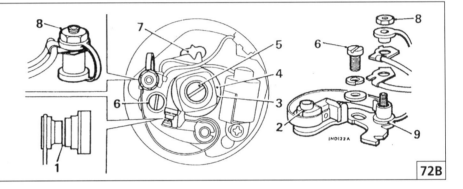

72B. This is the first type of 'quick-fit' points assembly which is a direct replacement for the old type of separate fixed and moving points. The pivot post (72B.2) is hollow and fits on the post which carried the old fixed point. The terminals on the wires from the capacitor and the low tension terminal are the same as the old type, but, instead of a separate insulating sleeve and washer, this assembly uses two linked insulating sleeves (72B.9).

72C. This is the latest type of 'quick-fit' points assembly for the Lucas 45D distributor where the wires from the capacitor and the coil slide into spring clips instead of being held by a nut.

72D. To set the points gap with any type of points, turn the centre shaft of the distributor until the heel of the moving point is on one of the four lobes of the centre cam. Slacken the screw holding the fixed point and adjust it until the correct feeler gauge will just slide between the two points. Tighten, but don't over-tighten the screw holding the fixed point. Test the gap with the heel of the moving point on the other three lobes of the cam. If you get a wide variation in the gaps, it means that the bearings of the distributor centre shaft are worn. The car will still run if you set the points on the cam lobe which gives the smallest gap but, for best

efficiency, the distributor should be replaced. Setting the gap with a feeler gauge is accurate enough to get the engine running but, for the best performance and economy, the gap should be tested and set using a dwell meter, see Job 33.

INSIDE INFORMATION: New points are covered with a protective film of grease which has to be cleaned off the points faces. Use a rag moistened in methylated spirit. Before fitting the new points, dribble a few drops of oil down inside the distributor base plate to lubricate the

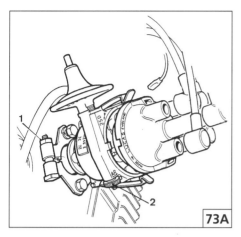

73A

mechanical advance and retard mechanism and smear just a trace of high melting point grease on the four lobes of the distributor cam. Take care not to get grease on the faces of the points. For some reason, many people seem to think that the screw holding the fixed point has to be forced home very tight with a large screwdriver. You often find screws on which the slot in the head has been mauled. If this is the case with your car, get a new screw when you buy the new points; you do not get a new one with the points set.

☐ Job 73. Ignition timing.

73A. In this line drawing of the Lucas 25D distributor (shown with the cap and leads partially removed), (73A.1) is the clamp bolt which you loosen to remove, or time, the distributor, and (73A.2) is the vernier timing adjustment for 'fine tuning' the timing. Some distributors are not fitted with a vernier adjuster. If yours has one, set it in the middle of its travel.

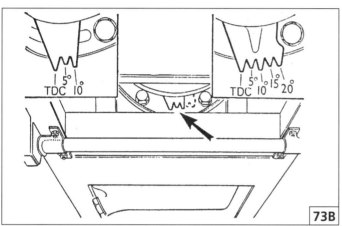

73B

Tighten the clamp bolt lightly, (73A.1) remove the distributor cap and turn the engine until the rotor arm is pointing towards the stud in the cap which feeds number 1 sparking plug and the contact points are just opening. Sometimes, this position is not easy to determine. It helps if you disconnect the low tension lead from the side of the distributor and connect a lamp and battery (any low voltage will do) between this lead and engine earth. The lamp will light when the points are closed and, as you turn the engine, the position when the points just open is indicated by the lamp going out.

73B. Now look at the front crankshaft pulley where you will see a notch in the rim and behind this, on the timing cover, a serrated pointer. Depending on the age of the engine, this will have three, five or six teeth, each tooth indicating a certain degree of ignition advance. Check that the notch in the pulley is opposite the correct degree of advance for your engine - see **Facts and Figures, Chapter 8.** If it is not, turn the engine until it is and return to the distributor. Without turning the engine, turn the vernier adjuster until the contact breaker points are just opening. If the vernier has insufficient travel, or if one is not fitted, slacken the distributor clamp bolt and rotate the distributor slightly. Tighten the clamp bolt after adjustment.

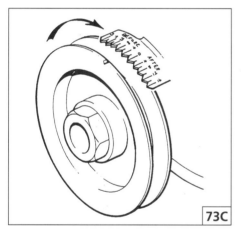

73C

73C. On 1493cc engines, the toothed scale is mounted over the top of the crankshaft pulley and has Top Dead Centre in the middle of the teeth, marked 0. The teeth each side of this show the degrees of advance (before) and retard (after) TDC.

73D. Static timing is sufficiently accurate to get the engine started and running but, for maximum efficiency and economy, the timing should be checked dynamically with a strobe lamp. You can either buy a strobe lamp at an accessory shop and follow the instructions or get a garage to check it for you.

73D

INSIDE INFORMATION: The size of the points gap affects the timing so always set the points gap before timing the ignition. Use a dwell meter to set the gap accurately before using a strobe lamp. If you buy a strobe lamp, get one with a Xenon light. The cheaper ones with a neon light work all right but the light is difficult to see in bright daylight and almost impossible to see in sunlight. It helps to see the timing marks if you rub a piece of chalk over them first.

When you have the distributor on the bench, you can check that the vacuum advance and retard is working. Sucking on the advance and retard pipe with your mouth is not often very efficient, nor pleasant, but you can make an efficient tester by reversing the washer in an ordinary bicycle pump so that it sucks instead of pumps. Attach the flexible connector on the end of the pump to the advance and retard pipe on the distributor and gently draw the pump handle back. As you do so, you should see the baseplate carrying the contact breaker move. Don't jerk the pump handle back hard or you could create enough suction to split the diaphragm in the distributor.

Job 74. Clean fuel filter and pump.

948cc AND 1493cc ENGINES ONLY

> *SAFETY FIRST!*
> *Disconnect the battery and read the precautions given in Chapter 1, Safety First! before doing any work on the fuel system.*

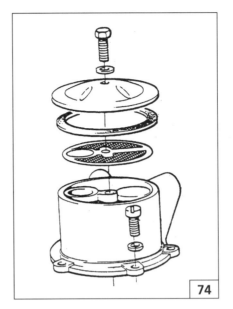

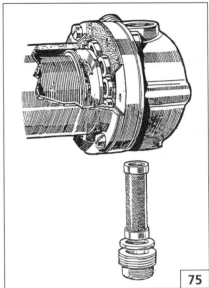

74. 948cc and 1493cc engines are fitted with an AC mechanical fuel pump with a filter under the top cover. Remove the centre bolt - don't lose the fibre washer - and lift the cover off. Underneath is a circular gasket and a flat gauze filter. If the filter is dirty, rinse it in clean petrol. Under the filter is the sediment bowl which you should clean out. Replace the filter, gasket and cover but don't over-tighten the centre bolt. The body of the pump is diecast, and the threads strip quite easily.

Job 75. Clean fuel pump filter.

1098cc AND 1275cc ENGINES ONLY

75. 1098cc and 1275cc engined cars have an SU electric fuel pump which contains a filter under a plug in the main body. Several types of SU pump have been fitted over the years, and it is quite possible that a later model pump has been fitted to an early car as an exchange unit, so we can only be general about the position of the filter. Our line drawing shows a typical position for it. Undo the plug, remove the filter, which may brass or plastic gauze, and rinse it in clean petrol before replacing.

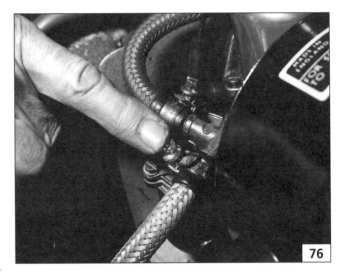

Job 76. Fuel connections.

76. Check all the fuel line connections from the pump to the carburettors to make sure there are no leaks and that the pipes are not chafing. IMPORTANT NOTE: on 1098cc and 1275cc cars fitted with SU electric pumps, the ignition must be switched on to pressurise the system before any leaks will show. On 948cc and 1493cc cars with AC mechanical fuel pumps, the engine must be running to pressurise the system.

Job 77. Top up carburettor dashpots.

77. Unscrew the dashpot caps on the SU carburettors and lift out the plungers. These plungers are dampers to stop the piston and needle in the carburettor fluttering and to hold the piston steady on hard acceleration. If they are dry you will get poor pick-up and poor acceleration. Top the dashpots up with engine oil or general lubricating oil to the top of the hollow stem of the piston.

☐ **Job 78. Set carburettors.**

SAFETY FIRST!
Read carefully the information in Chapter 1, Safety First! especially that regarding the safety hazards surrounding petrol (gasoline). In addition, note that you will have to run the engine with the air cleaners removed. There is a very slight risk of carburettor flashback, so don't get your face or your clothing too close. Also, have a workshop-sized fire extinguisher handy and make sure it is a type which can be used on petrol fires. If a fire should break out, turn off the ignition immediately to stop the engine and fuel pump and prevent any more petrol being pumped through. Because of the fire risk, and because of the very real danger of exhaust fumes, carry out the next part of this work out of doors.

Many owners fight shy of setting up twin carburettors but the job can be done at home with the simplest of tools and a little care. It helps if you have a carburettor balancing tool, but the job can be done without it. What is essential is that the sparking plugs, contact breaker points, ignition timing and valve clearances are all set correctly. You should by now have dealt with the ignition jobs, but if your tappets are clattery, attend to Job 114 to set the clearances correctly before carrying out this work.

The first job is to ensure that the pistons are free in the carburettor dashpots. Remove the air cleaners and, with your finger, lift each carburettor piston in turn and let it drop. It should fall smoothly and stop at the bottom with a slight 'clunk'. If it sticks or hesitates, you need to take the dashpot off for cleaning. Before you do this, check the throttle spindles for wear by trying to rock them.

INSIDE INFORMATION: There is a lot of uninformed talk about wear at the throttle spindles. Serious wear will affect the efficiency of the carburettor all the time, but slight wear will allow air leaks only at tick-over when the depression at the throttle spindles is high. Once past fast tick-over, slight wear at the spindles will have no measurable effect.

78A. Some cars will be fitted with carburettors that have three holding screws for the dashpot, and these three screws will be offset so that the dashpot can be fitted in one position only. However, some carburettors have only two screws, or three equally-spaced screws, so there is a danger of putting the dashpot back in a different position. To be on the safe side, mark the side of the dashpot and the body of the carburettor with Tippex or a felt-tipped pen before taking out the screws. Lift the dashpot up slowly after removing the screws. Inside you will find the piston and a long, whippy coiled spring. If you are not careful, this will bounce off on to

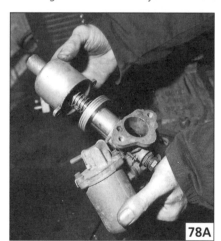

the floor and, if it gets distorted, you will need a new one. One end of the spring will have a smaller diameter coil than the rest. This is the end which fits inside the piston.

78B. Pistons usually stick in the dashpots because they need cleaning. Use only petrol or methylated spirit to clean the inside of the dashpot and the grooved ring of the piston. Don't use anything abrasive, even as mild as metal polish. Be careful not to bend the needle while you are cleaning and testing the piston drop. You will have now two types of needle in the piston, one rigid and one spring loaded so that it is 'floating'.

When you have cleaned it the piston and dashpot thoroughly you can test by the piston drop. Plug the two large air transfer holes in the piston with something like Plasticine, hold the dashpot upside down, put the piston in and put a nut, bolt and washer through one of the dashpot holes. Lift the piston until it touches the washer and let it drop. It should drop easily and smoothly, and should take between five and seven seconds. Remember to remove the Plasticine plugs afterwards.

78C. **CARBURETTORS WITH RIGID, NON-FLOATING NEEDLES.** If the piston drop is OK with the dashpot off the carburettor, it should also be OK when the dashpot is bolted back on, and the jet adjusting nut is in its highest position. You may find, however, that you do not get an audible 'clonk' at the end of the drop when the jet adjusting nut is in its lowest position. This is a sign that the jet needs centring. First, disconnect the rod between the jet lever and the jet head, then undo the union holding the nylon

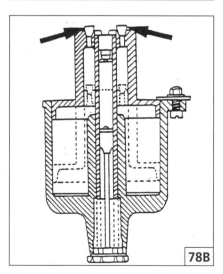

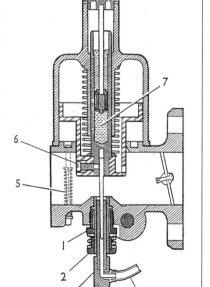

feed tube into the base of the float chamber and withdraw both the jet and the tube together. Don't try to separate them. Undo the jet adjusting nut and take off the lock spring. Replace the adjusting nut without the spring, screw it to its topmost position and replace the jet and feed tube.

Slacken off the large jet locking nut until you can just rotate the jet bearing with finger pressure. Now, with the damper removed, press down on the top of the piston with a pencil or something similar to press the piston down on to the jet bridge. Tighten the locking nut and try the piston drop with the adjusting nut fully up and fully down. If the piston still hesitates, repeat the centring until it falls smoothly and stops with a clonk. Remember to replace the locking spring and connect the feed tube to the float chamber after this operation. Set the jet adjusting nut so that, when you look down inside with the dashpot and piston off, the top of the jet is just level with the bridge piece. This will give a good starting point for setting the mixture.

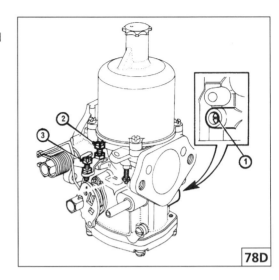
78D.

78D. On later HIF carburettors, mixture adjustment is by the mixture adjustment screw (78D.1) - turn it by small increments in or out until the fastest, smoothest engine speed is obtained. Now set the idle speed using the throttle adjusting screw (78D.2). Finally adjust the fast idle speed by pulling out the choke until the arrow on the carburettor fast idle cam is aligned with the adjustment screw. Turn the adjusting screw (78D.3) as necessary to obtain the specified fast idle speed. (Illustration, courtesy Rover Cars)

☐ **Job 79. Balancing the carburettors.**

For this job, the engine needs to be ticking over at its normal operating temperature, so warm it up before you start. Disconnect the choke cable from the carburettors.

79A. There's no mystique about twin carburettors, they're just two carburettors joined by spindles to operate as one. Before any adjustments can be made, they should be freed from each other by slackening the spindle clamps on the throttle and choke linkages illustrated.

79A.

INSIDE INFORMATION: A simple, very cheap, but invaluable tool for this job is a length of hose - heater hose or even garden hose is ideal - about 12 inches (30 cm) long. You use this to balance the air flow through the carburettors.

Before you can set the mixture, you have to balance the air flow. With the engine ticking over, and the air cleaners removed, hold one end of the hose to each air intake in turn and listen to the hiss. You are not listening for loudness, you are listening for pitch. With a little practice, you will be surprised how easy it is to detect a change in pitch of the hiss as you move from one intake to the other. Slacken the pinch bolts connecting the throttle and choke shafts to each carburettor as

79B.

described above, and bring the hiss at both intakes to the same pitch by turning the idle speed screw of one carburettor either in or out. When they are both at the same pitch, unscrew each one by an equal amount to bring the engine speed down to its slow idle revs as specified in *Chapter 8, Facts and Figures.*

79B. It would be really helpful to buy a carburettor balancer such as the type marketed by Gunson's used here. This accurately measures the air flow through each carburettor and takes the guess work out of the job, although a trained ear could judge the 'hiss' of the inlet air. All balancing meters fit onto the carburettor intake and measure the ingoing air velocity on a scale. First check that each carburettor is running at the same speed by placing the balancer over the intake of one carburettor, then the other. Turn the throttle adjusting screws as necessary until the intake air passing through each carburettor is the same, as indicated on the balancer scale. Once they're balanced, turn the throttle adjusting screws on both carburettors by the same amount so that the idle speed is as specified in *Chapter 8, Facts and Figures.* Turning both the screws by equal amounts alters the tickover while keeping the carburettors in balance. Carry out the mixture adjustments as described earlier. Re-check the idle speed and when satisfied, re-tighten the spindles ensuring that there is a small gap between the peg at the end of the spindle and the lower part of the fork. The gap size is not critical but that both are identical is.

☐ Job 80. Setting the mixture.

80. With the engine ticking over, but before replacing the air cleaners, put a long, thin screwdriver or length of stiff wire in the intake of the front carburettor and lift the piston by about 1/32 inch (1 mm). If the engine speed increases, it indicates that the mixture strength of the front carburettor is too rich. If the speed immediately decreases, it indicates that the mixture is too weak. If the speed momentarily increases very slightly, then settles down, the mixture strength is correct. Adjust the mixture strength by raising (to weaken) or lowering (to richen) the jet adjusting nut, indicated in our picture.

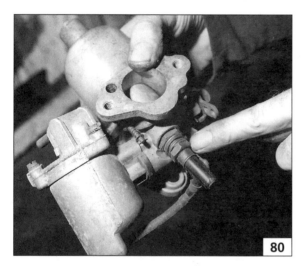

80

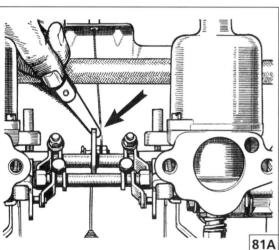

81A

When the mixture on the front carburettor is correct, check the mixture on the rear carburettor. You will probably have to check the mixture at each carburettor several times because the carburettors are interdependent. You may also find that, when the mixture is correct, the engine idle speed has increased. Bring it back to specification by unscrewing each slow running adjustment screw by the same amount.

When the mixture is correct, the exhaust note should be regular and even. If it is irregular, with misfiring and a colourless exhaust, the mixture is too weak. If there is a regular, rhythmic type of misfire in the exhaust beat, together with sooty smoke, the mixture is too rich.

☐ Job 81. Throttle and choke linkages.

81A. The throttle on each carburettor is operated by a lever and a pin, in a forked lever attached to the throttle spindle. There must be a clearance between the fork and the pin when the engine is stopped and the throttle is closed, to prevent any load from the accelerator linkage and return springs being imposed on the carburettor throttle butterflies. Deal with each carburettor in turn. To set this clearance, with the throttle shaft pinch bolts still free, put a 0.012 inch (0.3 mm) feeler gauge between the throttle shaft stop at the top and the carburettor heat shield. Move the shaft throttle lever downwards until the pin rests lightly on the lower arm of the fork on the carburettor throttle lever. Tighten the clamp bolt of the throttle shaft lever at this position. Do the same for the other carburettor and remove the feeler gauge. The pins should now have clearance in the forks, so you can tighten the throttle shaft pinch bolts. (Illustration, courtesy Rover Cars)

81B. Reconnect the choke cable and check first that the carburettor jets are against the jet adjusting nuts when the choke control is pushed fully in.

81C. Then pull out the choke control on the dash about a quarter of an inch, until the linkage is just about to move the carburettor jets. Adjust the fast idle screws of both carburettors to give the idle speed specified in *Chapter 8, Facts and Figures.*

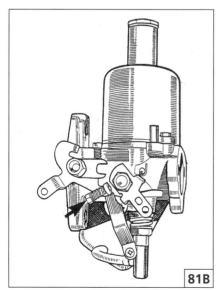

81B

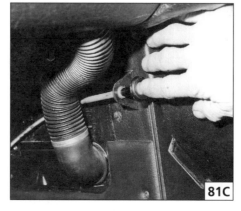

81C

☐ Job 82. Exhaust emissions.

SPECIALIST SERVICE. Have a properly equipped garage such as an MoT test station, carry out an exhaust emissions check. Note the comments in *Chapter 7, Getting Through the MoT,* regarding the difficulty of getting SU carburettors through the MoT emissions test.

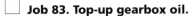

6,000 mile Mechanical and Electrical - Around the Car

First, carry out Jobs 8 to 17, then 19, 20 and 38.

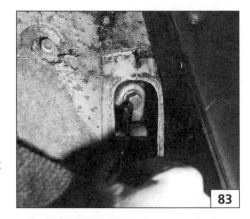

☐ Job 83. Top-up gearbox oil.

83. Lift up the carpet on the left hand side of the gearbox tunnel and remove the large rubber dust cover to gain access to the gearbox level/filler plug. Wipe round it before removing it so that you do not get dirt into the gearbox. If necessary, top up with the correct grade of oil, to the bottom of the threads.

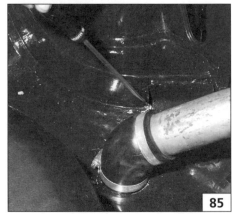

☐ Job 84. Adjust headlamps.

SPECIALIST SERVICE: You can adjust your own headlamps up to a point (see Job 12), but not with sufficient accuracy to avoid dazzling other road users and, at the same time, give you the best lighting of the road. For this job, take the car to a properly equipped garage, such as an MoT test station, for them to adjust the beams with a beam setter.

☐ Job 85. Fuel filler pipe.

85. Check the fuel filler pipe connections for tightness and leaks.

☐ Job 86. Front wheel alignment (tracking).

SPECIALIST SERVICE: The front wheels can go out of alignment in general use, particularly if you hit pot holes in the road or bump the kerb. Specialist aligning equipment is needed to check and reset it, so you cannot do this job at home. If the alignment is not correct, the steering will be less precise and the front tyres will wear out very quickly.

☐ Job 87. Rear ride height.

87. With the car on level ground and the tyres correctly inflated, measure the distance on each side of the car between the ground and the underside of the wheel arch. The measurements should be almost the same each side. If there is a large discrepancy, look for tired or broken springs - and also check the front springs as a weak or broken front spring can also affect the rear ride heights.

☐ Job 88. Front ride height.

Check the front ride height as described in Job 87.

☐ Job 89. Fuel filler cap.

89. Check that the sealing ring on the fuel filler cap is in good condition. A faulty seal is an MoT failure!

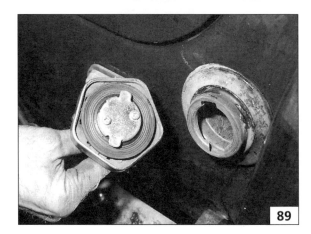

☐ Job 90. Check wheel tightness.

Check the tightness of wheel nuts - see Job 51.

6,000 mile Mechanical and Electrical - Under the Car

First carry out Jobs 39 to 54

☐ Job 91. Front fuel lines.

Check all the fuel lines beneath the front end of the car, taking note that corrosion starts at areas exposed to blasting by road dirt, and around and underneath clips.

☐ Job 92. Front brake lines.

Check all the brake pipes and flexible hoses under the front end of the car, again paying particular attention under clips where corrosion often starts. Bend each flexible hose back on itself quite sharply and look for cracks in the surface of the rubber. If you find signs of cracking, the hose needs replacing, so seek SPECIALIST SERVICE.

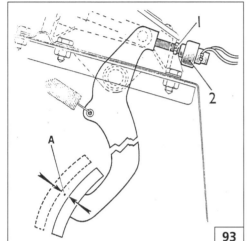

93

☐ Job 93. Adjust brake pedal travel.

EXPORT MODEL CARS ONLY

93. On some cars intended for export, the mounting for the brake stop lamp switch also controlled the footbrake pedal travel. To adjust the pedal travel, slacken the stop lamp switch locknut and turn the switch one way or the other to obtain 1/8 inch free play at the foot pedal. Remember to retighten the locknut.

☐ Job 94. Exhaust manifold.

94. Check the front exhaust manifold and downpipe connections for security and leaks. You will often find it useful to discard the old clamp and fit a new one, with exhaust sealant wiped around the inside before fitting.

INSIDE INFORMATION: An easy way to locate any leaks in the exhaust system is to get a helper to hold a rag over the end of the tailpipe while the engine is ticking over. Any leaks will show up as a hissing sound. Never carry out this check in the garage, always out of doors.

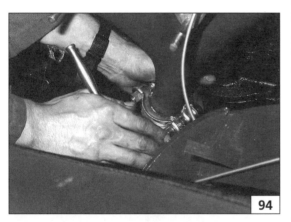

94

☐ Job 95. Front dampers.

95. Check the front dampers for any signs of leaks and, if necessary, top them up with the correct grade of oil. If you find leaks, the damper needs replacing, but always replace dampers in pairs, never singly, even if only one is faulty.

Also check the damper bushes and replace if worn.

INSIDE INFORMATION: The filler plug on the front dampers is easy to see but not so easy to undo because of the limited room to swing a spanner. You need a socket with quite a long extension to make the job easy.

☐ Job 96. Clutch hydraulics.

Check the clutch hydraulic lines for corrosion or leaks. A slight leak from the slave cylinder isn't easy to spot, so pull back the rubber boot and look for evidence of hydraulic fluid, particularly if the clutch master cylinder needed frequent topping up.

> **SAFETY FIRST!**
> *Lower the front of the car to the ground and then raise the rear of the car after carefully reading the information at the start of this chapter on lifting and supporting the car.*

95

☐ Job 97. Rear brake pipes.

Check all the rear brake pipes and flexible hoses for signs of corrosion or deterioration, paying particular attention under clips where corrosion often starts. Bend the flexible hose back on itself quite sharply and look for signs of surface cracking. If you find any, the hose needs replacing so seek **SPECIALIST SERVICE.**

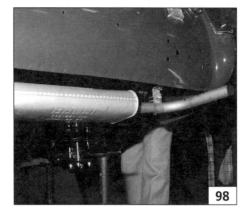

☐ Job 98. Exhaust.

98. Check the rear of the exhaust system for security and leaks.

INSIDE INFORMATION: Mounting rubbers frequently break, putting strain on the manifold joint and causing leaks.

☐ Job 99. Rear damper and spring mountings.

99A. Check the rear dampers for security and leaks and use a pry bar or a tyre lever to check that the rubber in the linkages has not perished. You cannot top up the rear dampers on a Midget without removing them as there is insufficient room under the floor. They should not need topping up unless they have leaked and, in that case, they need replacing. Always replace dampers in pairs even if only one is faulty.

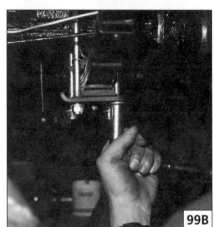

99B. Also check the spring-to-axle, bolts (four per side) for tightness.

☐ Job 100. Universal joints.

100. Check the security and tightness of the universal joint nuts. Some universal joints are the sealed for life type but others have grease nipples, If yours have nipples, grease them. Also grease the nipple on the sliding splines of the propshaft.

☐ Job 101. Rear axle oil.

101. Inspect the level and, if necessary, top up the rear axle oil with the correct grade of lubricant, see *Chapter 8, Facts and Figures,* for the correct grade. It is not particularly easy to top up the oil, but it can be done with a long spout on the oil bottle. Fill the axle through the level plug until oil *just* dribbles out of the hole, then replace the filler plug.

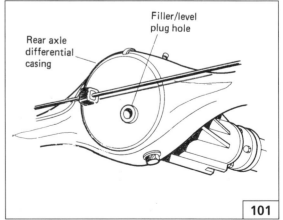

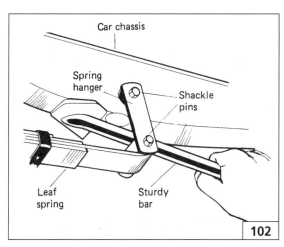

102

☐ Job 102. Rear springs.

102. Brush the rear springs clean of road dirt and check them for broken leaves. There is no need to oil the springs or spray them with any lubricant; they have interleaving that makes this unnecessary. Do, however, check the bushes at both ends of the springs, as shown, and renew if movement is found.

6,000 mile Mechanical and Electrical - Road Test

Carry out jobs 61 to 64.

6,000 mile Bodywork and Interior - Around the Car

First carry out Jobs 18 to 24 and 55 to 60.

☐ Job 103. Bonnet release and stay.

103A. Smear the jaws of the bonnet catch liberally with grease and put a large blob of grease on the end of the inner cable where it comes out of the outer casing to prevent water creeping down.

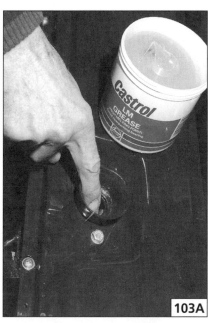

103A

103B. Lubricate the bonnet release catch.

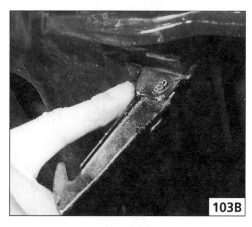

103B

103C. Lubricate the bonnet stay and check that the automatic locking mechanism works and holds properly. A stay which collapses when you have your head under the bonnet can cause a nasty accident.

103C

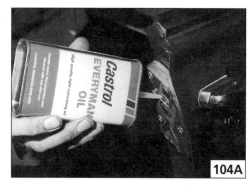

104A

☐ Job 104. Body fittings.

104A. Lubricate the door and boot lock mechanisms.

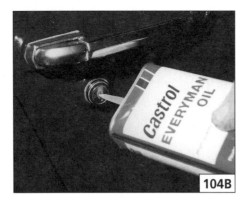

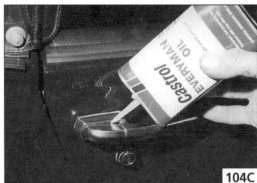

104B. Squirt a small amount of oil in the key holes to prevent the tumblers seizing.

104C. Lubricate the door release press buttons and work them a few times to distribute the oil inside.

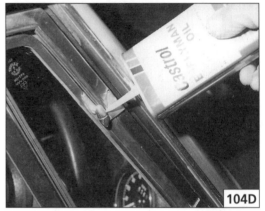

104D. Lubricate the hinges and locks of the opening quarter lights and operate them a few times to make sure they are not stiff.

INSIDE INFORMATION: If the quarter light is impossibly stiff and noisy, remove the door trim and spray releasing fluid up, onto the spring beneath the bottom pivot.

Job 105. Seats and seat belts.

105. Check the seats for security by trying to rock them and check the seat adjustment mechanism. Examine the seat belts for chafing and tug hard at them to check their fixings to the body. With inertia seat belts, check the inertia lock. On some types this can be done just by giving the belt a sharp tug, but others operate only when the car is under hard deceleration. Test this type on the road but make sure there are no pedestrians nor any other traffic about.

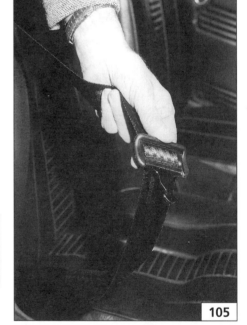

6,000 miles Bodywork - Under the Car

SAFETY FIRST!
Raise the car off the ground only after reading carefully the information at the start of this chapter on lifting and supporting the car.

Job 106. Rustproofing under the body.

Renew wax treatment to wheel arches and underbody areas. Refer to *Chapter 5, Rustproofing,* for details.

Job 107. Clear drain holes.

107. Check and clear the drain holes in the doors, boot and sills.

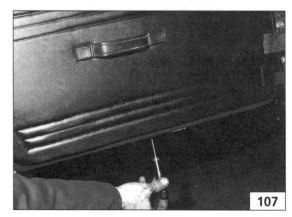

You can learn a lot about the condition of an engine from looking at the spark plugs. The following information and photographs, reproduced here with grateful thanks to NGK, show you what to look out for.

1. Good Condition

If the firing end of a spark plug is brown or light grey, the condition can be judged to be good and the spark plug is functioning at its best.

4. Overheating

When having been overheated, the insulator tip can become glazed or glossy, and deposits which have accumulated on the insulator tip may have melted. Sometimes these deposits have blistered on the insulator's tip.

6. Abnormal Wear

Abnormal electrode erosion is caused by the effects of corrosion, oxidation, reaction with lead, all resulting in abnormal gap growth.

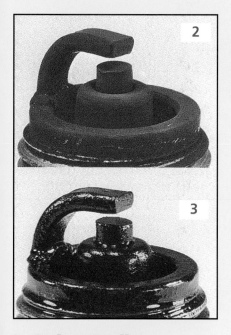

2. Carbon Fouling

Black, dry, sooty deposits, which will eventually cause misfiring and can be caused by an over-rich fuel mixture. Check all carburettor settings, choke operation and air filter cleanliness. Clean plugs vigorously with a brass bristled wire brush.

3. Oil Fouling

Oily, wet-looking deposits. This is particularly prone to causing poor starting and even misfiring. Caused by a severely worn engine but do not confuse with wet plugs removed from the engine when it won't start. If the "wetness" evaporates away, it's not oil fouling.

5. Normal Wear

A worn spark plug not only wastes fuel but also strains the whole ignition system because the expanded gap requires higher voltage. As a result, a worn spark plug will result in damage to the engine itself, and will also increase air pollution. The normal rate of gap growth is usually around 'half-a-thou.' or 0.0006 in. every 5,000 miles (0.01 mm. every 5,000 km.).

7. Breakage

Insulator damage is self-evident and can be caused by rapid heating or cooling of the plug whilst out of the car or by clumsy use of gap setting tools. Burned away electrodes are indicative of an ignition system that is grossly out of adjustment. Do not use the car until this has been put right.

12,000 Miles - or Every Twelve Months, Whichever Comes First

12,000 mile Mechanical and Electrical - Emission Control Equipment

☐ **Job 108. Crankcase breather.**

EARLY CARS ONLY

108. Early engines had two parts to the emission control system, the oil filler cap with an integral air filter, and a flat-topped breather valve on the left hand side of the rocker cover. The filler cap and breather are renewed only as a complete assembly, but the breather valve can be dismantled for cleaning. (Illustration, courtesy Rover Cars)

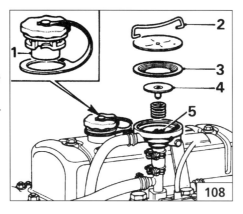

108

109A

Dismantle the valve, clean the rubber diaphragm with methylated spirit and the metal parts with a degreasing solvent such a methylated spirit. If there are stuck-on deposits on the metal parts which are difficult to remove, boil them first in an old saucepan with a little detergent. If the diaphragm is perished, or any parts are damaged, renew them. Make sure that the metering valve fits in the cruciform guides and that the diaphragm seats properly.

Most models, including all UK cars with plastic oil filler caps, take in their air through the oil filler cap, which contains an integral filter, in which case the filler cap should now be replaced. A blocked filler/filter cap will cause the car to burn oil, put out smoke and display several symptoms of a worn-out engine. A new cap comes a lot less expensive!

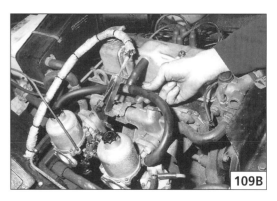

109B

☐ **Job 109. Breather hoses and connectors.**

109A. Check the hoses to the breather valve. On earlier engines, shown here, there is a single pipe.

109B. On later models, the pipe goes to the carbs. via a Y-piece, which is also prone to fracturing. If pipes are blocked it is almost certain that the breather connection on the engine is also blocked. Renew the hoses and clear the obstruction.

☐ **Job 110. Overhaul emission control equipment.**

US MODELS ONLY

It is important to note that US models had different quantities of emission control equipment fitted, according to year of manufacture. In most territories, it is illegal to tamper with or remove this equipment.

110A. ADSORPTION CANISTER: You have to take out the canister (110A.2) in order to renew the filter. Disconnect the three pipes at the top and one at the bottom of the canister, unscrew the clip that holds the canister in place and lift it away. Remove the screw that holds the bottom of the canister in place and take out the air filter pad secured by the end cap of the canister. Fit a new filter pad. When refitting the canister, make sure that the purge pipe that runs from the engine rocker cover (110A.3) is connected to the centre connection on the top of the canister. (Illustration, courtesy Rover Cars)

1.	Lower hose connection	5.	Oil separator
2.	Adsorption canister	6.	Breather hose
3.	Rocker cover connection	7.	Breather hose-to-carbu-
4.	Oil filler cap		rettor connections

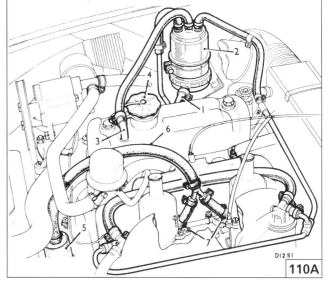

110A

SECOND FUEL FILTER: Some cars fitted with an evaporative loss control system are equipped with two in-line fuel filters in order to ensure that no residue can enter and damage the system. Ensure that both are changed at 12,000 miles/twelve months. After changing the filter/s, turn on the ignition and ensure that there are no fuel leaks.

AIR PUMP BELT: Change the air pump drive belt. When correctly tensioned, the belt should deflect by about 1/2 inch (12 mm) half way along the longest part of the belt between the pulleys. Retighten the mounting bolts to a torque of 10 lb ft (1.38 kg m). Check all pipes and connections for soundness. Replace if necessary. Faulty air pumps usually become excessively noisy.

1. Charcoal absorption canister
2. Vapour lines
3. Purge line
4. Restricted connection
5. Sealed oil filler cap
6. Oil separator/flame trap (arrester)
7. Fuel pipe
8. Fuel pump
9. Running-on control valve
10. Running-on control pipe
11. Air manifold
12. Air pump
13. Diverter valve
14. Check valve
15. Diverter valve pipe

16. Air temperature control valve
17. Hot air hose
18. Exhaust gas/recirculation valve
19. EGR valve flame trap
20. EGR valve line to carburettor choke cam
21. EGR valve pipe
22. Distributor flame trap
23. Distributor flame trap line carburettor
24. Flame trap line to distributor vacuum unit

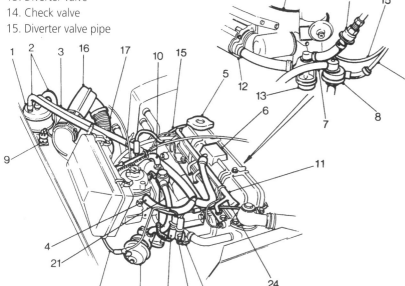

110B

INSIDE INFORMATION: Try disconnecting the air pump belt then running the engine again, to see if the noise is actually coming from the pump.

SPECIALIST SERVICE. If you suspect the air pump of any other fault, seek specialist advice for diagnosis, rebuild or for the cost of a replacement.

AIR PUMP FILTER: Some systems fitted with an air pump have a renewable type of paper air filter. Replace it.

TEST CHECK VALVE: Some systems fitted with an air pump have a check valve on the inlet side. Check it by removing, then trying to blow through from one end and then the other. The valve should only allow air to pass from the 'inlet' end, not the air pump end. If it does so, discard and replace.

FUEL FILLER CAP: Check the condition of the fuel filler cap seal. Replace the seal if it appears damaged.

EMISSION SYSTEM, GENERAL: **SPECIALIST SERVICE.** Have a specialist run a check over the emission control and evaporative loss control system for leaks and correct operation of all the valves and components that cannot be checked without specialist equipment.

110B. The ex-Triumph 1493cc engine has a very different looking system but the general principles are similar. **SPECIALIST SERVICE.** Have your dealer check the system over annually to ensure that you remain street-legal.

12,000 mile Mechanical and Electrical - The Engine Bay

First, carry out Jobs 2 to 6, 26 to 37 and 65 to 82.

☐ Job 111. Oil leaks.

Check over the engine carefully for oil leaks, paying particular attention to the area round the crankshaft seals at the front and back of the sump, the mechanical fuel pump, if fitted, the front timing cover and the rocker cover. Generally speaking, leaks will mean dismantling and new gaskets. You will be fitting a new gasket to the rocker cover as part of Job 118 but, if you find leaks at other places and do not feel competent to carry out the dismantling necessary to renew the gasket, seek SPECIALIST SERVICE.

☐ Job 112. Clean radiator.

Remove the front grille, and clean any muck and dead flies from the radiator matrix.

☐ Job 113. Water pump.

Check water pump for leaks. Early cars had a water pump with a greasing plug at the top just behind the fan. Remove the plug, fit a grease nipple and give it just two strokes of the grease gun. Remove the nipple and replace the plug.

☐ **Job 114. Valve clearances.**

114. Remove the rocker cover and check the valve clearances. The valve clearances must be set with the tappet on the heel of the cam to give the greatest clearance. The easiest way to set the engine for this is to remember the Rule of Nine. Remove the sparking plugs to make turning the engine easier, then turn the engine with a spanner on the front of the crankshaft until number 8 valve is fully open. Then set the clearance on valve number 1 (8 plus 1 equals 9). Next, turn the engine until number 7 valve is fully open and set the clearance on valve number 2 (7 plus 2 equals 9). Carry on until all the valve clearances have been set. Set the clearances by slackening the locknut at the end of the rocker arm and turning the adjuster screw until a feeler gauge of the correct thickness (see *Chapter 8, Facts and Figures*) is a firm sliding fit between the top of the valve and the rocker arm.

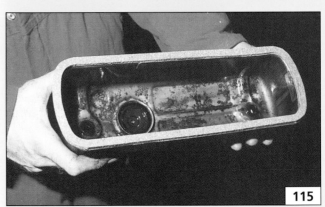
114

INSIDE INFORMATION: If, after setting the clearances accurately, the tappets are still noisy it probably means that the pads at the ends of the rocker arms are indented, giving a false reading. You can buy a tool at most accessory shops with which you can set the clearances to allow for this indentation.

Alternatively, you can do it with two feeler gauges. First, put any feeler gauge in the gap and screw the adjuster down until the feeler is tight. Then back the adjusting screw off, counting the turns and part turns carefully, until a feeler of the correct thickness will just slide in on top of the first feeler. You now know the number of turns back-off to give the correct clearance, so remove both feelers, screw the adjusting screw down until there is no clearance and back it off by the same number of turns and part turns.. You will now have the correct clearance.

115

☐ **Job 115. Rocker cover.**

115. Clean the inside of the rocker cover and remove all traces of the old gasket. Fit a new gasket.

INSIDE INFORMATION: Fasten the gasket to the rocker cover with gasket jointing compound but don't get any on the face of the gasket. Then, if you have to remove the rocker cover later, the gasket will stay with the cover instead of getting torn or squeezed out of shape.

116

☐ **Job 116. Cylinder compressions.**

SAFETY FIRST!
Take off the HT lead that runs from the coil to the centre of the distributor cap so that there is no danger of the engine firing nor of electric shock. Carry out this work outside, and make sure that the gearbox is in neutral.

Ensure that the engine oil is up to the recommended level and that the engine is at operating temperature. Remove the sparking plugs.

116. Screw the compression tester into each plug hole in turn. Open the throttle fully and crank the engine over on the starter motor. Make a note of the maximum reading on the pressure gauge. Check each cylinder in turn and compare the results. If the engine is in good condition there should not be a variation in the readings of more than 5 or 6 psi, 10 at the most.

INSIDE INFORMATION. If you get a low reading on two adjacent cylinders it is an indication that the cylinder head gasket is leaking between the two. If you get low, varied readings, put a teaspoonful of oil in each plug hole and test again. If the readings come up and show much less variation, it means that the pistons rings are worn or sticking and the oil has made a temporary seal. If there is little or no difference in the readings compared with the first test, it means that the valves in the cylinder head are worn and need reseating.

12,000 mile Mechanical and Electrical - Around the Car

> First, carry out Jobs 19 to 25, 38 and 83 to 90.

☐ Job 117. Test dampers.

117. With the car on level ground, 'bounce' each corner in turn and note how the car recovers from the bounce. It should return evenly and smoothly from being pushed down. If it continues to bounce, it means that the dampers are weak and worn out, Always renew dampers in pairs.

12,000 mile Mechanical and Electrical - Under the Car

> First carry out Job 25, 39 to 54 and 91 to 101.

> *SAFETY FIRST!*
> *Raise the front of the car off the ground after reading carefully the information at the start of this chapter on lifting and supporting the car.*

117

☐ Job 118. Wishbone bushes.

118. Check with a pry bar or tyre lever for wear in the front suspension bushes. If you find too much movement, or the ends of the rubber bushes have gone soggy and soft, seek SPECIALIST ADVICE as removing the front suspension spring can be very hazardous.

☐ Job 119. Kingpins and hubs.

119A. With the wheel just clear of the ground, and before you put axle stands under the car, use a long lever to try to lift the wheel bodily up and down:

118

> *SAFETY FIRST!*
> *Keep well clear of the car when you do this in case you lever enough to make it fall from the jack. The wheel should be only an inch or so off the ground.*

119B. With the car safely on axle stands, grasp the wheel at the top and bottom and try to rock it. If there is any movement, either with the lever or when rocking the wheel, either the king pins or the front hubs could be worn. Seek SPECIALIST ADVICE.

While you are carrying out this job, if you feel any play at the road wheel, ask an assistant to look underneath to see whether it is king pins or hubs. In either case you need **SPECIALIST SERVICE**.

119A

119B

☐ Job 120. Check anti-roll bar mountings.

120. Worn anti-roll bar mountings (at the chassis) and bushes (at the suspension wishbones) will cause handling to deteriorate. Two (rusted-in!) bolts hold each mounting rubber block in place. They are split, so easy to replace once the bolts are undone.

120

☐ Job 121. Front callipers.

Examine the front brake callipers to check for leaks, Any sign of leaks means that the calliper must be overhauled or renewed.

☐ Job 122. Lubricate steering rack.

On early cars only there is an oil nipple on the steering rack - left hand side of the rack housing on right hand drive cars and right hand side of the housing on left hand drive cars. Give it 10 strokes maximum with a gun filled with the correct grade of oil - NOT grease.

124A

☐ Job 123. Check steering free play.

Check for excessive free play at the steering wheel. If it is present, find out why or seek SPECIALIST SERVICE. See *Chapter 7, Getting Through the MoT,* for what is and what isn't acceptable.

☐ Job 124. Check ball joints.

Check for excessive free play in the ball joints.

124A. With the wheel free of the ground, grasp it at each side and try turning it from side to side. If you feel free play, check whether this is in the ball joints at the inner ends of the steering rack, or the track rod ends.

124B. You can feel even a small amount of free play at a track rod end ball joint by putting your hand over it while a helper turns the wheel from side to side.

Now carry out Jobs 41 to 45.

Lower the front of the car to the ground and raise the rear.

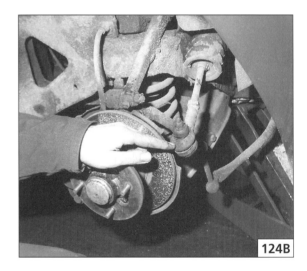

124B

SAFETY FIRST!
Raise the rear of the car only after reading carefully the information at the start of this chapter on lifting and supporting the car.

☐ **Job 125. Rear brake inspection.**

SAFETY FIRST! and SPECIALIST SERVICE:
*Obviously, a car's brakes are among its most important safety related items. Do not dismantle your car's brakes unless you are fully competent to do so. If you have not been trained in the this work, but wish to carry out the work described here, we strongly recommend that a qualified mechanic or a garage checks your work before you use the car on the road. See the section on BRAKES AND ASBESTOS in **Chapter 1, Safety First** for further important information.*
Lockheed, the suppliers of original equipment for Sprites and Midgets, recommend that, after fitting new brake shoes, avoid heavy braking - except in an emergency - for the first 150-200 miles (250-300 km.)

125A

Early cars. Remove the dust cover in the brake drum and turn the drum until you can see the brake shoe adjusting screw. Unscrew the adjuster as far as it will go before trying to remove the brake drum.

On later cars, the rear brake shoe adjuster is a small shaft with a squared end at the rear of the back plate. Unscrew it, away from the back plate, as far as it will go before trying to remove the drum. Use a proper brake adjusting tool for this, rather than a spanner, as it is thicker and less likely to round off the squared end.

125B

125A. Remove the drum by taking out the two cross-head screws (cars with bolt-on wheels) or four bolts (cars with wire wheels).

125B. If the drum does not want to move, tap *very carefully* round its rim with a hide-faced hammer then pull free.

125C

125C. Check the lining thickness. The maker's recommendation is that new shoes are fitted when the linings are worn down to 3/32 inch or less. Remember that it will be another 12,000 miles before you inspect them again, so we would recommend 1/8 inch as a minimum. The car's linings here are being compared with new ones. As you can see, there is plenty of life in them yet.

125D. Lift back the rubber boot on the hydraulic wheel cylinder and check for any leakage of brake fluid. If you find any, the cylinder needs overhauling or replacing. Unless you are competent in this work, seek **SPECIALIST SERVICE.**

The hub flange at the rear of a Sprite or Midget is quite large which makes replacing the brake shoes rather awkward. Attempt it only if you are competent to do so. Whether you renew the shoes or not, squirt all the mechanism and the back plate liberally with a proprietary brake cleaner to remove the dust. Do not blow this off with an air blast as the dust is harmful if inhaled.

125D

125E. On early cars, undo the small coil springs (125E.1), (push and twist) which hold the shoes to the back plate. Then pull the ends out of the hydraulic cylinder, disengage the handbrake lever (125E.5), and the long spring (125E.2), and lift the shoes off from the fixed location complete with the shorter spring (125E.3). Do not lose the snail cam adjuster (125E.4). Fit the new shoes in the reverse order after lightly greasing the fixed pivot points and the snail cam adjuster with brake grease, NEVER with ordinary high melting point grease. Smear just a trace of brake grease on the edges of the shoes where they rub on the back plate, but be careful not to get grease on the linings or the brake drum.

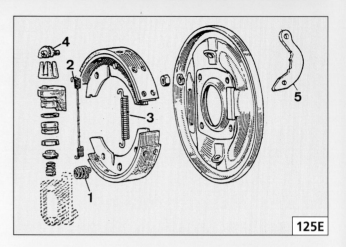

125E

125F. On later cars, lever the shoes away from the ends of the hydraulic cylinder and disengage the spring with long hooks (125F.1). Disengage the handbrake lever (125F.3), then slide the shoes out of the fixed pivot points and lift them away. If the adjuster (125F.5), was hard to turn, it can be screwed right through the back plate from the rear and the threads greased before replacing. Fit the new shoes in the reverse order after lightly greasing the fixed pivot points with high melting point grease. Smear just a trace of high melting point grease on the edges of the shoes where they rub on the back plate, but be careful not to get grease on the linings. (Illustrations courtesy AP Lockheed.)

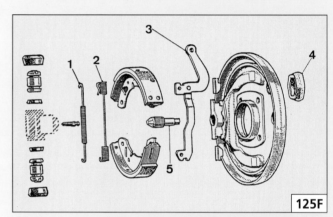

125F

INSIDE INFORMATION: However careful you are, there is always a danger of contaminating the new linings with oil from dirty fingers. Cover the linings with masking tape before you start and remove it only after the new shoes are in place.

125G. When you fit the drum back on you may have to tap the shoes up and down slightly to centralise them before the drum will go on. Once the drums are on, you can centralise the shoes properly by treading hard on the brake pedal several times before adjusting the shoes.

After adjusting the brakes, refit the wheels and lower the car to the ground.

125G

12,000 mile Mechanical and Electrical - Road Test

Carry out a road test as detailed in Jobs 61 to 64.

12,000 mile Bodywork and Interior - Around the Car

First, carry out Jobs 18 to 24, 55 to 60 and 102 to 105.

☐ Job 126. Seat runners.

126. Remove the seat cushions and lubricate the seat runners and catch. Check the seat frame fixings (arrowed) for security. It is best to use a non-staining silicone grease to avoid soiling the carpets.

In the case of early cars, seat bases lift straight out.

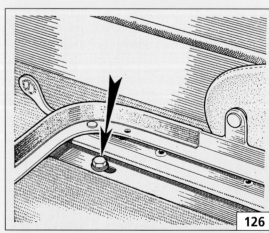

126

128

129

Job 127. Toolkit and jack.

Check that you have at least the minimum toolkit - wheel chocks, wheel brace or hide hammer, jack and warning triangle - for changing a wheel at the roadside if necessary. Note: MG Sports Cars does not recommend using the side sill body jack on Sprites and Midgets because of the danger of straining the jack mountings in the sills. Their advice is to buy an independent hydraulic jack.

Job 128. Wire wheel splines.

WIRE WHEELED CARS ONLY

128. Remove each wheel in turn and wash any dirt and old grease off the wheel splines, cones and spinners, both on the hub and the wheel. Check the splines for damage or deformation. 'Sharp' splines are worn and should be replaced. Should they fail - and they might - you will be left without brakes on that wheel - highly dangerous! Lubricate the splines, cones and spinner threads with fresh grease.

Job 129. Wire wheel spokes.

WIRE WHEELED CARS ONLY

129. With the weight of the spokes off the wheel, run round the spokes tapping them lightly with a screwdriver. They should all give out a 'ting' - ideally at more or less the same pitch. If you find any bent spokes, or spokes which give a dull 'tonk' instead of a sharp 'ting' when tapped, seek **SPECIALIST SERVICE** at a wheel specialist.

12,000 mile Bodywork - Under the Car

First carry out Jobs 25 and 60, bearing in mind that Job 130 entails a more thorough wax coating treatment.

Job 130. Top-up rustproofing.

Renew and top-up the wax coating to the sills, box sections, insides of doors and underside of car. See *Chapter 5, Rustproofing,* for full details.

24,000 Miles - or Every Twenty Four Months, Whichever Comes First

The Service Jobs listed below should be carried out in addition to the regular 12,000 mile/twelve month Service Jobs shown previously. They cover the areas which experience has shown can give trouble in the longer term or, in some cases, they cover areas that may prevent trouble starting in the first place. Most of them don't appear on manufacturer's service schedules, but they are the sort of jobs that can make the difference between a car that is reliable and one that gives trouble out of the blue.

24,000 mile Mechanical and Electrical - The Engine Bay

Job 131. Engine mountings.

Check the engine mountings at the sides of the engine and also at the rear of the gearbox. Look for rubber which has become distorted or which has deteriorated and become soggy because of oil spillage. Damaged or soggy mountings need replacing.

☐ Job 132. Drain and refill cooling system.

SAFETY FIRST!
Work on the cooling system only when the engine is cold. If you drain a system when the engine is hot, the remaining coolant inside can boil over and release scalding water and steam.

132A. Remove the pressure caps and the filler plugs, open the heater valve and drain the system. On early cars there is a drain tap at the bottom of the radiator but, on later cars, the radiator has to be drained by undoing the bottom radiator hose.

132B. On later cars there is a drain tap, or a drain plug, at the back of the block on the right hand side.

After draining the system, flush it through with cold water. With the caps and plugs still out, put a garden hose into the bottom radiator hose and plug it with

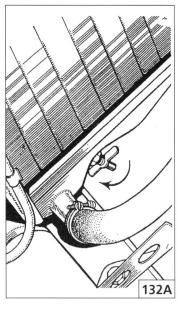

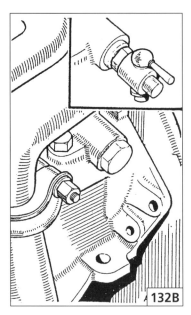

rags. Turn on the water and let it run till no more sediment or discoloured water comes out. Open and close the heater tap from time to time to help the water surge through and flush the heater. If you suspect the heater is heavily sedimented, disconnect the hoses and flush it through separately. After the block is flushed, fit and plug the hosepipe in the bottom radiator connection and reverse flush the radiator. If the radiator is heavily sedimented you may have to take it out, turn it upside down and reverse flush it away from the car.

Refill the system, first checking in *Chapter 8, Facts and Figures,* to establish the capacity of the cooling system. Mix sufficient water and antifreeze in a 50/50 solution. Close the drain taps and replace the drain plugs, reconnect the hoses and fill the system gradually through the filler plugs - on the radiator for 948cc, 1098cc and 1275cc engines and on the thermostat housing on 1493cc engines. Continue filling until the expansion bottle is half full. Squeeze the bottom radiator hose from time to time to help expel trapped air.

Replace the filler plug and pressure cap, start the engine and let it run to circulate the coolant. Wait for the engine to cool right down, then check the coolant level again. Check it yet again when it has cooled down after a run on the road.

SAFETY FIRST!
Keep your hands and clothing well away from the fan belt and fan when the engine is running. Do not wear loose clothing.

INSIDE INFORMATION: Remember that antifreeze, even in diluted form, will attack paintwork. Be particularly careful when flushing and if you have to disconnect the heater hoses. Any spilt antifreeze should be washed off immediately with plenty of cold water.

☐ Job 133. Radiator pressure cap.

Renew the radiator pressure cap even it looks in good condition. The spring weakens in time and releases coolant earlier than it should so your engine could overheat. Check the poundage of the new cap to make sure it is the same as the old one. It should be stamped on the top.

☐ Job 134. Fan belt.

Renew fan belt. The risk of fan belt breakage is higher than the cost of automatic replacement at this interval.

24,000 mile Mechanical and Electrical - Under the Car

SAFETY FIRST!
Raise the car, front or back as necessary, only after reading carefully the information at the start of this chapter on lifting and supporting the car.

☐ Job 135. Flushing oil.

On older engines where you don't know the service history it could be a good idea to drain and flush the oil at this service. Generally, though, flushing will not be necessary on engines which have had regular oil changes. Drain the old oil, but leave the oil filter in place. Fill the engine with proprietary flushing oil and follow the instructions on the can. Generally these will say run the engine for five

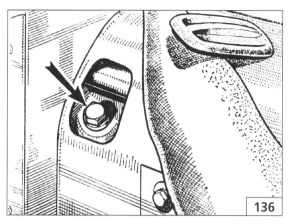

minutes or so after it reaches its normal operating temperature. Don't rev the engine unduly, and never drive it on the road, with flushing oil in the sump. Drain the flushing oil out, change the filter and refill with new oil as detailed in Job 41.

Job 136. Gearbox oil

136. Drain and replace the gearbox oil. The quantity and grade to use can be found in *Chapter 8, Facts and Figures,* and *Appendix 1.* After filling, run the engine for a few moments with the gear lever in neutral and the clutch engaged, then check the level again. Wear gloves when draining the old oil.

Job 137. Suspension mountings.

137. Check the tightness of all the bolts of the front suspension including those holding the bottom of the spring pan. At the rear, check the shackle bolts as shown here, and use a pry bar to check the shackle bushes.

Job 138. Brake discs.

Except on cars with front drums, check the thickness of the front brake discs. Some manuals tell you to use a micrometer but, if the disc has worn thin enough to warrant replacing, it is unlikely to have worn without ridges and these can give a completely false micrometer reading. A safer guide is the general condition of the discs and the size of the ridge at the top outside the area on which the pads have been operating. If in doubt, seek **SPECIALIST SERVICE** but, as a good safety rule, replace any discs that look badly worn. Fit new pads as well to bring the braking back to top-line condition.

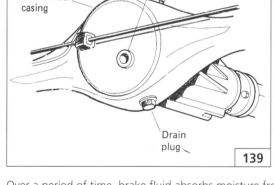

Job 139. Rear axle oil.

139. Place a suitable container under the back of the car and drain the rear axle oil. Remember to wear gloves. Refill with the correct grade of oil, *see Chapter 8, Facts and Figures.*

Job 140. Renew brake fluid.

SAFETY FIRST! and SPECIALIST SERVICE.
Obviously, a car's brakes are among its most important safety related items. DO NOT dismantle your car's brakes unless you are fully competent to do so. If you have not been trained in this work, but wish to carry out the work described here, we strongly recommend that you have a garage or qualified mechanic check your work before using the car on the road. See also the section on BRAKES AND ASBESTOS in Chapter 1, for further important information.

Over a period of time, brake fluid absorbs moisture from the air and, should the fluid at the callipers or wheel cylinders get very hot with prolonged braking, this water can boil and cause a vapour lock - in other words, completely inoperative brakes! **If this job is not carried out properly it can result in brakes which could let you down without warning.**

Do not carry out this job unless you have been trained to do it, and do not attempt it without the workshop manual as procedures differ on different models of car. We strongly recommend that you regard this as a **SPECIALIST SERVICE** and leave the job to your MG specialist or Rover dealer. They have equipment which can do the job quickly and thoroughly.

Job 141. Brake drums.

Remove the rear brake drums, and front drums if fitted, and check them for ridging and scoring. Even if no ridges are present, check for crazing or 'Chinese writing' on the surface where the linings have been rubbing. If ridging, scoring or crazing is severe, renew the drums or, if they are suitable, have them skimmed by a specialist. Hang the drum up on a piece of string and tap it with a screwdriver. It should ring true like bell. If the ring sounds flat and dull, the drum is cracked and needs replacing. Do not use the car until it is replaced.

CHAPTER THREE

☐ Job 142. Brake back plates.

While the drums are off, clean the brake back plates with a proprietary brake cleaner to prevent brake squeal and seizure. The dust inside a brake drum can be very harmful if inhaled. Do not dust it off before spraying on the cleaner.

First read the SAFETY FIRST! and SPECIALIST SERVICE note at the beginning of Job 140.

24,000 mile Bodywork and Interior - Around the Car

☐ Job 143. Window regulators.

143. Remove the trim from the inside of the doors and check and lubricate the window regulating mechanism. Apply silicone grease to the window channelling inside the door.

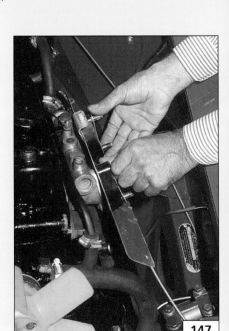
143

☐ Job 144. Door gear.

While the trim is off, lubricate the inside of the door locks and mechanism.

☐ Job 145. Lamp seals.

Remove all the lamp lenses and the headlamp rims and check the condition of the rubber seals. Renew any that are split or perished.

36,000 Miles - or Every Thirty Six Months, Whichever Comes First

Carry out all the Jobs listed under earlier service heading before carrying out these tasks.

☐ Job 146. Overhaul ignition.

Renew the distributor cap and high tension leads. Using the old cap and the recess for the locating tag as a guide, mark the turrets of the new cap 1, 2, 3 and 4, either with numbers on slips of masking tape or with typewriter correcting fluid, so you do not fit the new leads in the wrong order.

INSIDE INFORMATION: If you make a mistake, or lose the order, you can set it again. Put the rotor arm on, but leave the cap off, and turn the engine, noting which way the rotor arm is turning, till number 1 cylinder is on its firing stroke. You can check this by removing the plug, putting your thumb over the plug hole and feeling for the pressure of compression. Alternatively, remove the rocker cover and check that both valves of number 1 cylinder have clearance. Turn the engine to top dead centre by checking the timing marks, offer up the new cap and check the stud to which the rotor arm is pointing. This will be the stud for number 1 lead. The firing order is 1, 3, 4, 2 so, going round the cap the same way as the rotor arm turns, the remaining four turrets will take the leads for number 3, number 4 and number 2 plugs.

☐ Job 147. Float chambers and heat shields.

147. Remove the float chambers from the carburettors and clean out any sediment. Also, check the heat shield - seen here being replaced, with carburettors off - and the two black emulsion blocks for completeness - and being there! Replace if necessary.

147

☐ Job 148. Front hubs.

148. Lever the grease retainer cap from the middle of the front hubs, clean it out and check that the small air hole in the centre is clear. Fill it with new high melting point grease and tap it back on. If no grease spurts out of the air hole as you tap the cap on, lever it off again, fill it again and tap it back in place.

148

CHAPTER 4
REPAIRING BODYWORK BLEMISHES

However well you look after your car, there will always be the risk of car park accident damage - or even worse! The smallest paint chips are best touched up with paint purchased from your local auto. accessory shop. If your colour of paint is not available, some auto. accessory shops offer a mixing scheme or you could look for a local paint factor in Yellow Pages. Take your car along to the paint factor and have them match the colour and mix the smallest quantity of cellulose paint that they will supply you with.

Larger body blemishes will need the use of body filler. You should only use a filler with a reputable name behind it, such as Isopon P38 Easy Sand and that's what we used to carry out this repair.

> **SAFETY FIRST!**
> **Always** *wear plastic gloves when working with any make of filler, before it has set. Always wear a face mask when sanding filler and wear goggles when using a power sander.*

4.1

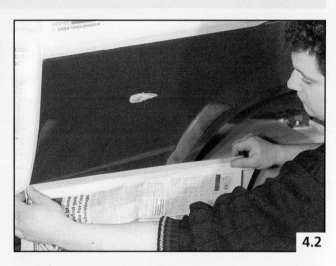

4.2

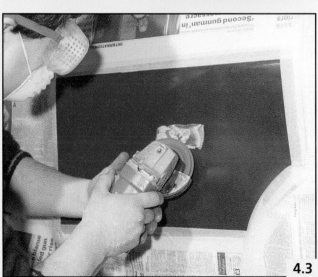

4.3

4.1 The rear of this car has sustained a nasty gash - the sort of damage for which you will certainly need to use body filler.

4.2 The first stage is to mask off. Try to find "natural" edges such as body mouldings or styling stripes and wherever you can, mask off body trim rather than having to remove it.

4.3 Isopon recommend that you remove all paint from the damaged area and for about 1 in. around the damaged area. Roughen the bare metal or surface with coarse abrasive paper - a power sander is best - and wipe away any loose particles. If you have access to professional spirit wipe, so much the better and the whole area should now be wiped down. If not, wipe over the area with white spirit (mineral spirit) and then wash off with washing-up liquid in water - *not* car wash detergent.

4.4 Use a piece of plastic on which to mix the filler and hardener, following the instructions on the can.

4.4

4.5 Mix the filler and hardener thoroughly until the colour is consistent and no traces of hardener can be discerned. It's best to use a piece of plastic or metal rather than cardboard because otherwise, the filler will pick up fibres from the surface of the card.

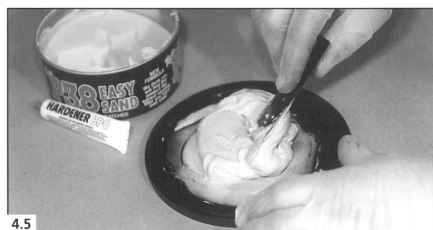

4.5

4.6 You can now spread the filler evenly over the repair.

4.7 If the damage is particularly deep, apply the paste in two or more layers, allowing the filler to harden before adding the next layer. The final layer should be just proud of the level required, but do not overfill as this wastes paste and will require more time to sand down. *(Courtesy Isopon)*

4.7

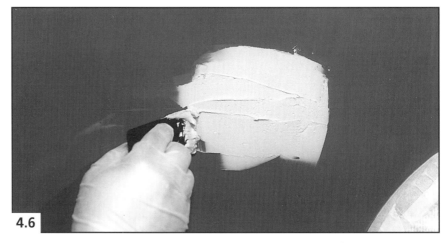

4.6

4.8 It is essential when sanding down that you wrap the sanding paper around a flat block. You can see from the scratch marks that the repair has been sanded diagonally in alternate directions until the filler is level with the surrounding panel but take care not to go deeply into the edges of the paint around the repair.

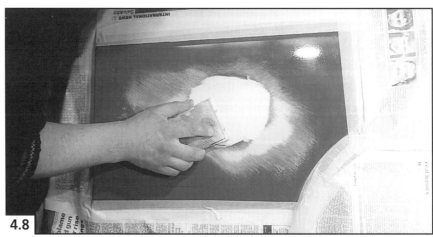

4.8

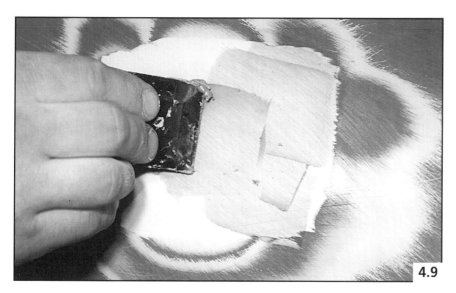

4.9 There will invariably be small pin holes even if, as in this case, the right amount of filler was applied first time. Use a tiny amount of filler scraped very thinly over the whole repair, filling in deep scratches and pin holes and then sanding off with a fine grade of sand paper - preferably dry paper rather than wet-or-dry because you don't want to get water on to the bare filler - until all of the core scratches from the earlier rougher sanding have been removed.

4.9

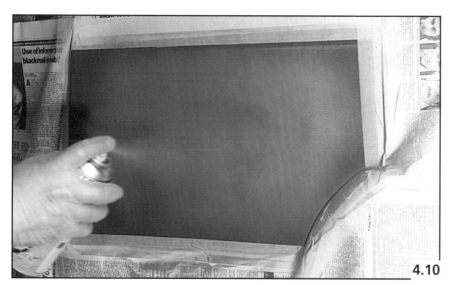

4.10 You can now use an aerosol primer to spray over the whole area of the repair but preferably not right up to the edges of the masking tape ...

4.10

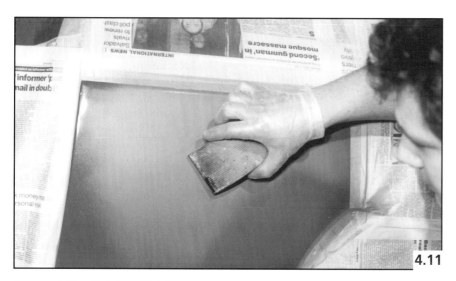

4.11 ... and you can now use wet-or-dry paper, again on a sanding block, to sand the primer paint since the Isopon is now protected from the water by the paint. If you do apply paint right up to the edge of the tape, be sure to 'feather' the edges of the paint, once it has dried off thoroughly (usually next day) so that the edges blend in smoothly to the surrounding surface, with no ridges.

4.11

SAFETY FIRST!

Always wear an efficient mask when spraying aerosol paint and only work in a well-ventilated area, well away from any source of ignition, since spray paint vapour, even that given off by an aerosol, is highly flammable. Ensure that you have doors and windows open to the outside when using aerosol paint but in cooler weather, close them when the vapour has dispersed otherwise the surface of the paint will "bloom", or take on a milky appearance. In fact, you may find it difficult to obtain a satisfactory finish in cold and damp weather.

4.12 Before starting to spray, ensure that the nozzle is clear. Note that the can must be held with the index finger well back on the aerosol button. If you let your finger overhang the front of the button, a paint drip can form and throw itself on to the work area as a paint blob. This is most annoying and means that you will have to let the paint dry, sand it down and start again.

4.13 One of the secrets of getting a decent coat of paint which doesn't run badly is to put a very light coat of spray paint on to the panel first, followed by several more coats, allowing time between each coat for the bulk of the solvent to evaporate. Alternate coats should go horizontally, followed by vertical coats as shown on the inset diagram.

4.14 If carried out with great care and skill, this type of repair can be virtually invisible. After allowing about a week for the paint to dry, you will be able to polish it with a light cutting compound, blending the edges of the repair into the surrounding paintwork.

4.12

Do note that if your repairs don't work out first time and you have to apply more paint on top of the fresh paint that you have already used, allow a week to elapse otherwise there is a strong risk of pickling or other reactions taking place. Also note that a prime cause of paint failure is the existence of silicone on the surface of the old paint before you start work. These come from most types of polish and are not all that easy to remove. Thoroughly wipe the panel down with white spirit before starting work and wash off with warm water and washing-up liquid to remove any further traces of the polish and the white spirit - but don't use the sponge or bucket that you normally use for washing the car otherwise you will simply introduce more silicones onto the surface!

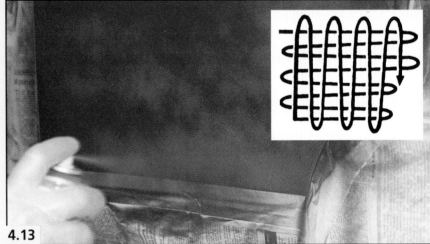
4.13

4.15 We are grateful to W. David & Sons Ltd, the makers of Isopon for their assistance with this section of the book and to CarPlan for their supply of the aerosol paints featured here. Isopon P38 is available in several different sizes of container and can easily be matched to the size of the repair that you have to carry out and all of the products shown here are readily available from high street motorists' stores.

4.14

4.15

CHAPTER 5 - RUSTPROOFING

When mechanical components deteriorate, they can cost you a lot of money to replace. But when your Sprite or Midget's bodywork deteriorates it can cost you the car, if the deterioration goes beyond the point where the car is economic to repair. Here's how to carry out preventative treatment and how to reapply it when the time comes. Please remember, however, that different models of Midget and Sprite have 'access' holes (they weren't put there for that, of course) in different places, so it isn't possible to be specific about which cars have to be drilled and which can use existing holes.

Do take note of the fact that in Britain, the Automobile Association has carried out research into rust-proofing materials and has found that inadequately applied materials do more harm than good. So do take great care that you apply rustproofing as thoroughly as possible - reaching every part of the car with a type of rustproofing fluid that creeps into each of the seams, into any rust that may have already formed on the surface and using an applicator that applies the fluid in a mist rather than in streams or blobs which unfortunately is all that some of the hand applicators we have seen seem to do.

Also, you should note that the best time to apply rustproofing materials to your car is in the summer when the warmer weather will allow the materials to flow better inside the hidden areas of the car's bodywork.

SAFETY FIRST!
Wear gloves a face mask and goggles when applying rustproofing material. Keep such materials away from your eyes but if you do get any into your eyes, wash out with copious amount of cold water and, if necessary, immediately seek medical advice. All rust-proofing materials are flammable and should be kept well away from all sources of ignition, especially when applying them. All such materials are volatile and in vaporised form are more likely to catch fire or explode. Do bear in mind that, if any welding has to be carried out on the car within a few months of rust-proofing materials being injected into it you must inform those who are carrying out the welding because of the fire risk. Cover all brake components with plastic bags so that none of the rustproofing material can get on to the brake friction materials and keep well away from the clutch bellhousing and from exhaust manifold and exhaust system. Always carry out this work out of doors since the vapour can be dangerous in a confined space.

INSIDE INFORMATION: i) All electric motors should be covered up with plastic bags so that none of the rustproofing fluids get into the motors (these include power windows and power aerials) and all win-dows should be fully wound up when injecting fluid inside the door panels. ii) Ensure that all drain channels are clear (see Job 107 in Chapter 3, Service Intervals Step-by-Step) so that any excess rust-

proofing fluid can drain out and also check once again that they are clear after you have finished carrying out the work to ensure that your application of the fluid has not caused them to be clogged up, other-wise water will get trapped in there, negating much of the good work you have carried out.

☐ Job 1. Wash Underbody

You will have to wash off the underside of the body, paying particular attention to the undersides of the wings and wheel arches, before you can start to apply new rustproofing. Scrape off any hard, thick deposits of mud, and any old flaking body sealant under the car. One of the quickest ways to do the job is to use a power washer with a long lance. Many garages have this equipment for customer use in a wash bay and this is a very efficient way of doing the job. You will, however, still have to go underneath with a scraper afterwards as even a power jet won't take off flaking body sealant. You will also have to wait up to a week for the underside of the car to dry thoroughly before applying new rustproofing.

2A

☐ Job 2. Equipment

2A. Gather together all the materials you need to do the job before you start. Bear in mind the safety equipment you will need referred to in Safety First! - see above. You will also

---

Our thanks are due to LMG Kent Ltd for help in preparing this chapter and for making a car available for photography.

need lifting equipment and axle stands - see *Chapter 1, Safety First!* for information on raising and supporting a car above the ground and also the introduction to *Chapter 3, Service Intervals Step-by-Step,* for the correct procedures to follow when raising your car with a trolley jack. You will need copious amounts of newspaper to spread on the floor because quite a lot of rustproofing fluid will run out of the box sections and other areas under the car and you may have to park your car over newspaper for a couple of days after carrying out this treatment. Remember that the vapour given off by the materials will continue for several days, so park your car in the open for a week or so if you can, rather than in an enclosed garage. Probably the best known makes of rust preventing fluid in the UK are Waxoyl and Dinitrol. MG specialists LMG at Bexlyheath in Kent, where we went for inside information on the vulnerable areas on a Midget, use Waxoyl, but it is a matter of personal choice. We have seen cars which had been treated with both these products quite a few years before and can say that, provided they are properly applied, topped up at regular intervals, and provided rust has not already gained a serious hold, either will do the job of protecting the car from further rusting for many years. Waxoyl kits come either with the one-hand applicator shown here or with a larger hand pump applicator which is more easy to use if you have a helper to pump while you hold the lance.

2B. A far more thorough coverage - indeed the only way you'll do the job properly - is by using an air compressor-fed injector gun. Here, the bonnet air intake on a Frogeye is being treated.

You'll need a drill large enough for the injector lance - but ensure you can buy grommets to match before you start drilling!

INSIDE INFORMATION: Except in a heat wave, it is essential to stand the container of rustproofer in a tub of hot water to keep it fluid. Top up the tub from time to time with more hot water while you are working. Not only will warm rustproofer penetrate seams better, it will flow through the applicator better and not clog so easily. Some people thin the rustproofer with white spirit, but many prefer warming it. Wash the gun and lances out with white spirit afterwards. If you let the rustproofer set, it is almost impossible to clean them.

Around the Car

Job 3. Chrome Trim

Some rustproofing fluids in aerosol cans are thin enough for injecting behind chromium trim strips and badges but some people find that they are inclined to leave a stain on the paintwork around the trim. As an alternative to a rustproofing fluid, you can use a water dispersant or a thin oil - see Job 59 in *Chapter 3, Service Intervals Step-by-Step.*

Job 4. Boot Lid

4. Inject rustproofing fluid in all the double skinned areas of the bootlid. You can do this with a lance or the plastic pipe of the applica-

tor or, as shown here, by using a long plastic spout on an oil can which you can keep for the job of rustproofing and topping up. Provided you keep Waxoyl warm, the oil can will inject it quite easily.

Job 5. Boot side box sections

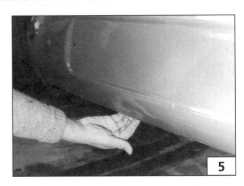

5. Unlike some cars, you don't have to drill holes inside a Midget's boot to get the fluid inside box sections and pressings. At the back of the floor where the box section curves round, there is a gap into which you can feed the nozzle of the applicator. At the other end of the box section where it meets the side panel, there is another gap where you can inject. Beware fumes when working inside a Frogeye boot!

Job 6. Boot side panels

6. Also at the side, insert your nozzle or lance down behind the openings in the side panels to give a good coating of rustproofing fluid deep into the well.

Job 7. Rear box pressing

7. Lastly inside the boot, there is a gap at the base of the box pressing right in the middle of the rear panel. You can inject fluid here and also in the central hole in the middle of the pressing a few inches above the base.

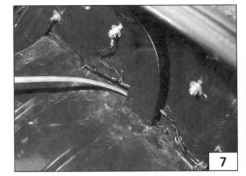

Job 8. Inside doors

8. Some rustproofing firms drill a hole in the end of the door, or use an existing drain hole, to inject rustproofing fluid. However, you will be able to make a better and more thorough job of it if you remove the interior trim so that you can see where the fluid is going.

Job 9. Bonnet pressing

9. Apply rustproofing fluid generously inside the inner pressing which supports the bonnet hinge. In the case of the 'Frogeye' Sprite, you will have excellent access, but the whole assembly must be treated meticulously. It is literally irreplaceable!

Job 10. Front bonnet pressing

Towards the front, inject fluid into the large cross section where the bonnet catch comes down, making sure that you reach right out to the side edges.

Job 11. Bonnet nose

11. Right at the front of the bonnet, inject fluid deep into the nose section. This is a very vulnerable section so make sure it is well coated.

Job 12. Sills

12A. Use the jacking point on the sills to inject fluid both fore and aft along the sills. Use a long pipe or lance, pushing this right in and then injecting as you withdraw it.

Afterwards, it is advisable to use a short lance or the oil can to make sure that the rustproofing fluid has penetrated round the tubular jacking point itself.

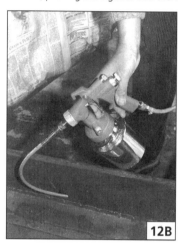

12B. You'll need to drill the inner sill to be certain of reaching the full length of the sill, in both directions.

Inside the Car

Job 13. Rear cross member

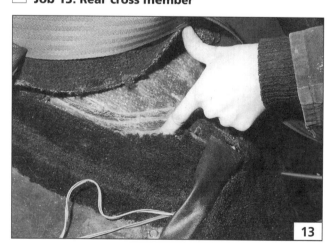

13. To complete the rustproofing inside the boot, you need to inject into the cross member just in front of the boot wall. The best place to get access to this is from inside where you have to lift the carpet and drill a hole in the top part of the box section. Use a rubber grommet to close the hole afterwards.

Job 14. Floor panels

14

14. These reinforcing members are crucial on the early, quarter-elliptic sprung cars. Because most rust proofing fluids never dry completely, most owners prefer not to coat over the inside of the floor panels. However, these are vulnerable because of condensation under the carpet, and from rain which inevitably gets in before you have had time to close the hood when a shower starts. As part of the rustproofing process, you should take out the seat runners and carpets, wire brush any existing rust, coat it with a rust killing paint, and then paint the inside of the floor with an undersealing body compound. Allow this to dry out for a day or two and then cover it with a sheet of polythene before replacing the carpet.

Job 15. Door pillars

While you have the carpets out, lift the trim on the door hinge pillar and shut pillar each side and inject rust proofing fluid into each pillar. The vulnerable area is at the base, so make sure the fluid coats this area thoroughly.

Beneath the Car

Job 16. Rear wheel arches

Make sure there is no mud trapped in the crevices underneath and spray fluid liberally round the inside of the wheel arch. Remember to wear goggles while you are spraying any part of the underside of the car.

Job 17. Front wheel arches

Spray liberally round the inside of the front wheel arches with particular attention to the areas around the headlamps and the bottom part of the front wing where it curves underneath. These are notorious areas for rust to start.

Job 18. Longitudinal box sections

18. On the longitudinal sections at the sides, both front and back, there are access holes, which should be closed by oval rubber plugs, though these are sometimes missing. If

18

they are, get new ones from your MG specialist dealer. Poke your lance or plastic pipe well into them along the section and inject fluid as you withdraw it.

Job 19. Rear floor box section

19

19. You will find two other access holes where the floor panel starts just in front of the rear axle. Repeat the treatment here.

Job 20. Rear floor pressings

Alongside the front anchorage for the rear springs there are large holes in the floor pressings where mud can collect and start rust forming. If your initial washing did not clear them out, scrape around inside to get as much of the mud out as you can then coat the inside of these sections liberally with fluid. On MkI and MkII Sprites and MkI Midgets, the quarter-elliptic spring boxes are a nightmare to cut out and replace, so rustproof thoroughly all around them. You could drill extra holes front the inside of the car into this triangular 'Toblerone'-shaped hollow box, above the rear floor.

Job 21. Above the rear axle

Over the top of the rear axle there are box sections which start by the top anchorage for the axle rebound strap. The front of these box sections is not completely closed, though you may have to enlarge the openings slightly to get the nozzle of your lance in. Push the tube of the lance fully in and spray while you withdraw it.

Job 22. Toe board cross member

The toe board cross member, where it joins the bulkhead pressing, is vulnerable to rusting at the outer bottom parts. If you reach up above the member you will feel an opening where you can inject rustproofing fluid. Make sure the inside of this section is well coated.

Job 23. Underside of floor panels

After making sure that there is no loose or flaking body sealing on the floor panels, coat them well with a body undersealing compound. When this has set - though it never dries rock hard - spray rustproofing fluid liberally over it and repeat this after washing at your rustproofing periods.

CHAPTER 6 - FAULT FINDING

This Chapter aims to help you to overcome the main faults that can affect the mobility or safety of your Land Rover. It also helps you to overcome the problem that has affected most mechanics - amateur and professional - at one time or another... Blind Spot Syndrome!

It goes like this: the vehicle refuses to start one damp Sunday morning. You decide that there must be no fuel getting through. By the time you've stripped the fuel pump, carburettor. fuel lines and "unblocked" the fuel tank, it's time for bed. And the next day, the local garage finds that your main HT lead has dropped out of the coil! Something like that has happened to most of us!

Don't jump to conclusions: if your engine won't start or runs badly, if electrical components fail, follow the logical sequence of checks listed here and detailed overleaf, eliminating each "check" (by testing, (not by "hunch") before moving on to the next. Remember that the great majority of failures are caused by electrical or ignition faults: only a minor proportion of engine failures come from the fuel system, follow the sequences shown here - and you'll have better success in finding that fault. Before carrying out any of the work described in this Chapter please read carefully *Chapter 1 Safety First!*

Engine won't start

1. Starter motor doesn't turn.

2. Starter motor turns slowly.

3. Starter motor noisy or harsh.

4. Starter motor turns engine but vehicle will not start. See 'Ignition System' box.

5. Is battery okay?

6. Can engine be rotated by hand?

7. Check battery connections for cleanliness/tightness.

8. Test battery with voltmeter.

9. Have battery 'drop' test carried out by specialist.

10. If engine cannot be rotated by hand, check for mechanical seizure of power unit, or pinion gear jammed in mesh with flywheel - 'rock' vehicle backwards and forwards until free. or apply spanner to square drive at front end of starter motor.

11. If engine can be rotated by hand, check for loose electrical connections at starter, faulty solenoid, or defective starter motor.

12. Battery low on charge or defective - recharge and have 'drop' test carried out by specialist.

13. Internal fault within starter motor - e.g. worn brushes.

14. Drive teeth on ring gear or starter pinion worn/broken.

15. Main drive spring broken.

16. Starter motor securing bolts loose.

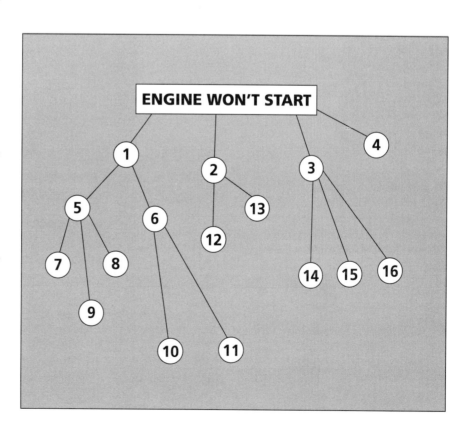

Ignition system

17. Check for spark at plug (remove plug and prop it with threads resting on bare metal of cylinder block). Do not touch plug or lead while operating starter.

18. If no spark is present at plug, check for spark at contact breaker points when 'flicked' open (ignition 'on'). Double-check to ensure that points are clean and correctly gapped, and try again.

19. If spark present at contact breaker points. Check for spark at central high tension lead from coil.

20. If spark present at central high tension lead from coil, check distributor cap and rotor arm; replace if cracked or contacts badly worn.

21. If distributor cap and rotor arm are okay, check high tension leads and connections - replace leads if they are old. carbon core type suppressed variety.

22. If high tension leads are sound but dirty or damp, clean/dry them.

23. If high tension leads okay, check/clean/dry/re-gap sparking plugs.

24. Damp conditions! Apply water dispellant spray to ignition system.

25. If no spark present at contact breaker points, examine connections of low tension leads between ignition switch and coil and from coil to contact breaker (including short low-tension lead within distributor).

26. If low tension circuit connections okay, examine wiring.

27. If low tension wiring is sound, is condenser okay! If in doubt, fit new condenser.

28. If condenser is okay, check for spark at central high tension lead from coil.

29. If no spark present at central high tension lead from coil, check for poor high tension lead connections.

30. If high tension lead connections okay, is coil okay? If in doubt, fit new coil.

31. If spark present at plug, is it powerful or weak? If weak, see '27'.

32. If spark is healthy, check ignition timing.

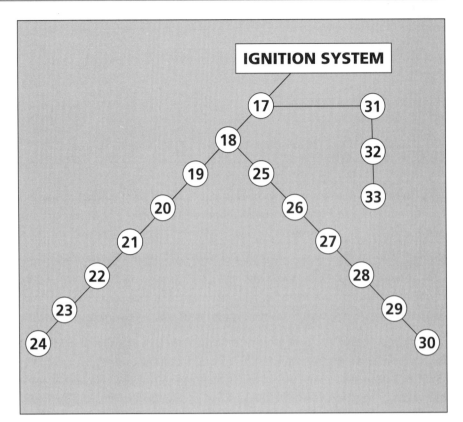

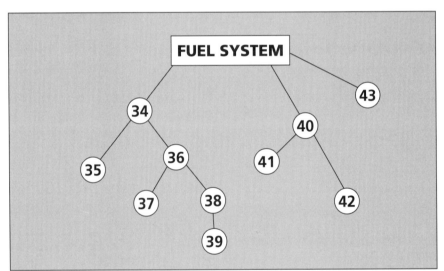

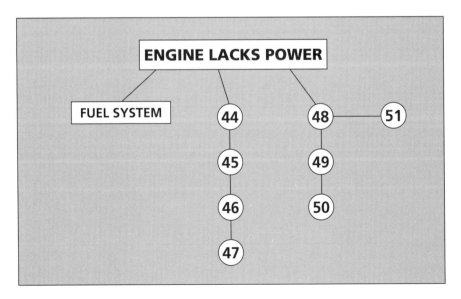

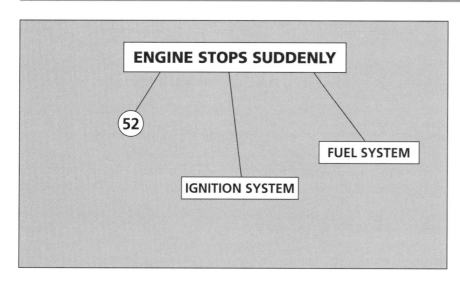

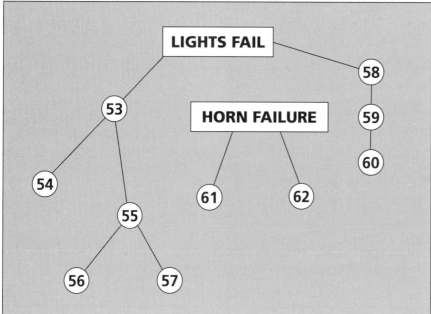

33. If ignition timing is okay, see 'Fuel System' box (see 36).

Fuel system

34. Check briefly for fuel at feed pipe to carb. (Disconnect pipe and turn ignition 'on', ensuring pipe is aimed away from hot engine and exhaust components and into a suitable container). If no fuel present at feed pipe, is petrol tank empty! (Rock vehicle and listen for 'sloshing' in tank as well as looking at gauge). If you have a twin-tank vehicle, make sure that the under-dash switch is correctly positioned.

35. If tank is empty, replenish!

FUEL SYSTEM - SAFETY FIRST!
*Before working on the fuel system, read **Chapter 1, Safety First!** Take special care to 1) only work out of doors . 2) wear suitable gloves and goggles and keep fuel out of eyes and away from skin: it is known to be carcinogenic. 3) if fuel does come into contact with skin, wash off straight away. 4) if fuel gets into your eyes, wash out with copious amounts of clean, cold water. Seek medical advice if necessary. 5) when draining fuel or testing for fuel flow. drain or pump into a sufficiently large container, minimising splashes. 6) don't smoke, work near flames or sparks or work when the engine or exhaust are hot.*

---

36. If there is petrol in the tank but none issues from the feed pipe from pump to carburettor, check that the small vent hole in the fuel filler cap is not blocked and causing a vacuum.

37. Check for a defective fuel pump. With outlet pipe disconnected AND AIMED AWAY FROM PUMP AND HOT EXHAUST COMPONENTS, ETC. as well as your eyes and clothes, and into a suitable container, turn the engine over and fuel should issue from pump outlet.

38. If pump is okay, check for blocked fuel filter or pipe, or major leak in pipe between tank and pump, or between pump and carb.

39. If the filter is clean and the pump operates, suspect blocked carburettor jet(s) or damaged/sticking float or incorrectly adjusted carburettor.

40. If fuel is present at carburettor feed pipe, remove spark plugs and check whether wet with unburnt fuel.

41. If the spark plugs are fuel-soaked, check that the automatic choke is operating as it should and is not jammed 'shut'. Other possibilities include float needle valve(s) sticking 'open' or leaking, float punctured, carburettor incorrectly adjusted or air filter totally blocked. Clean plugs before replacing.

42. If the spark plugs are dry, check whether the float needle valve is jammed 'shut'.

43. Check for severe air leak at inlet manifold gasket or carburettor gasket, incorrectly set valve clearances.

Engine lacks power

44. Engine overheating. Check oil temperature gauge (where fitted). Low oil pressure light may come on.

45. Thermostat not opening/closing at the correct temperatures or the cooling air flaps not operating because they've seized. If you car's carburation has an air inlet connected to a heater chamber on the exhaust manifold check that: i) the pipe is in place and not split and, ii) any thermostatic valve or flap is operating correctly. If not the car can stop and restart intermittently because of inlet icing in freezing weather.

46. If thermostat/air flaps okay, check oil level BEWARE - DIPSTICK AND OIL MAY BE VERY HOT. Also, check for loss of coolant. WAIT UNTIL THE ENGINE HAS FULLY COOLED BEFORE ATTEMPTING TO REMOVE RADIATOR CAP. USE A RAG TO PROTECT HANDS WHEN RELEASING CAP, AND KEEP FACE WELL CLEAR IN CASE COOLANT SPRAYS OUT. If low of coolant, check hoses and connections, water pump and cylinder block for leaks. Rectify and top up system.

47. If oil level okay, check for slipping fan belt, cylinder head gasket 'blown', partial mechanical seizure of engine, blocked or damaged exhaust system.

48. If engine temperature is normal, check cylinder compressions.

49. If cylinder compression readings low, add a couple of teaspoons of engine oil to each cylinder in turn. and repeat test. If readings don't improve. suspect burnt valves/seats.

50. If compression readings improve after adding oil as described, suspect worn cylinder bores, pistons and rings.

51 . If compression readings are normal, check for mechanical problems. For example, binding brakes, slipping clutch partially seized transmission etc.

Engine stops suddenly

52. Check for sudden ingress of water/snow onto ignition components, in adverse weather conditions. Sudden failure is almost always because of an ignition fault. Check for simple wiring and connection breakdowns.

Lights fail

53. Sudden failure - check fuses.

54. If all lamps affected, check switch and main wiring feeds.

55. If not all lamps are affected, check bulbs on lamps concerned.

56. If bulbs appear to be okay, check bulb holder(s), local wiring and connections.

57. If bulb(s) blown, replace!

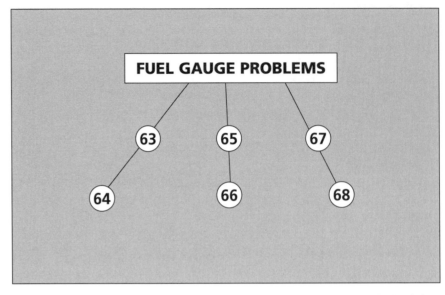

FUEL GAUGE PROBLEMS

63   65   67

64   66   68

58. Intermittent operation, flickering or poor light output - check earth (ground) connections(s).

59. If earth(s) okay, check switch.

60. If switch okay, check wiring and connections.

Horn failure

61. If horn does not operate, check fuse, all connections (particularly earths/grounds) and cables. Remove horn connections, check and clean. Use 12v test lamp to ascertain if power getting to horn.

62. If horn will not stop(!), disconnect the horn and check for earthing of cable between button and horn unit, and the wiring in the horn switch housing.

Fuel gauge problems

63. Gauge reads 'empty' - check for fuel in tank.

64. If fuel is present in tank, check for earthing and wiring from tank to gauge. and for wiring disconnections.

65. Gauge permanently reads 'full', regardless of tank contents. Check wiring and connections as in '66'.

66. If wiring and connections all okay, sender unit/fuel gauge defective.

67. With wiring disconnected, check for continuity between fuel gauge terminals. Do NOT test gauge by short-circuiting to earth. Replace unit if faulty.

68. If gauge is okay, disconnect wiring from tank sender unit and check for continuity between terminal and case. Replace sender unit if faulty.

CHAPTER 7
GETTING THROUGH THE MOT

Taking your beloved Sprite or Midget for the annual MoT test can be rather like going to the dentist - you're not sure what to expect and the result could be painful - not only to your pocket. However, it needn't be like that...

This Chapter is for owners in Britain whose cars need to pass the MoT test. The Test was first established in 1961 by the then-named Ministry of Transport: the name of the Test remains, even though the name of the government department does not.

The information in this Chapter could be very useful to non-UK owners in helping to carry out a detailed check of a car's condition - such as when checking over a car that you might be interested in buying, for instance. But it is MOST IMPORTANT that UK owners check for themselves that legislation has not changed since this book was written and that non-UK owners obtain information on the legal requirements in their own territory - and that they act upon them.

Part I: Pass the MoT

The aim of this chapter is to explain what is actually tested on an Midget or Austin-Healey Sprite and (if it is not obvious) how the test is done. This should enable you to identify and eliminate problems before they undermine the safety or diminish the performance of your car and long before they cause the expense and inconvenience of a test failure.

SAFETY FIRST!
*The MoT tester will follow a set procedure and we will cover the ground in a similar way, starting inside the car, then continuing outside, under the bonnet, underneath the car etc. When preparing to go underneath the car, do ensure that it is jacked on firm level ground and then supported on axle stands or ramps which are adequate for the task. Wheels which remain on the ground should have chocks in front of and behind them, and while the rear wheels remain on the ground, the hand brake should be firmly ON. For most repair and replacement jobs under a car these normal precautions will suffice. However, the car needs to be even more stable than usual when carrying out these checks. There must be no risk of it toppling off its stands while suspension and steering components are being pushed and pulled in order to test them. Read carefully **Chapter 1, Safety First!** for further important information on raising and supporting a vehicle above the ground.*

The purpose of the MoT test is to try to ensure that vehicles using British roads reach minimum standards of safety. Accordingly, it is an offence to use a car without a current MoT certificate. Approximately 40 per cent of vehicles submitted for the test fail it, but many of these failures could be avoided by knowing what the car might fail on, and by taking appropriate remedial action before the test proper is carried out. It is also worth noting that a car can be submitted for a test up to a month before the current certificate expires - if the vehicle passes, the new certificate will be valid until one year from the date of expiry of the old one, provided that the old certificate is produced at the time of the test.

It is true that the scope of the test has been considerably enlarged in the last few years, with the result that it is correspondingly more difficult to be sure that your MG will reach the required standards. In truth, however, a careful examination of the car in the relevant areas, perhaps a month or so before the current certificate expires, will highlight components which require attention, and enable any obvious faults to be rectified before you take the car for its test.

If the car is muddy or particularly dirty (especially underneath) it would be worth giving it a thorough clean a day or two before carrying out the inspection so that it has ample time to dry. Do the same before the real MoT test. A clean car makes a better impression on the examiner, who can refuse to test a car which is particularly dirty underneath.

MoT testers do not dismantle assemblies during the test but you may wish to do so during your pre-test check-up for a better view of certain wearing parts, such as the rear brake shoes for example. See *Chapter 3, Service Intervals Step-by-Step* for information on how to check the brakes.

Tool Box

Dismantling apart, few tools are needed for testing. A light hammer is useful for tapping panels underneath the car when looking for rust. If this produces a bright metallic noise, then the area being tapped is sound. If the noise produced is dull, the area contains rust or filler. When tapping sills and box sections, listen also for the sound of debris (that is, rust flakes) on the inside of the panel. Use a screwdriver to prod weak parts of panels. This may produce holes of course, but if the panels have rusted to that extent, you really ought to know about it. A strong lever (such as a tyre lever) can be useful for applying the required force to suspension joints etc. when assessing whether there is any wear in the joints.

You will need an assistant to operate controls and perhaps to wobble the road wheels while you inspect components under the car.

Two more brief explanations are required before we start our informal test. Firstly, the age of the car determines exactly which lights, seat belts and other items it should have. Frequently in the next few pages you will come across the phrase "Cars first used ..." followed by a date. A car's "first used date" is either its date of first registration, or the date six months after it was manufactured, whichever was earlier. Or, if the car was originally used without being registered (such as a car which has been imported to the U.K. or an ex-H.M. Forces car etc.) the "first used date" is the date of manufacture.

Secondly, there must not be excessive rust, serious distortion or any fractures affecting certain prescribed areas of the bodywork. These prescribed areas are load-bearing parts of the bodywork within 30 cm (12 in.) of anchorages or mounting points associated with testable items such as seat belts, brake pedal assemblies, master cylinders, servos, suspension and steering components and also body and fuel tank mountings. Keep this rule in mind while inspecting the car, but remember also that even if such damage occurs outside a prescribed area, it can cause failure of the test. Failure will occur if the damage is judged to reduce the continuity or strength of a main load-bearing part of the bodywork sufficiently to have an adverse effect on the braking, steering, or any other safety aspect.

The following notes are necessarily abbreviated, and are for assistance only. They are not a definitive guide to all the MoT regulations. It is also worth mentioning that the varying degrees of discretion of individual MoT testers can mean that there are variations between the standards as applied. However, the following points should help to make you aware of the aspects which will be examined. Now, if you have your clipboard, checklist and pencil handy, let's make a start...

The 'Easy' Bits

Checking these items is straightforward and should not take more than a few minutes - it could avoid an embarrassingly simple failure.

Lights

Within the scope of the test are headlamps, side and tail lights, brake lamps, direction indicators, and number plate lamps (plus rear fog lamps on all cars first used on or after 1 April, 1980, and any earlier cars subsequently so equipped, and also hazard warning lamps on any car so fitted). All must operate, must be clean and not significantly damaged; flickering is also not permitted. The switches should also all work properly Pairs of lamps should give approximately the same intensity of light output, and operation of one set of lights should not affect the working of another - such trouble is usually due to bad earthing.

Indicators should flash at between 60 and 120 times per minute (rev the engine to encourage them, if a little slow, although the examiner might not let you get away with it!) Otherwise, renew the (inexpensive) flasher unit and check all wiring and earth connections.

Interior reminder lamps, such as for indicators, rear fog lamps and hazard warning lamps should all operate in unison with their respective exterior lamps.

Head light aim must be correct - in particular, the lights should not dazzle other road users. An approximate guide can be obtained by shining the lights against a vertical wall, but final adjustment may be necessary by reference to the beam checking machine at the MoT station - if necessary, you may have to ask the examiner to adjust the lights so that they comply.

Reflectors must be unbroken, clean, and not obscured - for example, by stickers.

Wheels and Tyres

Check the wheels for loose nuts, cracks, and damaged rims. Missing wheel nuts or studs are also failure points, naturally enough.

There is no excuse for running on illegal tyres. The legal requirement is that there must be at least 1.6 mm of tread depth remaining, over the central three-quarters of the width of the tyre all the way around. From this it can be deduced that there is no legal requirement to have

1.6 mm. (1/16 in.) of tread on the shoulders of the tyre, but in practice, most MoT stations will be reluctant to pass a tyre in this condition. In any case, for optimum safety - especially wet grip - you would be well advised to change tyres when they wear down to around 3 mm (118 in.) or so depth of remaining tread.

Visible tread wear indicator bars, found approximately every nine inches around the tread of the tyre are highlighted when the tread reaches the critical 1.6 mm. point.

Tyres should not show signs of cuts or bulges, rubbing on the bodywork or running gear, and the valves should be in sound condition, and correctly aligned.

Cross-ply and radial tyre types must not be mixed on the same axle, and if pairs of cross-ply and radial tyres are fitted, the radials must be on the rear axle.

Windscreen

The screen must not be damaged (by cracks, chips, etc.) or obscured so that the driver does not have a clear view of the road. Permissible size of damage points depends on where they occur. Within an area 290 mm. (nearly 12 in.) wide, ahead of the driver, and up to the top of the wiper arc, any damage must be confined within a circle less than 10 mm. (approx. 0.4 in.) in diameter. This is increased to 40 mm. (just over 1.5 in.) for damage within the rest of the screen area swept by the wipers.

Washers and Wipers

The wipers must clear an area big enough to give the driver a clear view forwards and to the side of the car. The wiper blades must be securely attached and sound, with no cracks or missing sections. The wiper switch should also work properly. The screen washers must supply the screen with sufficient liquid to keep it clean, in conjunction with the use of the wipers.

Mirrors

If your MG was first used before 1 August, 1978, it needs to have only one rear view mirror. Later cars must have at least two, one of which must be on the driver's side. The mirrors must be visible from the driver's seat, and not be damaged or obscured so that the view to the rear is affected. Therefore cracks, chips and discolouration can mean failure.

Horn

The horn must emit a uniform note which is loud enough to give adequate warning of approach, and the switch must operate correctly. Multitone horns playing notes in sequence are not permitted, but two tones sounding together are fine.

Seat Security

The seats must be securely mounted, and the frames should be sound.

Number (Registration) Plates

Both front and rear number plates must be present, and in good condition, with no breaks or missing numbers or letters. The plates must not be obscured, and the digits must not be re-positioned to form names, for instance.

Vehicle Identification Numbers (VIN)

Midgets first used on or after 1 August, 1980 are obliged to have a clearly displayed VIN - Vehicle Identification Number (or old-fashioned 'chassis number' for older cars), which is plainly legible. See *Chapter 8, Facts and Figures* for the correct location on your car.

Exhaust System

The entire system must be present, properly mounted, free of leaks and should not be noisy - which can happen when the internal baffles fail. Proper repairs by welding, or exhaust cement, or bandage are acceptable, as long as no gas leaks are evident. Then again, common sense, if not the MoT, dictates that exhaust bandage should be only a very short-term emergency measure. For safety's sake, fit a new exhaust if yours is reduced to this.

Seat Belts

Belts are not needed on Midgets or Sprites first used before 1 January, 1965. On cars after this date - and earlier examples, if subsequently fitted with seat belts - the belts must be in good condition (i.e. not frayed or otherwise damaged), and the buckles and catches should also operate correctly. Inertia reel types, where fitted, should retract properly.

Belt mountings must be secure, with no structural damage or corrosion within 30 cm. (12 in.) of them.

Part II: Detailed Checks

You've checked the easy bits - now it's time for the detail. Some of the easy bits referred to above are included here, but this is intended as a more complete check list to give your car the best possible chance of gaining a First Class Honours, MoT Pass.

Inside the Car

☐ 1. The steering wheel should be examined for cracks and for damage which might interfere with its use, or injure the driver's hands. It should also be pushed and pulled along the column axis, and also up and down, at 90 degrees to it. This will highlight any deficiencies in the wheel and upper column mounting/bearing, and also any excessive end float, and movement between the column shaft and the wheel. Rotate the steering wheel in both directions to test for free play at the

wheel rim - this shouldn't exceed approximately 13 mm. (0.5 in.), assuming a 380 mm. (15 in.) diameter steering wheel. Look, too, for movement in the steering column fasteners, and visually check their condition and security. They must be sound, and properly tightened.

☐ 2. Check that the switches for headlamps, sidelights, direction indicators, hazard warning lights, wipers, washers and horn, are in good working order and check that the telltale lights or audible warnings are working where applicable.

☐ 3. Make sure that the windscreen wipers operate effectively with blades that are secure and in good condition. The windscreen washer should provide sufficient liquid to clear the screen in conjunction with the wipers.

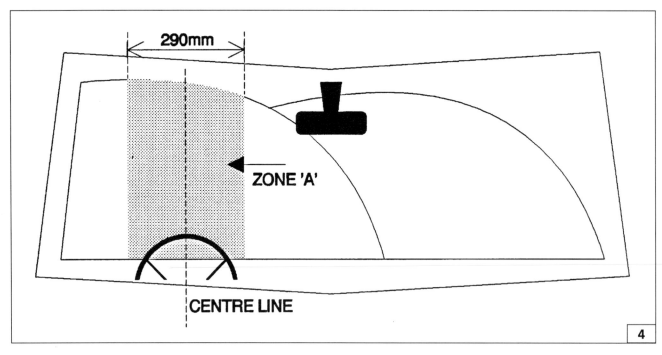

☐ 4. Check for windscreen damage, especially in the area swept by the wipers. From the MoT tester's point of view, Zone A is part of this area, 290 mm (11.5 in.) wide and centred on the centre of the steering wheel. Damage to the screen within this area should be capable of fitting into a 10 mm (approx. 0.4 in.) diameter circle and the cumulative effect of more minor damage should not seriously restrict the driver's view. Windscreen stickers or other obstructions should not encroach more than 10 mm (approx 0.5 in.) into this area. In the remainder of the swept area the maximum diameter of damage or degree of encroachment by obstructions is 40 mm (approx. 1.6 in.) and there is no ruling regarding cumulative damage. Specialist windscreen companies can often repair a cracked screen for a lot less than the cost of replacement.

☐ 5. The horn control should be present, secure and readily accessible to the driver, and the horn(s) should be loud enough to be heard by other road users. Gongs, bells and sirens are not permitted (except as part of an anti-theft device) and two (or more) tone horns (which alternate between two or more notes) are not permitted at all. On cars first used after 1 August 1973, the horn should produce a constant, continuous or uniform note which is neither harsh nor grating.

☐ 6. There must be one exterior mirror on the driver's side of the vehicle and either an exterior mirror fitted to the passenger's side or an interior mirror. The required mirrors should be secure and in good condition.

☐ 7. Check that the hand brake operates effectively without coming to the end of its working travel. The lever and its mechanism must be complete, securely mounted, unob-structed in its travel and in a sufficiently good condition to remain firmly in the 'On' position even when knocked from side to side. The 30 cm rule applies in the vicinity of the hand brake lever mounting.

☐ 8. The foot brake pedal assembly should be complete, unobstructed, and in a good working condition, including the pedal rubber (which should not have been worn smooth). There should be no excessive movement of the pedal at right angles to its normal direction (indicating a badly worn pedal bearing or pivot). When fully depressed, the pedal should not be at the end of its travel. The pedal should not feel spongy (indicating air in the hydraulic system), nor should it tend to creep downwards while held under pressure (which indicates a faulty master cylinder).

☐ 9. Seats must be secure on their mountings and seat backs must be capable of being locked in the upright position.

☐ 10. On Midgets and Sprites first used on or after 1 January 1965, but before 1 April 1981, the driver's and front passenger's seats need belts, but these can be simple diagonal belts rather than the three-point belts (lap and diagonal belts for adults with at least three anchorage points) required by later cars. (For safety's sake, however, we do not recommend this type of belt.) Examine seat belt webbing and fittings to make sure that all are in good condition and that anchorages are firmly attached to the car's structure. Locking mechanisms should be capable of remaining locked, and of being released if required, when under load. Flexible buckle stalks (if fitted) should be free of corrosion, broken cable strands or other weaknesses.

☐ 11 . Check that on retracting seat belts the webbing winds into the retracting unit automatically, albeit with some manual assistance to start with.

☐ 12. Note the point raised earlier regarding corrosion around seat belt anchorage points. The MoT tester will not carry out any dismantling here, but he will examine floor mounted anchorage points from underneath the car if that is possible.

☐ 13. Before getting out of the car, make sure that both doors can be opened from the inside.

Outside the Car

☐ 14. Before closing the driver's door check the condition of the inner sill. Usually the MoT tester will do this by applying finger or thumb pressure to various parts of the panel while the floor covering remains in place. For your own peace of mind, look beneath the sill covering, taking great care not to tear any rubber covers. Then close the driver's door and make sure that it latches securely and repeat these checks on the nearside inner sill and door.

Now check all of the lights, front and rear, (including the number plate lights) while your assistant operates the light switches.

☐ 15. As we said earlier, you can carry out a rough and ready check on head lamp alignment for yourself, although it will certainly not be as accurate as having it done for you at the MoT testing station. Drive your car near to a wall, as shown.

Check that your tyres are correctly inflated and the car is on level ground.

Draw on the wall, with chalk:

a horizontal line about 2 metres long, and at same height as centre of head lamp lens.

two vertical lines about 1 metre long, each forming a cross with the horizontal line and the same distance apart as the head lamp centres.

another vertical line to form a cross on the horizontal line, midway between the others.

Now position your car so that:

it faces the wall squarely, and its centre line is in line with centre line marked on the wall.

the steering is straight. - head light lenses are 3.8 metres (12.5 ft) from the wall.

Switch on the headlamps' main and dipped beams in turn, and measure their centre points. You will be able to judge any major discrepancies in intensity and aim prior to having the beams properly set by a garage with beam measuring equipment.

Headlamps should be complete, clean, securely mounted, in good working order and not adversely affected by the operation of another lamp, and these basic requirements affect all the lamps listed below. Headlamps must dip as a pair from a single switch. Their aim must be correctly adjusted and they should not be affected (even to the extent of flickering) when lightly tapped by hand. Each head lamp should match its partner in terms of size, colour and intensity of light, and can be white or yellow.

☐ 16. Side lights should show white light to the front and red light to the rear. Lenses should not be broken, cracked or incomplete.

☐ 17. Vehicles first used before 1 April 1986 do not have to have a hazard warning device, but if one is fitted, it must be tested, and it must operate with the ignition switch either on or off. The lights should flash 60-120 times per minute, and indicators must operate independently of any other lights.

☐ 18. Check your stop lights. Pre-1971 cars need only one, but when two are fitted, both are tested, so you will not get away with one that works and one that doesn't! Stop lamps should produce a steady red light when the foot brake is applied.

☐ 19. There must be two red rear reflectors - always fitted by the manufacturers, of course - which are clean, and securely and symmetrically fitted to the car.

☐ 20. Cars first used on or after 1 April 1980 must have one rear fog lamp fitted to the centre or offside of the car and, so far as fog lamps are concerned, the MoT tester is interested in this lamp on these cars only. It must comply with the basic requirements (listed under headlamps) and emit a steady red light. Its tell-tale lamp, inside the car, must work to inform the driver that it is switched on.

☐ 21 . There must be a registration number plate at the front and rear of the car and both must be clean, secure, complete

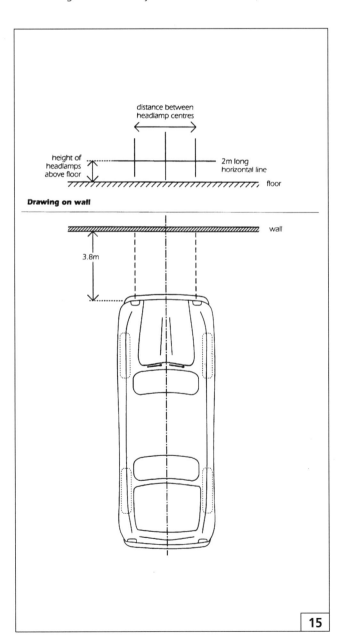

distance between headlamp centres

height of headlamps above floor

2m long horizontal line

floor

Drawing on wall

wall

3.8m

15

and unobscured. Letters and figures must be correctly formed and correctly spaced and not likely to be misread due to an uncovered securing bolt or whatever. The year letter counts as a figure. The space between letters and figures must be at least twice that between adjacent letters or figures.

☐ 22. Number plate lamps must be present, working, and not flickering when tapped by hand, just as for other lamps. Where more than one lamp or bulb was fitted as original equipment, all must be working.

The MoT tester will examine tyres and wheels while walking around the car and again when he is under the car.

☐ 23. Front tyres should match each other and rear tyres should match each other, both sets matching in terms of size, aspect ratio and type of structure. For example, you must never fit tyres of different sizes or types, such as cross-ply or radial, on the same 'axle' - both front wheels counting as 'on the same axle' in this context. Cross-ply or bias belted tyres should not be fitted on the rear axle, with radials on the front, neither should cross-ply tyres be fitted to the rear, with bias belted tyres on the front.

☐ 24. Failure of the test can be caused by a cut, lump, tear or bulge in a tyre, exposed ply or cord, a badly seated tyre, a re-cut tyre, a tyre fouling part of the vehicle, or a seriously damaged or misaligned valve stem which could cause sudden deflation of the tyre. To pass the test, the grooves of the tread pattern must be at least 1.6 mm deep throughout a continuous band comprising the central three-quarters of the breadth of tread, and round the entire outer circumference of the tyre.

All of the following photographs and the information in this section have been supplied with grateful thanks to Dunlop/SP Tyres.

☐ 24A. Modern tyres have tread wear indicators built into the tread groves (usually about eight of them spread equidistantly around the circumference). These appear as continuous bars running across the tread when the original pattern depth has worn down to 1.6 mm. There will be a distinct reduction in wet grip well before the tread wear indicators start to show, and you should replace tyres before they get to this stage, even though this is the legal minimum in the UK.

☐ 24B. Lumps and bulges in the tyre wall usually arise from accidental damage or even because of faults in the tyre construction. You should run your hand all the way around the side wall of the tyre, with the car either jacked off the ground, or moving the car half a wheels revolution, so that you can check the part of the tyre that was previously resting on the ground. Since you can't easily check the insides of the tyres in day-to-day use, it is even more important that you spend time carefully checking the inside of each tyre - the MoT tester will certainly do so! Tyres with bulges in them must be scrapped and replaced with new, since they can fail suddenly, causing your car to lose control.

☐ 24C. Abrasion of the tyre side wall can take place either in conjunction with bulging, or by itself, and this invariably results from an impact, such as the tyre striking the edge of a kerb or a pothole in the road. Once again, the tyre may be at imminent risk or failure and you should take advice from a tyre specialist on whether the abrasion is just superficial, or whether the tyre will need replacement.

NEW TYRE · TWI · **ILLEGAL TYRE** · 24A

24B

24C

24D

☐ 24D. All tyres will suffer progressively from cracking, albeit in most cases superficially, due to the effects of sunlight. If old age has caused the tyres on your car to degrade to this extent, replace them.

☐ 24E. If the outer edges of the tread are worn noticeably more than the centre, the tyres have-been run under inflated which not only ruins tyres, but causes worse fuel consumption, dangerous handling and is, of course, illegal.

24E

24F

Over-inflation causes the centre part of the tyre to wear more quickly than the outer edges. This is also illegal but in addition, it causes the steering and grip to suffer and the tyre becomes more susceptible to concussion damage.

☐ 24F. Incorrect wheel alignment causes one side of the tyre to wear more severely than the other. If your car should ever hit a kerb or large pothole, it is worthwhile having the wheel alignment checked since this costs considerably less than new front tyres.

☐ 25. Road wheels must be secure and must not be badly damaged, distorted or cracked, or have badly distorted bead rims (perhaps due to kerbing), or loose or missing wheel nuts, studs or bolts.

☐ 26. Check the bodywork for any sharp edges or projections, caused by corrosion or damage, which could prove dangerous to other road users, including pedestrians.

☐ 27. Check that the fuel cap fastens securely and that its sealing washer is neither torn nor deteriorated, or its mounting flange damaged sufficiently to allow fuel to escape (for example, while the car is cornering).

Under the Bonnet

☐ 28. The car should have a Chassis Number or Vehicle Identification Number fitted to the bodywork. The modern VIN plate is required on all vehicles first used on or after 1 August 1980. This can be on a plate secured to the vehicle or, etched or stamped on the bodywork. Others have a more traditional 'chassis number' which the tester will need to refer to. See *Chapter 8, Facts and Figures* for information on where they should be located on your car.

☐ 29. Check the steering column and neck clamp bolts for wear and looseness by asking your assistant to turn the steering wheel from side to side while you watch what happens under the bonnet. More than 13 mm (approx. 0.5 in.) of free play at the perimeter of the steering wheel, on the Midget's or Sprite's rack and pinion system, due to wear in the steering components, is sufficient grounds for a test failure. Note that the 13 mm criterion is based on a steering wheel of 380 mm (15 in.) diameter and will be less for smaller steering wheels. Also check for the presence and security of retaining and locking devices in the steering column assembly.

☐ 30. While peering under the bonnet check that hydraulic master cylinders and reservoirs are securely mounted and not severely corroded or otherwise damaged. Ensure that caps are present, that fluid levels are satisfactory and that there are no fluid leaks.

☐ 31. Also check that the servo is securely mounted and not damaged or corroded to an extent that would impair its operation. Vacuum pipes should be sound, that is, free from kinks, splits and excessive chafing and not collapsed internally.

☐ 32. Still under the bonnet, make a thorough search for evidence of excessive corrosion, severe distortion or fracture in any load bearing panelling within 30 cm (12 in.) of important mounting points such as the master cylinder/servo mounting, front suspension mountings etc.

Under the Car Front End

☐ 33. Have an assistant turn the steering wheel from side to side while you watch for movement in the steering rack mountings (make sure too that they are secure), and within the ball joints. While in this vicinity, visually examine the rack gaiters - no leaks should be evident, and the rubbers must not be split. The ball joint dust covers should also be in sound condition. Ensure that all split pins, locking nuts and so on are in place and correctly fastened, throughout the steering and suspension systems.

> **SAFETY FIRST!**
> On some occasions there is no alternative but for your assistant to sit in the car whilst you go beneath. Therefore: I) Place the car ramps as well as axle stands beneath the car's structure so that it cannot fall. 2) Don't allow your assistant to move vigorously or get in or out of the car while you are beneath it If either of these are problematical, DON'T CARRY OUT THIS CHECK leave it to your garage.

☐ 34. Closely examine the wishbone support rubber bushes - they should not be severely squashed or breaking up. The rubber bushes supporting the anti-roll bar also require close scrutiny. Next, employ a suitable lever (such as a long screwdriver or tyre lever) to test for excessive movement in each rubber bush.

☐ 35. With the front of the car raised, and securely supported on axle stands (with the wheels clear of the ground), grasp each front wheel/tyre in turn at top and bottom, and attempt to 'rock' the wheel in and out. If more than just perceptible movement is evident at the rim, this could be due to wear in the king (swivel) pins and bushes, or in the front wheel bearings. Repeat the test while an assistant applies the foot brake. This will effectively lock the hub to the stub axle assembly, so any movement remaining will be in the king pins and bushes.

☐ 36. Spin each front wheel in turn, listening for roughness in the bearings. There must be none.

☐ 37. Visually inspect the shock absorbers and front coil springs. The lever arm type shock absorbers employed on the Midget can leak from the joints between the body of the unit and the operating arms - check each joint very carefully for wear, as well; leaks mean failure. Check also the small upper trunnion bushes (two on each side) where the shock absorber arm joins the top of the king pin. The coil springs must be sound and free from cracks or other visible damage.

☐ 38. With the wheels on the ground again, push down firmly a couple of times on each front wing of the car, then let go at the bottom of a stroke. The car should rise and then fall to approximately its original level. Continuing oscillations will earn your MG a failure ticket for worn front dampers.

Under the Car - Rear Suspension

☐ 39. Check the condition and alignment of the spring leaves, and ensure that the central leaf retaining bolt is sound. On early cars with quarter-elliptical springs, check the condition and security of the chassis mounting. Watch in particular for cracks in the main leaf. Look closely too at the condition of the spring eye bushes - these must be sound, as must the shackle assemblies. The lever arm rear shock absorbers can suffer from leaks around the operating arm - check carefully. Look too for deterioration in the bushes at each end of the link rod connecting the shock absorber with the spring, on each side of the car, and check that all mounting bolts and fixings are tight.

☐ 40. A bounce test can be carried out, as for the front shock absorbers, as an approximate check on how efficient or otherwise the damping effect is.

☐ 41. With the back of the car raised on axle stands (both rear wheels off the ground), rotate the rear wheels and check, as well as you can, for roughness in the bearings, just as you did at the front.

Brakes

☐ 42. The MoT brake test is carried out on a special rolling-road set-up, which measures the efficiency in terms of percentage. For the foot brake, the examiner is looking for 50 per cent; the hand brake must measure 25 per cent. Frankly, without a rolling road of your own, there is little that you can do to verify whether or not your car will come up to the required figures. What you can do, though, is carry out an entire check of the brake system, which will also cover all other aspects the examiner will be checking, and be as sure as you can that the system is working efficiently.

☐ 43. The MoT examiner will not dismantle any part of the system, but you can do so. So, take off each front wheel in turn, and examine the front brake discs (look for excessive grooving/crazing), the calliper pistons/dust seals (look for signs of fluid leakage and deterioration of the seals), and the brake pads - ideally, replace them if less than approximately 3 mm. (1/8th in.) friction material remains on each pad. At the rear, remove each brake drum and check the condition of the linings (renew if worn down to anywhere near the rivet heads), the brake drum (watch for cracking, ovality and serious scoring, etc.) and the wheel cylinders. Check the cylinder's dust covers to see if they contain brake fluid. If so, or if it is obvious that the cylinder(s) have been leaking, replace them or - ONLY if the cylinder bore is in perfect condition - fit a new seal kit. Carry out this check at the front on early cars with drum front brakes.

IMPORTANT! See *Chapter 3, Service Intervals, Step-by-Step* for important information, including *SAFETY FIRST!* information before working on your car's brakes.

☐ 44. Ensure that the rear brake adjusters (where fitted) are free to rotate (i.e. not seized!). If they are stuck fast, apply a little penetrating oil to the backs of the adjusters (but only from behind the backplate, not inside the brake drum where there would be some risk of getting oil onto the brake shoes), and gently work the adjuster backwards and forwards with a brake adjuster spanner. Eventually the adjusters should free, and a little brake grease can be applied to the threads to keep them in this condition. With the rear brakes correctly adjusted, check hand brake action. The lever should rise three or four clicks before the brake operates fully - if it goes further, the cable requires adjustment. Ensure too that the hand brake lever remains locked in the 'on' position when fully applied, even if the lever is knocked sideways.

☐ 45. As a very approximate check on brake operation, with the car securely supported with either both front or both rear wheels clear of the ground, get an assistant to apply the foot brake, then attempt to rotate each wheel in turn - they should not, of course, move. Repeat the test with the hand brake applied, but on the rear wheels only this time...

☐ 46. Closely check the state of ALL visible hydraulic and fuel-line pipework. If any section of the steel tubing shows signs of corrosion, replace it, for safety as well as to gain an MoT pass. Look too for leakage of fluid around pipe joints, and from the master cylinder. The fluid level in the master cylinder reservoir must also be at its correct level - if not, find out why and rectify the problem. Bend the flexible hydraulic hoses through 180 degrees (by hand) near each end of each pipe, checking for signs of cracking. If any is evident, or if the front pipes have been chafing on the tyres, wheels, steering or suspension components, replace them with new items, re-routing them to avoid future problems. Also, where fuel line retaining clips were fitted by the manufacturer, they must be present and effective.

☐ 47. Have an assistant press down hard on the brake pedal while you check all flexible pipes for bulges. As an additional check, firmly apply the foot brake and hold the pedal down for a few minutes. It should not slowly sink to the floor (if it does, you have a hydraulic system problem). Press and release the pedal a few times - it should not feel 'spongy' (due to the presence of air in the system). If there is the risk of any problems with the braking system's hydraulics, have a qualified mechanic check it over before using the car.

☐ 48. A test drive should reveal obvious faults (such as pulling to one side, due to a seized calliper piston, for example), but otherwise all will be revealed on the rollers at the MoT station...

Bodywork Structure

A structurally deficient car is a dangerous vehicle, and rust can affect many important areas, including the inner and outer sills (which literally hold the car together, especially on Midgets or Sprites), floor pans and the quarter panels, and in front of the rear wheels. Examine these areas, also the inner wings and reinforcing sections at the upper, and the rear corners underneath the front wings, since weakness here will bring MoT disappointment. See *Chapter 3, Service Intervals Step-by-Step* for illustrations.

☐ 49. Essentially, fractures, cracks or serious corrosion in any load bearing panel or member (to the extent that the affected sections are weakened) need to be dealt with. In addition, failure will result from any deficiencies in the structural metalwork within 30 cm. (12 in.) of the seat belt mountings, and also the steering and suspension component attachment points. Repairs made to any structural areas must be carried out by continuous seam welding, and the repair should restore the affected section to at least its original strength.

☐ 50. The MoT examiner will be looking for metal which gives way under squeezing pressure between finger and thumb, and will use his wicked little Corrosion Assessment Tool (i.e. a plastic-headed hammer), which in theory at least should be used for detecting rust by lightly tapping the surface. If scraping the surface of the metal shows weakness beneath, the car will fail.

☐ 51. Note that the security of doors and other openings must also be assessed, including the hinges, locks and catches. Corrosion damage or other weakness in the vicinity of these items can mean failure. It must be possible to open both doors from inside and outside the car.

Exterior Bodywork

☐ 52. Check for another area which can cause problems. Look out for rust, or accident damage, on the exterior bodywork, which leaves sharp/jagged edges and which may be liable to cause injury. Ideally, repairs should be carried out by welding in new metal, but for nonstructural areas, riveting a plate over a hole, bridging the gap with glass fibre/body filler or even taping over the gap can be legally acceptable, at least as far as the MoT test is concerned.

Fuel System

☐ 53. Another recent extension of the regulations brings the whole of the fuel system under scrutiny, from the tank to the engine. The system should be examined with and without the engine running, and there must be no leaks from any of the components. The tank must be securely mounted, and the filler cap must fit properly - temporary caps are not permitted.

Emissions

0h dear - even the thought of this aspect can cause headaches. In almost every case, a proper engine tune will help to ensure that your car is running at optimum efficiency, and there should be no difficulty in passing the test, unless your engine, the distributor or the carburettors really are well worn. However, Midgets can be more difficult than most in this regard - see below.

☐ 54. For cars first used before 1 August, 1973*, the only test carried out is for visual smoke emission. The engine must be fully warmed up, allowed to idle, then revved slightly. If smoke emitted is regarded by the examiner as being excessive, the car will fail. Often smoke emitted during this test is as a result of worn valve stem seals, allowing oil into the combustion chambers during tickover, to be blown out of the exhaust as blue smoke when the engine is revved. In practice, attitudes vary widely between MoT stations on this aspect of the test.

☐ 55. For cars first used between 1 August, 1973* and 31 July, 1983, a smoke test also applies. Again, the engine must be fully warmed up, and allowed to idle, before being revved to around 2,500 rpm for 20 seconds (to purge the system). If dense blue or black smoke is emitted for more than five seconds, the car will fail. In addition, the exhaust gas is analysed. A maximum of 6 per cent carbon monoxide (CO),

and 1,200 parts per million (ppm) hydrocarbons is allowable. The percentage of these gases are established using an exhaust gas analyser - home user versions are available for testing CO readings.

☐ 56. Normally, if the CO reading is within limits, the hydrocarbon emissions will be acceptable but, unfortunately, some cars fitted with twin S.U. carburettors (MGs included) give excessive hydrocarbon percentage readings when checked with the engine idling - EVEN WITH NEW CARBURETTORS. Therefore, many cars were failing the test and in some cases their owners were persuaded to spend vast sums of money on replacement carburettors they didn't need, and which in any case had a marginal effect on the hydrocarbon levels in the exhaust gas.

Therefore, a little-known, but vitally important, exemption was introduced by the Vehicle Inspectorate Executive Agency, in the form of Special Notice SN 18/19, Section 2. Copies should have been circulated to all MoT Testing Stations, but an unofficial survey by members of the MG Owners' Club revealed that many examiners were apparently unaware of the exemption. Under this, it is acknowledged that some vehicles were unable to meet the specified hydrocarbon limit, even when new. These vehicles include twin-carburettor MGs and Sprites. If such vehicles meet the CO requirements at normal idling speed, but fail the hydrocarbon test at the same speed, the hydrocarbon test should be repeated at an engine speed of 2,000 rpm, using the throttle, NOT cold start/cold running mechanisms to increase the engine speed. If the hydrocarbon reading is then 1,200 ppm or less, the car will pass. So, if you should have difficulties in this respect, politely show the examiner this book, and quote SN 18/19, Section 2.

INSIDE INFORMATION: It helps the CO levels at low speeds if the vacuum advance pipe to the distributor is temporarily disconnected and the end of the pipe leading to the inlet manifold blocked off - temporarily again. If all else fails, it's worth a try.

* Emissions regulations are under constant review so check current dates and requirements at your local MoT testing station

CHAPTER 8 - FACTS & FIGURES

This chapter serves two main purposes. First, we show you how to find the identification numbers on your car and then we show you which settings you will need to use in order to carry out the servicing.

The "Data" sections of this chapter will also make essential reading when you come to carrying out the servicing on your car since you will then need to know things like valve clearances, spark plug gap, torque settings and a whole host of other adjustments and measurements that you will need to carry out in the course of maintaining your car.

PART I - IDENTIFICATION NUMBERS

For location of the numbers and plates mentioned in this section please refer to the illustrations in **Chapter 2, Buying Spares.**

BMC and British Leyland used to recommend that, when parts were being purchased, the correct identification numbers were quoted and, as we said earlier, with the passage of time and the possibility of replacement of major components such as engine or gearbox, this becomes even more important.

You won't have individual part numbers, but always quote the VIN number (Vehicle Identification Number). It is also wise to quote the engine, gearbox or rear axle numbers if you need parts for these as, over the years, these may have been replaced with later units of a slightly different specification. It is also not unknown for engines from Morris Minors, A30s and other A-Series engined cars to have found their way into Sprites and Midgets

SPRITES - All models

The most important number of all is the car's chassis number or VIN (Vehicle Identification Number). This is found under the bonnet stamped on a plate fixed to the left hand inner wheel arch valance.

The engine number is stamped on a plate fixed to the right hand side of the cylinder block just under the front sparking plug.

The gearbox number is stamped on the left hand side of the casing or, on early models, the top of the casing.

The rear axle number is stamped on the front left hand side of the rear axle tube near to the spring anchorage.

The body number is stamped on a plate fixed to the left hand front door pillar.

MIDGETS

Vehicle Identification Numbers are in the same location as those on Sprites.

On 1,493cc cars the engine number is stamped into the metal of the block instead of being on a plate.

PART II - WHAT THE NUMBERS MEAN

CHASSIS NUMBERS

The chassis, or VIN, number consists of a prefix followed by an individual identification number. The prefix identifies the model as follows:

Sprite

Prefix	Model	Production
H-AN5	Mk 1 948 cc	March 1958-April 1961
H-AN6	Mk 2 948 cc	May 1961-September 1962
H-AN7	Mk 2 1,098 cc	October 1962-February 1964
H-AN8	Mk 3 1,098 cc	March 1964 - September 1966
H-AN9	Mk 4 1,275 cc	October 1966 - September 1969
H-AN10	Mk 4 1,275 cc	October 1969 - December 1970
A-AN10	Mk 4 1,275 cc	January 1971 - June 1971

The H part of the prefix was changed to A when the Healey name was dropped.

Midget

Prefix	Model	Production
GAN-1	Mk 1 948 cc	June 1961 - September 1962
GAN-2	Mk 1 1,098 cc	October 1962 - February 1964
GAN-3	Mk 2 1,098 cc	March 1964 - September 1966

GAN-4   Mk 3 1,275 cc   October 1966 - September 1969
GAN-5   Mk 3 1,275 cc   October 1969 - September 1964
GAN-6   Midget 1,493 cc October 1964 - November 1979

The dates given are dates of production. Dates of first registration may vary because of the time lag in deliveries to dealers.

ENGINE NUMBERS

A-Series engines, fitted to all models except GAN-6 cars, had three prefix groups before the serial number indicating the cubic capacity and model, gearbox and ancillary equipment, and compression ratio.

First prefix group

9C	948 cc, Sprite Mk 1
9CG	948 cc, Sprite Mk 2 and Midget Mk 1
10CG	1,098 cc, Sprite Mk 2 and Midget Mk 1
10CC	1,098 cc, Sprite Mk 3 and Midget Mk 2
12CC	1,275 cc, Sprite Mk 4 and Midget Mk 3
12CE	1,275 cc, Sprite Mk 4 and Midget Mk 3

12CD, 12CJ &12V prefixes denoted special equipment, usually emission control, to comply with various export market regulations.

Second prefix group

U	Gearbox with central shift
Da	Close ratio gearbox with central shift

Third prefix group

H	High compression
L	Low compression

So a typical engine number might read 10CG-Da-H-1234 indicating a 1,098 cc high compression ratio engine with a serial number 1234, fitted with a close ratio central shift gearbox and used in a Sprite Mk 2 or a Midget Mk 1.

PART II - CAPACITIES

ENGINE

Firing order

All engines   1,3,4,2 (No. 1 cylinder next to radiator)

Valve clearances (exhaust and inlet)

948, 1,098 and 1,275 cc   0.012 in. (0.30 mm) cold
1,493 cc   0.010 in (0.00 mm) cold

IGNITION SYSTEM

Distributor

948 cc	Lucas DM2P4
1,098 cc	Lucas 25D4
1,275 cc	Lucas 23D4 or 25D4 (with vacuum advance)
1,493 cc	Lucas 45D4

Direction of distributor rotation

All models   Anticlockwise

Contact breaker gap

All engines   0.014 to 0.016 in (0.36 0.40 mm)

Coil

948 cc	Lucas LA12
1,098 cc	Lucas LA12
1,275 cc to engine No. 12CC/Da/H16300	Lucas 11C12
1,275 cc from engine No. 12CE/Da/H101	Lucas HA12
1,493 cc	Lucas 15C6

Static ignition timing

948 cc	4° BTDC
1,098 cc	5° BTDC
1,275 cc	7° BTDC
1,493 cc	7-10° BTDC

Stroboscopic ignition timing

948 cc	6° BTDC @ 600 engine rpm
1,098 cc	8° BTDC @ 600 engine rpm
1,275 cc (23D4 distributor)	22° BTDC @ 1200 rpm (Vacuum disconnected & plugged)
1,275 cc (25D4 distributor)	13° BTDC @ 1000 rpm (Vacuum disconnected & plugged)
1,493 cc	10° BTDC @ 650 engine rpm (Vacuum disconnected & plugged)

Dwell angle

948, 1,098 & 1,275 cc	60° + 3 o
1,493 cc	51° + 5 o

ELECTRICAL EQUIPMENT

Voltage

All models   12 volt

Polarity

948 cc	Positive earth
1,098 cc	Positive earth
1,275 cc to engine No. 12CC/Da/H16300	Positive earth
1,275 cc from engine No. 12CE/Da/H101	Negative earth
1,493 cc	Negative earth

Battery

948 cc	Lucas BT7A or BT27A
1,098 cc	Lucas N9 or NZ9
1,275 cc	Lucas N9 or NZ9 Later cars Lucas A9/AZ9 or A11/AZ11)
1,493 cc	

Dynamo

948 cc	Lucas C39
1,098 cc	Lucas C40
1,275 cc	Lucas C40
1,493 cc	

Control unit

948 cc	Lucas RB106/2
1,098 cc	Lucas RB106/2
1,275 cc	Lucas RB106
	(Later Lucas RB340)

Alternator

Later 1,275 cc	Lucas 16ACR
1,493 cc	Lucas 16ACR

Starter

948 cc	Lucas N35G/1
1,098 cc	Lucas M35G
1,275 cc	Lucas M35G or M35J
1,493 cc	Lucas M35J

Fuses

All A-Series engines	Two fuses, both 35 amp
1,493 cc	

FUEL SYSTEM

Carburettor

948 cc type 9C	Twin SU type HS1
Other 948, 1,098 & 1,275 cc	Twin SU type HS2
Jet	0.90 in (2.29 mm)
Needle	
948 cc	Standard V3, Rich V2, Weak GX
Early 1,098 cc	Standard GY, Rich M, Weak GG
Later 1,098 cc	Standard AN, Rich H6, Weak GG
1,275 cc	Standard AN, Rich H6, Weak GG
Piston spring	
948 cc	Light blue
1,098 & 1,275 cc	Blue
1,493 cc	Twin SU type HS4

Fuel pump

948 cc	AC type Y mechanical
1,098 & 1,275 cc	SU AUF 200, 206 or 216 electrical
1,493 cc	AC type RA1 mechanical

COOLING SYSTEM

Pressure cap setting

948 & 1,098 cc	7 psi
1,275 cc	7 psi (early models), 15 psi (later models)
1,493 cc	15 psi

Thermostat operating temperature

948 cc	65 - 70° C (149 - 158° F)
1,098 cc & 1,275 cc	82° C (180o F)
1,493 cc	82° C (180o F)

Fanbelt tension

All models	0.5 in (13 mm) deflection in middle of longest run.

BRAKES

Type	Lockheed hydraulic
Front	
948 cc	7 in diameter drums
1,098 cc, 1,275 cc &	
1,493 cc	8.25 in diameter discs
Rear	
All models	7 in diameter drums
Fluid type	

CLUTCH

All models	Hydraulic, non-adjustable
Fluid type	

LUBRICATION SYSTEM

Recommended lubricants
see Appendix 1.

Engine oil pressure (hot)

	Idling	Normal running
948 cc	30-60 psi	10-25 psi
1,098 cc	30-60 psi	10-25 psi
1,275 cc	40-70 psi	20 psi
1,493 cc	40-60 psi	10-25 psi

CAPACITIES

Cooling system

948 cc	10.5 pints (5.97 litres)
1,098 cc	
1,275 cc	
1,493 cc	7.5 pints (4.3 litres)

Engine oil including filter

948 cc	6.5 pints (3.7 litres)
1,098 cc	6.5 pints (3.7 litres)
1,275 cc	6.5 pints (3.7 litres)
1,493 cc	8 pints (4.5 litres)

Gearbox

948 cc	2.25 pints (1.3 litres)
1,098 cc	2.25 pints (1.3 litres)
1,275 cc	2.25 pints (1.3 litres)
1,493 cc	1.5 pints (0.85 litres)

Rear axle

948 cc	1.75 pints (1 litre)
1,098 cc	1.75 pints (1 litre)
1,275 cc	1.75 pints (1 litre)
1,493 cc	1.75 pints (1 litre)

Steering rack

All models	1/3 pint (0.19 litre)

GENERAL DATA

Tyre pressures (normal running)

	Front	Rear
All models		
520-13S cross-ply	18 psi (1.27 kg/cm2)	20 psi (1.41 kg/cm2)
145-SR13 radial-ply	22 psi (1.55 kg/cm2)	24 psi (1.69 kg/cm2)

Steering alignment

(Sometimes called toe-in or tracking)

All models, static laden   0-0.125 in (0-3.17 mm) toe-in

MAIN TORQUE WRENCH SETTINGS

Cylinder head nuts

948 cc, 1,098 cc	40 lb ft (5.5 kg m)
1,275 cc, plain studs	42 lb ft (5.8 kg m)
1,275 cc, studs stamped 22 or with small drill point	50 lb ft (6.9 kg m)
1,493 cc	46 lb ft (6.4 kg m)

Note: on 948 cc, 1,098 cc & 1,275 cc engines the outer nuts holding the rocker shaft pedestals are also cylinder head nuts. If the rocker shaft is removed, the engine coolant must be drained first, and all the cylinder head nuts loosened to avoid head distortion. When replacing, tighten the cylinder head nuts and the inner nuts for the rocker shaft pedestals in the order shown. The inner nuts for the pedestals are tightened to a torque of 25 lb ft (3.4 kg m)

Connecting rod caps

948 cc, 1,098 cc	35 lb ft (4.8 kg m)
1,275 cc plain nuts	45 lb ft (6.2 kg m)
1,275 cc Nyloc nuts	32-34 lb ft (4.4- 4.7 kg m)
1,493 cc	40/45 lb ft (5.5-6.2 kg m)

Main bearing caps

948 cc & 1,098 cc	60 lb ft (8.3 kg m)
1,275 cc	65 lb ft (9 kg m)

Road wheel nuts

all models	45 lb ft (6.2 kg m)

REPLACEMENT BULB WATTAGE

	Sprite Mk 1	Sprite Mk 2 & 3 Midget Mk 1 & 2	Later models
Headlamps	50/40	60/45	60/45
Sidelamps	6	6	-
Sidelamp/direction indicator	-	-	6/21
Stop/tail	21/6	21/6	21/6
Direction indicator	21	21	21
Number plate	6	6	6
Side marker	-	-	6
Reverse	-	-	18
Panel lamps	2.2	2.2	2.2
Warning lamps	2.2	2.2	2
Brake warning lamp	-	-	1.5
Courtesy & luggage lamps	-	-	6

CHAPTER 9 - TOOLS & EQUIPMENT

Although good tools are not cheap, if you reckon their cost against what you would otherwise spend on professional servicing and repairs, your arithmetic should show you that it doesn't take long to recoup your outlay - and then to start showing a profit!

In fact, there is no need to spend a fortune all at once - most owners who do their own servicing acquire their implements over a long period of time. However, there are some items you simply cannot do without in order properly to carry out the work necessary to keep your car on the road. Therefore, in the following lists, we have concentrated on those items which are likely to be valuable aids to maintaining your car in a good state of tune, and to keep it running sweetly and safely and in addition we have featured some of the tools that are 'nice-to-have' rather than 'must have' because as your tool chest grows, there are some tools that help to make servicing just that bit easier and more thorough to carry out.

Two vital points - firstly always buy the best quality tools you can afford. 'Cheap and cheerful' items may look similar to more expensive implements, but experience shows that they often fail when the going gets tough, and some can even be dangerous. With proper care, good quality tools will last a lifetime, and can be regarded as an investment. The extra outlay is well worth it, in the long run.

A fairly basic kit will tackle most servicing needs, plus some items of workshop equipment, plus some handy 'tuning' aids that have become available to the DIY market over recent years at affordable prices.

There are further items which can undoubtedly make life easier, and save money - but they could be a wee bit costly in the first place. Perhaps the answer is to share their benefits (and so their cost!) with like-minded DIY friends.

Over the years, there have been various nut/bolt/spanner designations. For many years British cars standardised on 'AF', a designation referring to the measurement 'across the flats' of the hexagon nut or bolt head, while the 'Foreigners' were 'Metric'. While there are still many 'AF' cars around, all modern cars are 'Metric' of course, apart from American cars. For the record, 'metric' sizes are also measured across their flats!. Be sure you know what designation applies to your car before you start buying. Your local motor accessory store should be able to advise - and if they can't shop elsewhere. Call your local main dealer to make sure, if necessary.

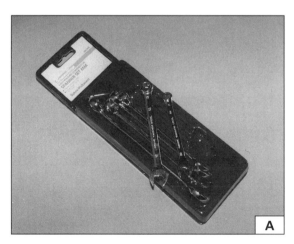

Spanners:

A. The two common types of spanner are the ring and the open-ended. The ring spanner grips practically all round the bolt, and is preferable where the bolt is really tight, for an open-ended spanner, merely straddling two flats of the bolt, could slip. On the other hand, the open-end is often quicker and easier to use - so this set of 'Combination' spanners, a ring at one end, open-ended the other, is a nice compromise!

Our thanks are due, for their kind assistance with this chapter, to Sykes-Pickavant Ltd, who supplied most of the hand tools shown here and in use in the servicing sections, similarly to Polcar-Belco Ltd, who supplied the 'Lock and Lift' trolley jack, and to Gunson Ltd, who supplied the tuning aids, again seen both here and in the servicing text.

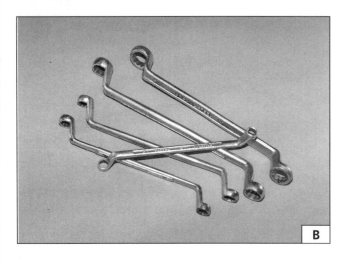

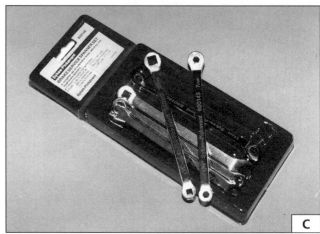

B. While the straight 'flatness' of the combinations (or of a conventional open-ended spanner) is often useful, there are occasions when only the offset, or 'swan neck' of the conventional ring spanner will do the job - like when having to operate over the top of one bolt in order to undo another.

Unlike the combinations, the conventional ring and open-ended spanners will have a different size at each end. Usually, the AF sizes will rise in sixteenths of an inch, and the metrics by one millimetre - the following sizes will probably cover most of your needs:
AF - 3/8 x 7/16, 1/2 x 9/16, 5/8 x 11/16, 13/16 x 7/8
Metric - 10 x 11, 12 x 13, 14 x 15, 16 x 17

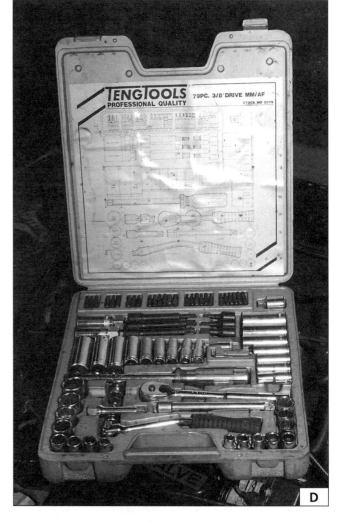

C. The sturdy specialist brake spanner, for brake adjusters or bleed nipples, is undeniably a wise buy, as mentioned in the brake servicing text. You might not need the set as shown here, but you can choose individual sizes to suit your car, such as 1/4 in. sq x 11/32 in. sq, or 1/4 in. hex x 5/16 in. AF, or perhaps 8 x 10mm hex - there are others.

D. It was once thought of as a luxury, but nowadays at least a basic socket set should figure highly on your shopping list, for it will cover your basic spanner sizes and can often solve difficult access or extra-leverage problems. This one is a fairly sophisticated Teng Tools set, and includes a number of useful extras, such as spark plug spanners and Allen key and screwdriver bits.

E. A torque wrench was also once a luxury, but nowadays it's practically essential, with specific torque settings quoted for many of the nuts and bolts used in modern car engineering. The example shown will cater for most applications, including adjustable wheel-bearing hub nuts, but even the next size up (30-150 lb/ft) in the DIY range will still fall short of the 200-odd lb/ft specified for some hub nuts!

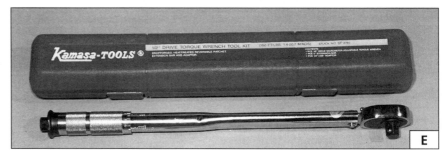

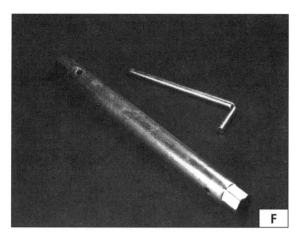

F. If you still need a plug spanner, and particularly if your engine features deep-set spark plugs, this Sykes-Pickavant 'extra long plug wrench', combining both 10mm and 14mm sizes, could be a boon. Some plugs are set deeper than the average length of a socket-set spark plug spanner, and if the socket set's extension bar is prone to leaving the spanner socket stuck on the plug, then you could have a problem ...

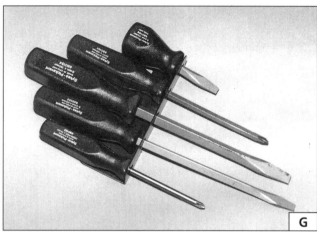

Screwdrivers:

G. You will need a selection of screwdrivers, both flat-bladed and cross-headed, long ones, short ones, slim ones, fat ones ...

Pliers:

H. Ordinary combination (or 'engineers') pliers are needed for general work, while a long-nosed pair are handy where access is tight. Their cutting edges are useful for stripping cable insulation, or for snipping wire or trimming split-pin lengths, but you might prefer a pair of specialist side-cutter pliers for such work.

I. Jolly useful as an extra pair of hands, or for gripping such as a rusty nut or bolt really tightly, is a self-grip wrench. This is a long-nose example, but there are also ordinary straight-jaw and round jaw versions.

Sundries:

J. You'll need hammers, including the useful 1lb ball-pein type, plus a hefty copper hammer and maybe a soft (plastic-headed) hammer, too.

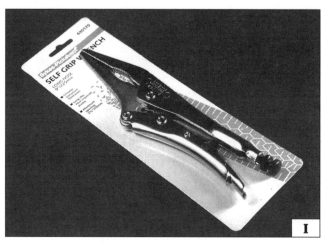

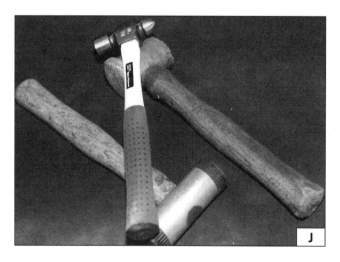

K. The wire brush should have brass bristles and as well as an ordinary set of feeler gauges, an 'ignition set' covers most plug and points gap sizes, and includes a points file and a gap setting tool.

L. You may need a grease gun, you will want an oil can, and an oil funnel, and a container of sufficient capacity in to which the engine oil can be drained.

M. You may also need a drain plug 'key' suitable for your car unless all the drain plugs are 'bolt'-type hexagons.

N. Well worthwhile, since some oil filters can be cussedly tight, is some sort of oil filter wrench - the chain-type by Sykes-Pickavant is a nice example.

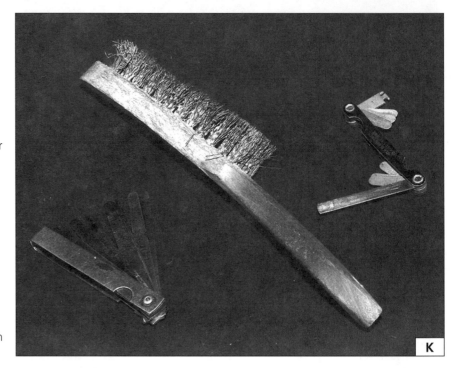

K

L

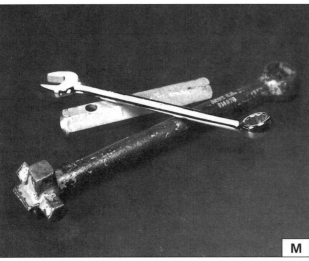

M

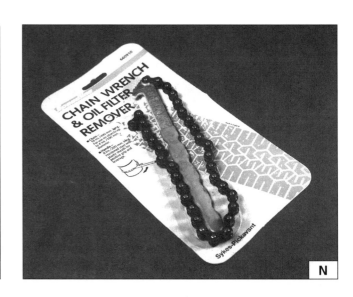

N

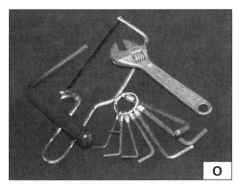

O. A separate set of hand-held Allen keys is a good idea (they come in metric or Imperial sizes), and an adjustable spanner and a 'Junior' hacksaw will have their uses.

P. For your weekly maintenance checks, you'll need a tyre pressure gauge, tyre tread depth gauge and a footpump - which might, like the example here, have an integral pressure gauge. And whether you're wheel-changing at home or roadside, you will welcome the extremely useful Sykes-Pickavant 'Wheelmaster' wrench, which can be extended to give enough leverage to shift those wheel nuts or bolts that the average car-kit wheelbrace wouldn't even look at - see 'Wheel-Change Routine' elsewhere in this book. Remember to carry it with you in the car!

Lifting:

Q. While the jack supplied with the car might be OK for emergency wheel-changes, you would soon tire of trying to use it for servicing operations. Here you need a good trolley jack, and one of the latest on the market is this 2-ton lifting capacity Belcar 'Lift and Lock' example which, as its name suggests, has a built-in fail-safe locking device in the event of hydraulic failure.

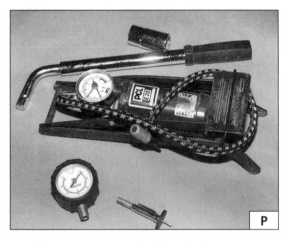

R. However, although their unique safety feature offers extra peace of mind, Belcar still warn that you should not venture beneath a car supported on a jack alone. Having raised it, you need to support it safely and securely. What you need now is definitely NOT house bricks (or any other such potentially dangerous items!) but rather axle stands or wheel-ramps. The adjustable-height stands are Paddy Hopkirk brand, the ramps are of both unknown vintage or make! If you don't need the wheels off, it can be argued that the ramps offer better stability - though you'll not always have the room (or the nerve!) to actually drive up onto them.

Tuning aids:

S. As we have said earlier in this chapter and within the servicing sections, the tuning aids that are now available to the DIY market have become practically invaluable 'musts' for the dedicated home mechanic. Any of the Gunson's collection shown here would soon prove their worth. Top of the tree, of course, is their 'Gastester Professional' - don't let its designation suggest that it's not for DIY use, for although it's expensive a group of friends sharing its cost would find their outlay well worth the benefits offered by the unit's Exhaust Gas 'CO' functions, plus its Voltage, Dwell and RPM modes. If it's pure 'multi-meter' you're after, then their 'Digimeter 320' is a tidy little hand-held unit, with clear digital read-outs for such as Volts (DC and household AC) and Amps, Ohms, RPM, and Dwell (degrees and per cent), and its sophistication extends to Frequency, Period and Pulsewidth testing (handy for fuel injection systems), as well as Diode, Resistance and Continuity testing. Also by Gunson's is the powerful 'Timestrobe' xenon timing light, the now not so new, but still novel 'Colortune' and (not shown) the 'Carbalancer', the latter two devices are also mentioned in the carburettor tuning text.

APPENDIX 1
RECOMMENDED CASTROL LUBRICANTS
FOR MG MIDGET & AUSTIN-HEALEY SPRITE

1. Engine

See Jobs 41 to 44
Castrol Classic XL 20W/50

2. Steering Rack

See Job 39
Castrol Hypoy EP 90

3. Front Suspension and Steering

See Job 50
Castrol LM Grease

4. Brake and Clutch Fluid

See Jobs 2, 3 and 140
Castrol Universal Brake & Clutch Fluid

5. Gearbox

See Jobs 83 and 136
Castrol Classic XL 20W/50

6. Universal Joints

See Job 100
Castrol LM Grease

7. Handbrake Cable and Linkage

See Job 54
Castrol LM Grease

8. Rear Axle

See Jobs 101 and 139
948 cc & 1098 cc - Castrol Hypoy EP 90
1275 cc - Castrol EPX 80W/90

9. Brake Mechanism - areas of metal-to-metal contact

See Jobs 125 and 141
Proprietary brand of high melting point brake grease such as Castrol PH Grease - not conventional high point melting grease.

10. General

Castrol Flick Easing Oil (aerosol)
Castrol Everyman Oil (in a can)
Castrol DWF - Ignition & HT Lead Moisture Repellant

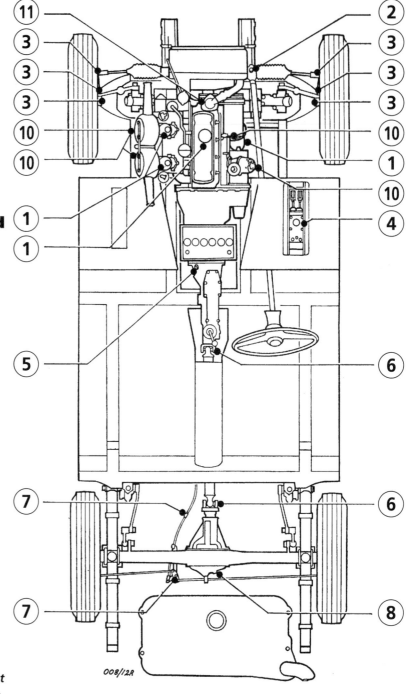

008/12R

11. Anti-freeze *(see Facts & Figures)*

Castrol Anti-Freeze and Summer Coolant

Issued by:
Castrol (UK) Ltd, Burmah Castrol House, Pipers Way, Swindon SN3 1RE

APPENDIX 2
AMERICAN AND BRITISH TERMS

It was Mark Twain who described the British and the Americans as, "two nations divided by a common language". such cynicism has no place here but we do acknowledge that our common language evolves in different directions. We hope that this glossary of terms, commonly encountered when servicing your car, will be of assistance to American owners and, in some cases, English speaking owners in other parts of the world, too.

American	British
Antenna	Antenna
Axleshaft	Halfshaft
Back-up	Reverse
Carburetor	Carburettor
Cotter pin	Split pin
Damper	Shock absorber
DC Generator	Dynamo
Defog	Demist
Drive line	Transmission
Driveshaft	Propeller shaft
Fender	Wing or mudguard
Firewall	Bulkhead
First gear	Bottom gear
Float bowl	Float chamber
Freeway, turnpike	Motorway
Frozen	Seized
Gas tank	Petrol tank
Gas pedal	Accelerator or throttle pedal
Gasoline, Gas or Fuel	Petrol or fuel
Ground (electricity)	Earth
Hard top	Fast back
Header	Exhaust manifold
Headlight dimmer	Headlamp dipswitch
High gear	Top gear
Hood	Bonnet
Industrial Alcohol or Denatured Alcohol	Methylated spirit
Kerosene	Paraffin
Lash	Free-play
License plate	Number plate
Lug nut	Wheel nut
Mineral spirit	White spirit
Muffler	Silencer
Oil pan	Sump
Panel wagon/van	Van
Parking light	Side light
Parking brake	Hand brake
'Pinging'	'Pinking'
Quarter window	Quarterlight
Recap (tire)	Remould or retread
Rocker panel	Sill panel

American	British
Rotor or disk (brake)	Disc
Sedan	Saloon
Sheet metal	Bodywork
Shift lever	Gear lever
Side marker lights, side turn signal or position indicator	Side indicator lights
Soft-top	Hood
Spindle arm	Steering arm
Stabiliser or sway bar	Anti-roll bar
Throw-out bearing	Release or thrust bearing
Tie-rod (or connecting rod)	Track rod (or steering)
Tire	Tyre
Transmission	Drive line
Trouble shooting	Fault finding/diagnosis
Trunk	Boot
Turn signal	Indicator
Valve lifter	Tappet
Valve cover	Rocker cover
Valve lifter or tappet	Cam follower or tappet
Vise	Vice
Windshield	Windscreen
Wrench	Spanner

Useful conversions:

	Multiply by
US gallons to Litres	3.785
Litres to US gallons	0.2642
UK gallons to US gallons	1.20095
US gallons to UK gallons	0.832674

Fahrenheit to Celsius (Centigrade) -
Subtract 32, multiply by 0.5555

Celsius to Fahrenheit -
Multiply by 1.8, add 32

SPECIALISTS & SUPPLIERS

APPENDIX 3
SPECIALISTS AND SUPPLIERS
FEATURED IN THIS BOOK

All of the products and specialists listed below have contributed in various ways to this book. All of the consumer products used are available through regular high street outlets.

Austin Healey Club. Send SAE to Colleen Holmes, Dept PC, 4 Saxby Street, Leicester, LE2 0AD
All Healeys including Frogeye and 'Spridget'-style Sprites.

Autoline (Dinitrol), Eagle House, Redstone Industrial Estate, Boston, Lincs, PE21 8EA. Tel: 01205 354500
Rust prevention treatment of various grades.

Automotive Chemicals Ltd, Bevis Green Works, Wallmersley, Bury, Lancs, BL9 8RE. Tel: 0161 797 5899
Aerosol spray paint.

Automotive Products, Tachbrook Road, Leamington Spa, Warwicks, CV31 3ER. Tel: 01926 472251
Manufacturers of AP Lockheed 'original equipment' brakes.

Maidstone Sports Cars, Apiary Business Park, Gravelly Bottom Road, Kingswood, Maidstone, Kent, ME17 3NH. Tel: 01622 842 998
Servicing and restoration of all MG models.

LMG Kent Ltd, 20 Upland Road, Bexleyheath, Kent, DA7 4NR. Tel: 0181 303 4811
Servicing, overhaul and restoration of all MG models plus new and used parts.

Castrol (UK) Ltd, Burmah House, Pipers Way, Swindon, Wiltshire, SN3 1RE. Tel: 01793 452222
Contact Castrol's Consumer Technical Department Help Line on the above number for assistance with lubrication recommendations.

Gunson Ltd, Coppen Road, Dagenham, Essex, RM8 1NU. Tel: 0181 984 8855
Electrical and electronic engine tuning equipment.

MG Car Club, Kimber House, PO Box 251, Abingdon, Oxon, OX14 1FF. Tel: 01235 555552
The original M.G. Car Club, founded 1930, hundreds of events for all models 1925-1995. Monthly magazine.

MG Owners Club, Octagon House, 2-4 Station Road, Swavesey, Cambridge, CB4 5QZ. Tel: 01954 231125
The largest car club in the world. Monthly magazine. Excellent for Midget owners.

Midget & Sprite Club. Send SAE to Nigel Williams, 7 King's Avenue Hanham, Bristol, BS15 3JN.
For all Sprites and Midgets from Frogeyes to 1500s.

NGK Spark Plugs (UK) Ltd, 7-8-9 Garrick Industrial Centre, Hendon, London, NW9 6AQ. Tel: 0181 202 2151
Top quality spark plugs.

Partco
See Yellow Pages for your local Partco centre (look under Motor Factors). Suppliers of most types of consumable and regular service items used in automotive repair.

SP Tyres UK Ltd, Fort Dunlop, Birmingham, B24 9QT. Tel: 0121 384 4444
Manufacturers of Dunlop tyres in both modern and period' patterns.

Sykes-Pickavant Ltd, Kilnhouse Lane, Lytham St.Annes, Lancashire, FY8 3DU. Tel: 01253 721291
Tools and equipment to cover almost every servicing and repair job on a car.

W David & Sons Ltd (Isopon), Ridgemount House, 1 Totteridge Lane, Whetstone, London, N20 0EY. Tel: 0181 445 0372
Manufacturers of Isopon filler and ancillaries - top quality products.

APPENDIX 4
SERVICE HISTORY

This Chapter helps you keep track of all the servicing carried out on your car and can even save you money! A car with a 'service history' is always worth more than one without. Although this book's main purpose is to give invaluable advice to anyone carrying out his or her own servicing, you could make full use of this section, even if you have a garage or mechanic carry out the work for you. It enables you to specify the jobs you want to have carried out to your car and, once again, it enables you to keep that all-important service history. And even if your car doesn't have a 'history' going back to when it was new, keeping this Chapter complete will add to your car's value when you come to sell it. Mind you, it obviously won't be enough to just to tick the boxes: keep all your receipts when you buy oil, filters and other consumables or parts. That way, you'll also be able to return any faulty parts if needs be.

IMPORTANT NOTE! The Service Jobs listed here are intended as a check list and a means of keeping a record of your car's service history. It is most important that you refer to *Chapter 3, Service Intervals, Step-by-Step* for full details of how to carry out each Job listed here and for essential SAFETY information, all of which will be essential when you come to carry out the work.

Wherever possible, the Jobs listed in this section have been placed in a logical order or placed into groups that will help you make progress on the car. We have tried to save you too much in the way of unnecessary movement by grouping Jobs around areas of the car and also - most important, this! - into groups of jobs that apply when the car is on the ground, when the front or rear of the car is off the ground, and so on. Therefore, at each Service Interval, you will see the work grouped into Jobs that need carrying out in the engine bay, around the car or under the car and another division into Bodywork and Interior Jobs, and Mechanical and Electrical Jobs.

You'll also see space at each Service Interval for you to write down the date, price and seller's name every time you buy consumables or accessories. And once again, do remember to keep your receipts! There's also space for you to date and sign the Service Record or for a garage's stamp to be applied.

As you move through the Service Intervals, you will notice that the work carried out at, say, 1,500 Miles or Every Month, whichever comes first, is repeated at each one of the following Service Intervals. The same applies to the 6,000 Miles or Every Six Months interval: much of it is repeated at 12,000 Miles or Every Twelve Months. Every time a Job or set of Jobs is 'repeated' from an earli-

er Interval, we show it in a tinted area on the page. You can then see more clearly which Jobs are unique to the level of Service Interval that you are on. And you may be surprised to find that all the major Service Intervals, right up to 36,000 Miles or Every Thirty Six Months contain Jobs that are unique to that Service Interval. That's why we have continued this Service History right up to the Thirty Six Month interval.

500 MILES, WEEKLY, OR BEFORE A LONG JOURNEY

This list is shown, complete, only once. It would have been a bit much to have provided the list 52 times over for use once a week throughout the year! They are, however, included with every longer Service list from 3,000 miles/Three months on so that each of the 'weekly' jobs is carried out as part of every Service.

500 miles Mechanical and Electrical - The Engine Bay

Job 1. Engine oil level

Job 2. Clutch fluid level

Job 3. Brake fluid level

Job 4. Battery electrolyte

Job 5. Windscreen washer reservoir

Job 6. Cooling system

Job 7. Inspect pressure cap

500 miles Mechanical and Electrical - Around the Car

Job 8. Check horns

Job 9. Windscreen washers

Job 10. Windscreen wipers

Job 11. Tyre pressures

Job 12. Check headlamps

Job 13. Check front sidelamps and indicators

Job 14. Check rear sidelamps

Job 15. Check number plate lamps

Job 16. Check reversing lamps

Job 17. **WIRE WHEELED CARS ONLY** Check wheel spinners

500 miles Bodywork and Interior - Around the Car

Job 18. Valet bodywork

1,500 MILES - OR EVERY MONTH, whichever comes first

These jobs are similar to the 500 Mile jobs but don't need carrying out quite so regularly. Once again, these jobs are not shown with a separate listing for each 1,500 miles/One Month interval but they are included as part of every 3,000 miles/Three Month Service list and for every longer Service interval.

1,500 miles Mechanical and Electrical - Around the Car

Job 19. Check tyres

Job 20. Check spare tyre

1,500 miles Bodywork and Interior - Around the Car

Job 21. Touch up paintwork

Job 22. Aerial/Antenna

Job 23. Valet interior

Job 24. Improve visibility

1,500 miles Bodywork - Under the Car

Job 25. Clean mud traps

3,000 MILES - OR EVERY THREE MONTHS, whichever comes first

All the Service Jobs in the tinted area have been carried forward from earlier service intervals and are to be repeated at this Service.

3,000 miles Mechanical and Electrical - The Engine Bay

First carry out all Jobs listed under earlier Service Intervals

☐ Job 1. Engine oil level

☐ Job 2. Clutch fluid level

☐ Job 3. Brake fluid level

☐ Job 4. Battery electrolyte

☐ Job 5. Windscreen washer reservoir

☐ Job 6. Cooling system

☐ Job 7. Inspect pressure cap

☐ Job 26. Adjust sparking plugs

☐ Job 27. Remove air trunking to the heater

☐ Job 28. Check HT circuit

☐ Job 29. Check ignition LT circuits

☐ Job 30. Distributor vacuum advance and retard pipe

☐ Job 31. **CONTACT BREAKER POINTS IGNITION ONLY** Distributor

☐ Job 32. Ignition timing

☐ Job 33. Setting ignition dwell

☐ Job 34. Generator/alternator belt

☐ Job 35. SU carburettors

☐ Job 36. Check air filters

☐ Job 37. Pipes and hoses

3,000 miles Mechanical and Electrical - Around the Car

First, carry out all Jobs listed under earlier Service Intervals

- [ ] Job 8. Check horns
- [ ] Job 9. Windscreen washers
- [ ] Job 10. Windscreen wipers
- [ ] Job 11. Tyre pressures
- [ ] Job 12. Check headlamps
- [ ] Job 13. Check front sidelamps and indicators
- [ ] Job 14. Check rear sidelamps
- [ ] Job 15. Check number plate lamps
- [ ] Job 16. Check reversing lamps
- [ ] Job 17. **WIRE WHEELED CARS ONLY** Check wheel spinners
- [ ] Job 19. Check tyres
- [ ] Job 20. Check spare tyre

- [ ] Job 38. Hand brake travel

3,000 miles Mechanical and Electrical - Under the Car

- [ ] Job 39. Steering rack
- [ ] Job 40. Track rod ends

Optional - Carry out Job 1

- [ ] Job 1. Engine oil level

or

- [ ] Job 41. Drain engine oil
- [ ] Job 42. Remove oil filter
- [ ] Job 43. Fit new oil filter
- [ ] Job 44. Pour in fresh oil
- [ ] Job 45. Check front discs
- [ ] Job 46. Check front brake pads
- [ ] Job 47. Renew front brake pads
- [ ] Job 48. **EARLY CARS WITH DRUM BRAKES ONLY** Adjust front brakes
- [ ] Job 49. Check front brake hoses
- [ ] Job 50. Lubricate front suspension
- [ ] Job 51. Refit front wheels
- [ ] Job 52. Adjust rear brakes
- [ ] Job 53. Rear check straps and bump stops
- [ ] Job 54. Lubricate hand brake linkage

3,000 miles Bodywork and Interior - Around the Car

First carry out all jobs listed under earlier Service Intervals

- [ ] Job 18. Valet bodywork
- [ ] Job 21. Touch up paintwork
- [ ] Job 22. Aerial/Antenna
- [ ] Job 23. Valet interior
- [ ] Job 24. Improve visibility

- [ ] Job 55. Wiper blades and arms
- [ ] Job 56. Check windscreen
- [ ] Job 57. Rear view mirrors
- [ ] Job 58. Check floors
- [ ] Job 59. Chrome trim and badges

3,000 miles Bodywork - Under the Car

First carry out all Jobs listed under earlier Service Intervals

- [ ] Job 25. Clean mud traps

- [ ] Job 60. Inspect underside

3,000 miles Mechanical and Electrical - Road Test

- [ ] Job 61. Clean controls
- [ ] Job 62. Check instruments and controls
- [ ] Job 63. Throttle pedal
- [ ] Job 64. Road test of brakes and steering

Date serviced:..

Carried out by:...
Garage Stamp or signature:

Parts/Accessories purchased (date, parts,
source) ....

....

....

....

....

6,000 MILES - OR EVERY SIX MONTHS, whichever comes first

All the Service Jobs in the tinted area have been carried forward from earlier service intervals and are to be repeated at this Service.

6,000 miles Mechanical and Electrical - The Engine Bay

First carry out all Jobs listed under earlier Service Intervals

- [ ] Job 2. Clutch fluid level
- [ ] Job 3. Brake fluid level
- [ ] Job 4. Battery electrolyte
- [ ] Job 5. Windscreen washer reservoir
- [ ] Job 6. Cooling system
- [ ] Job 27. Remove air trunking to the heater
- [ ] Job 28. Check HT circuit
- [ ] Job 29. Check ignition LT circuits
- [ ] Job 34. Generator/alternator belt
- [ ] Job 36. Check air filters
- [ ] Job 37. Pipes and hoses

- [ ] Job 65. Cooling system
- [ ] Job 66. Check coolant
- [ ] Job 67. Check water pump
- [ ] Job 68. Lubricate heater controls
- [ ] Job 69. Check fuse box
- [ ] Job 70. **EARLY CARS ONLY** Lubricate dynamo
- [ ] Job 71. Fit new sparking plugs
- [ ] Job 72. Renew contact breaker points and capacitor
- [ ] Job 73. Ignition timing
- [ ] Job 74. **948 cc AND 1493 cc ENGINES ONLY** Clean fuel filter and pump
- [ ] Job 75. **1098 cc AND 1275 cc ENGINES ONLY** Clean fuel pump filter
- [ ] Job 76. Fuel connections
- [ ] Job 77. Top up carburettor dashpots
- [ ] Job 78. Set carburettors
- [ ] Job 79. Balancing the carburettors
- [ ] Job 80. Setting the mixture
- [ ] Job 81. Throttle and choke linkage
- [ ] Job 82. **SPECIALIST SERVICE** Exhaust emissions

6,000 miles Mechanical and Electrical - Around the Car

First carry out all jobs listed under earlier Service Intervals.

- [ ] Job 8. Check horns
- [ ] Job 9. Windscreen washers
- [ ] Job 10. Windscreen wipers
- [ ] Job 11. Tyre pressures
- [ ] Job 12. Check headlamps
- [ ] Job 13. Check front sidelamps and indicators
- [ ] Job 14. Check rear sidelamps
- [ ] Job 15. Check number plate lamps
- [ ] Job 16. Check reversing lamps
- [ ] Job 17. **WIRE WHEELED CARS ONLY** Check wheel spinners
- [ ] Job 19. Check tyres
- [ ] Job 20. Check spare tyre
- [ ] Job 38. Hand brake travel

- [ ] Job 83. Top-up gearbox oil
- [ ] Job 84. Adjust headlamps
- [ ] Job 85. Fuel filler pipe
- [ ] Job 86. Front wheel alignment (tracking)
- [ ] Job 87. Rear ride height
- [ ] Job 88. Front ride height
- [ ] Job 89. Fuel filler cap
- [ ] Job 90. Check wheel tightness

6,000 miles Mechanical and Electrical - Under the Car

First carry out all jobs listed under earlier Service Intervals

- [ ] Job 39. Steering rack
- [ ] Job 40. Track rod ends
- [ ] Job 41. Drain engine oil
- [ ] Job 42. Remove oil filter
- [ ] Job 43. Fit new oil filter
- [ ] Job 44. Pour in fresh oil
- [ ] Job 45. Check front discs
- [ ] Job 46. Check front brake pads
- [ ] Job 47. Renew front brake pads
- [ ] Job 48. **EARLY CARS WITH DRUM BRAKES ONLY** Adjust front brakes
- [ ] Job 49. Check front brake hoses
- [ ] Job 50. Lubricate front suspension
- [ ] Job 51. Refit front wheels
- [ ] Job 52. Adjust rear brakes
- [ ] Job 53. Rear check straps and bump stops
- [ ] Job 54. Lubricate hand brake linkage

- [ ] Job 91. Front fuel lines
- [ ] Job 92. Front brake lines
- [ ] Job 93. **EXPORT MODEL CARS ONLY** Adjust brake pedal travel
- [ ] Job 94. Exhaust manifold
- [ ] Job 95. Front dampers
- [ ] Job 96. Clutch hydraulics
- [ ] Job 97. Rear brake pipes
- [ ] Job 98. Exhaust
- [ ] Job 99. Rear dampers and spring mountings
- [ ] Job 100. Universal joints
- [ ] Job 101. Rear axle oil
- [ ] Job 102. Rear springs

6,000 miles Mechanical and Electrical Road Test

First, carry out all jobs listed under earlier Service Intervals

- [ ] Job 61. Clean controls
- [ ] Job 62. Check instruments and controls
- [ ] Job 63. Throttle pedal
- [ ] Job 64. Road test of brakes and steering

6,000 miles Bodywork and Interior - Around the Car

First, carry out all jobs listed under earlier Service Intervals

- [ ] Job 18. Valet bodywork
- [ ] Job 21. Touch up paintwork
- [ ] Job 22. Aerial/Antenna
- [ ] Job 23. Valet interior
- [ ] Job 24. Improve visibility
- [ ] Job 55. Wiper blades and arms
- [ ] Job 56. Check windscreen
- [ ] Job 57. Rear view mirrors
- [ ] Job 58. Check floors
- [ ] Job 59. Chrome trim and badges

- [ ] Job 103. Bonnet release and stay
- [ ] Job 104. Body fittings
- [ ] Job 105. Seats and seat belts

6,000 miles Bodywork - Under the Car

First, carry out all jobs listed under earlier Service Intervals

- [ ] Job 25. Clean mud traps
- [ ] Job 60. Inspect underside

- [ ] Job 106. Rustproofing under the body

Be sure to carry out Job 107 after Job 106

- [ ] Job 107. Clear drain holes

Date serviced:...............................

Carried out by:...............................

Garage Stamp or signature:

Parts/Accessories purchased (date, parts, source) ....
....
....
....
....

9,000 MILES - OR EVERY NINE MONTHS, whichever comes first

All the Service Jobs at this Service Interval have been carried forward from earlier Service Intervals and are to be repeated at this Service.

9,000 miles Mechanical and Electrical - The Engine Bay

- [ ] Job 1. Engine oil level
- [ ] Job 2. Clutch fluid level
- [ ] Job 3. Brake fluid level
- [ ] Job 4. Battery electrolyte
- [ ] Job 5. Windscreen washer reservoir
- [ ] Job 6. Cooling system
- [ ] Job 7. Inspect pressure cap
- [ ] Job 26. Adjust sparking plugs
- [ ] Job 27. Remove air trunking to the heater
- [ ] Job 28. Check HT circuit
- [ ] Job 29. Check ignition LT circuits
- [ ] Job 30. Distributor vacuum advance and retard pipe
- [ ] Job 31. **CONTACT BREAKER POINTS IGNITION ONLY** Distributor
- [ ] Job 32. Ignition timing
- [ ] Job 33. Setting ignition dwell
- [ ] Job 34. Generator/alternator belt
- [ ] Job 35. SU carburettors
- [ ] Job 36. Check air filters
- [ ] Job 37. Pipes and hoses

9,000 miles Mechanical and Electrical - Around the Car

First carry out all jobs listed under earlier Service Intervals.

- [ ] Job 8. Check horns
- [ ] Job 9. Windscreen washers
- [ ] Job 10. Windscreen wipers
- [ ] Job 11. Tyre pressures
- [ ] Job 12. Check headlamps
- [ ] Job 13. Check front sidelamps and indicators
- [ ] Job 14. Check rear sidelamps
- [ ] Job 15. Check number plate lamps
- [ ] Job 16. Check reversing lamps
- [ ] Job 17. **WIRE WHEELED CARS ONLY** Check wheel spinners
- [ ] Job 19. Check tyres
- [ ] Job 20. Check spare tyre
- [ ] Job 38. Hand brake travel

9,000 miles Mechanical and Electrical - Under the Car

- [ ] Job 39. Steering rack
- [ ] Job 40. Track rod ends

  Optional - Carry out Job 1
- [ ] Job 1. Engine oil level

  or
- [ ] Job 41. Drain engine oil
- [ ] Job 42. Remove oil filter
- [ ] Job 43. Fit new oil filter
- [ ] Job 44. Pour in fresh oil
- [ ] Job 45. Check front discs
- [ ] Job 46. Check front brake pads
- [ ] Job 47. Renew front brake pads
- [ ] Job 48. **EARLY CARS WITH DRUM BRAKES ONLY** Adjust front brakes
- [ ] Job 49. Check front brake hoses
- [ ] Job 50. Lubricate front suspension
- [ ] Job 51. Refit front wheels
- [ ] Job 52. Adjust rear brakes
- [ ] Job 53. Rear check straps and bump stops
- [ ] Job 54. Lubricate hand brake linkage

9,000 miles Bodywork and Interior - Around the Car

First, carry out all jobs listed under earlier Service Intervals

- [ ] Job 18. Valet bodywork
- [ ] Job 21. Touch up paintwork
- [ ] Job 22. Aerial/Antenna
- [ ] Job 23. Valet interior
- [ ] Job 24. Improve visibility
- [ ] Job 55. Wiper blades and arms
- [ ] Job 56. Check windscreen
- [ ] Job 57. Rear view mirrors
- [ ] Job 58. Check floors
- [ ] Job 59. Chrome trim and badges

9,000 miles Bodywork - Under the Car

First, carry out all jobs listed under earlier Service Intervals

- [ ] Job 25. Clean mud traps
- [ ] Job 60. Inspect underside

9,000 miles Mechanical and Electrical - Road Test

First, carry out all jobs listed under earlier Service Intervals

- [ ] Job 61. Clean controls
- [ ] Job 62. Check instruments and controls
- [ ] Job 63. Throttle pedal
- [ ] Job 64. Road test of brakes and steering

Date serviced:....................................

Carried out by:..................................
Garage Stamp or signature:

Parts/Accessories purchased (date, parts, source) ....
....
....
....
....

12,000 MILES - OR EVERY 12 MONTHS, whichever comes first

All the Service Jobs in the tinted areas have been carried forward from earlier service intervals and are to be repeated at this Service.

12,000 miles Mechanical and Electrical - Emission Control Equipment

- [ ] Job 108. **EARLY CARS ONLY** Crankcase breather
- [ ] Job 109. Breather hoses and connectors
- [ ] Job 110. **US MODELS ONLY** Overhaul emission control equipment

12,000 miles Mechanical and Electrical - The Engine Bay

First carry out all Jobs listed under earlier Service Intervals

- [ ] Job 2. Clutch fluid level
- [ ] Job 3. Brake fluid level
- [ ] Job 4. Battery electrolyte
- [ ] Job 5. Windscreen washer reservoir
- [ ] Job 6. Cooling system
- [ ] Job 27. Remove air trunking to the heater
- [ ] Job 28. Check HT circuit
- [ ] Job 29. Check ignition LT circuits
- [ ] Job 34. Generator/alternator belt
- [ ] Job 36. Check air filters
- [ ] Job 37. Pipes and hoses
- [ ] Job 65. Cooling system
- [ ] Job 66. Check coolant
- [ ] Job 67. Check water pump
- [ ] Job 68. Lubricate heater controls
- [ ] Job 69. Check fuse box
- [ ] Job 70. **EARLY CARS ONLY** Lubricate dynamo
- [ ] Job 71. Fit new sparking plugs
- [ ] Job 72. Renew contact breaker points and capacitor
- [ ] Job 73. Ignition timing
- [ ] Job 74. **948 cc AND 1493 cc ENGINES ONLY** Clean fuel filter and pump

- [ ] Job 75. **1098 cc AND 1275 cc ENGINES ONLY** Clean fuel pump filter
- [ ] Job 76. Fuel connections
- [ ] Job 77. Top up carburettor dashpots
- [ ] Job 78. Set carburettors
- [ ] Job 79. Balancing the carburettors
- [ ] Job 80. Setting the mixture
- [ ] Job 81. Throttle and choke linkage
- [ ] Job 82. **SPECIALIST SERVICE** Exhaust emissions

- [ ] Job 111. Oil leaks
- [ ] Job 112. Clean radiator
- [ ] Job 113. Water pump
- [ ] Job 114. Valve clearances
- [ ] Job 115. Rocker cover
- [ ] Job 116. Cylinder compressions

12,000 miles Mechanical and Electrical - Around the Car

First, carry out all jobs listed under earlier Service Intervals

- [ ] Job 19. Check tyres
- [ ] Job 20. Check spare tyre
- [ ] Job 38. Hand brake travel
- [ ] Job 83. Top-up gearbox oil
- [ ] Job 84. Adjust headlamps
- [ ] Job 85. Fuel filler pipe
- [ ] Job 86. Front wheel alignment (tracking)
- [ ] Job 87. Rear ride height
- [ ] Job 88. Front ride height
- [ ] Job 89. Fuel filler cap
- [ ] Job 90. Check wheel tightness

- [ ] Job 117. Test dampers

12,000 miles Mechanical and Electrical - Under the Car

First carry out all jobs listed under earlier Service Intervals

- [ ] Job 39. Steering rack
- [ ] Job 40. Track rod ends
- [ ] Job 41. Drain engine oil
- [ ] Job 42. Remove oil filter
- [ ] Job 43. Fit new oil filter
- [ ] Job 44. Pour in fresh oil
- [ ] Job 45. Check front discs
- [ ] Job 46. Check front brake pads
- [ ] Job 47. Renew front brake pads
- [ ] Job 48. **EARLY CARS WITH DRUM BRAKES ONLY** Adjust front brakes
- [ ] Job 49. Check front brake hoses
- [ ] Job 50. Lubricate front suspension
- [ ] Job 51. Refit front wheels
- [ ] Job 52. Adjust rear brakes
- [ ] Job 53. Rear check straps and bump stops
- [ ] Job 54. Lubricate hand brake linkage
- [ ] Job 91. Front fuel lines
- [ ] Job 92. Front brake lines
- [ ] Job 93. **EXPORT MODEL CARS ONLY** Adjust brake pedal travel
- [ ] Job 94. Exhaust manifold
- [ ] Job 95. Front dampers
- [ ] Job 96. Clutch hydraulics
- [ ] Job 97. Rear brake pipes
- [ ] Job 98. Exhaust
- [ ] Job 99. Rear dampers and spring mountings
- [ ] Job 100. Universal joints
- [ ] Job 101. Rear axle oil
- [ ] Job 102. Rear springs

- [ ] Job 118. Wishbone bushes
- [ ] Job 119. Kingpins and hubs
- [ ] Job 120. Check anti-roll bar mountings
- [ ] Job 121. Front callipers
- [ ] Job 122. Lubricate steering rack
- [ ] Job 123. Check steering free play
- [ ] Job 124. Check ball joints
- [ ] Job 125. Rear brake inspection

12,000 miles Mechanical and Electrical Road Test

First, carry out all jobs listed under earlier Service Intervals

- [ ] Job 61. Clean controls
- [ ] Job 62. Check instruments and controls
- [ ] Job 63. Throttle pedal
- [ ] Job 64. Road test of brakes and steering

12,000 miles Bodywork and Interior - Around the Car

First, carry out all jobs listed under earlier Service Intervals

- [ ] Job 18. Valet bodywork
- [ ] Job 21. Touch up paintwork
- [ ] Job 22. Aerial/Antenna
- [ ] Job 23. Valet interior
- [ ] Job 24. Improve visibility
- [ ] Job 55. Wiper blades and arms
- [ ] Job 56. Check windscreen
- [ ] Job 57. Rear view mirrors
- [ ] Job 58. Check floors
- [ ] Job 59. Chrome trim and badges
- [ ] Job 103. Bonnet release and stay
- [ ] Job 104. Body fittings
- [ ] Job 105. Seats and seat belts

- [ ] Job 126. Seat runners
- [ ] Job 127. Toolkit and jack
- [ ] Job 128. **WIRE WHEELED CARS ONLY** Wire wheel splines
- [ ] Job 129. **WIRE WHEELED CARS ONLY** Wire wheel spokes

12,000 miles Bodywork - Under the Car

First, carry out all jobs listed under earlier Service Intervals

- [ ] Job 25. Clean mud traps
- [ ] Job 60. Inspect underside
- [ ] Job 106. Rustproofing under the body

  Be sure to carry out Job 107 after Job 106
- [ ] Job 107. Clear drain holes

- [ ] Job 130. Top-up rustproofing

Date serviced:...

Carried out by:...
Garage Stamp or signature:

Parts/Accessories purchased (date, parts, source) ....
....
....
....
....

15,000 MILES - OR EVERY 15 MONTHS, whichever comes first

All the Service Jobs at this Service Interval have been carried forward from earlier Service Intervals and are to be repeated at this Service.

15,000 miles Mechanical and Electrical - The Engine Bay

- [ ] Job 1. Engine oil level
- [ ] Job 2. Clutch fluid level
- [ ] Job 3. Brake fluid level
- [ ] Job 4. Battery electrolyte
- [ ] Job 5. Windscreen washer reservoir
- [ ] Job 6. Cooling system
- [ ] Job 7. Inspect pressure cap
- [ ] Job 26. Adjust sparking plugs
- [ ] Job 27. Remove air trunking to the heater
- [ ] Job 28. Check HT circuit
- [ ] Job 29. Check ignition LT circuits
- [ ] Job 30. Distributor vacuum advance and retard pipe
- [ ] Job 31. **CONTACT BREAKER POINTS IGNITION ONLY** Distributor
- [ ] Job 32. Ignition timing
- [ ] Job 33. Setting ignition dwell
- [ ] Job 34. Generator/alternator belt
- [ ] Job 35. SU carburettors
- [ ] Job 36. Check air filters
- [ ] Job 37. Pipes and hoses

15,000 miles Mechanical and Electrical - Around the Car

First carry out all jobs listed under earlier Service Intervals.

- [ ] Job 8. Check horns
- [ ] Job 9. Windscreen washers
- [ ] Job 10. Windscreen wipers
- [ ] Job 11. Tyre pressures
- [ ] Job 12. Check headlamps
- [ ] Job 13. Check front sidelamps and indicators
- [ ] Job 14. Check rear sidelamps
- [ ] Job 15. Check number plate lamps
- [ ] Job 16. Check reversing lamps
- [ ] Job 17. **WIRE WHEELED CARS ONLY** Check wheel spinners
- [ ] Job 19. Check tyres
- [ ] Job 20. Check spare tyre
- [ ] Job 38. Hand brake travel

15,000 miles Mechanical and Electrical - Under the Car

- [ ] Job 39. Steering rack
- [ ] Job 40. Track rod ends

    Optional - Carry out Job 1
- [ ] Job 1. Engine oil level

    or
- [ ] Job 41. Drain engine oil
- [ ] Job 42. Remove oil filter
- [ ] Job 43. Fit new oil filter
- [ ] Job 44. Pour in fresh oil
- [ ] Job 45. Check front discs
- [ ] Job 46. Check front brake pads
- [ ] Job 47. Renew front brake pads
- [ ] Job 48. **EARLY CARS WITH DRUM BRAKES ONLY** Adjust front brakes
- [ ] Job 49. Check front brake hoses
- [ ] Job 50. Lubricate front suspension
- [ ] Job 51. Refit front wheels
- [ ] Job 52. Adjust rear brakes
- [ ] Job 53. Rear check straps and bump stops
- [ ] Job 54. Lubricate hand brake linkage

15,000 miles Bodywork and Interior - Around the Car

First, carry out all jobs listed under earlier Service Intervals

- [ ] Job 18. Valet bodywork
- [ ] Job 21. Touch up paintwork
- [ ] Job 22. Aerial/Antenna
- [ ] Job 23. Valet interior
- [ ] Job 24. Improve visibility
- [ ] Job 55. Wiper blades and arms
- [ ] Job 56. Check windscreen
- [ ] Job 57. Rear view mirrors
- [ ] Job 58. Check floors
- [ ] Job 59. Chrome trim and badges

15,000 miles Bodywork - Under the Car

First, carry out all jobs listed under earlier Service Intervals

- [ ] Job 25. Clean mud traps
- [ ] Job 60. Inspect underside

15,000 miles Mechanical and Electrical - Road Test

First, carry out all jobs listed under earlier Service Intervals

- [ ] Job 61. Clean controls
- [ ] Job 62. Check instruments and controls
- [ ] Job 63. Throttle pedal
- [ ] Job 64. Road test of brakes and steering

Date serviced:...

Carried out by:..
Garage Stamp or signature:

Parts/Accessories purchased (date, parts,

source)..

....

....

....

....

All the Service Jobs at this Service Interval have been carried forward from earlier Service Intervals and are to be repeated at this Service.

18,000 miles Mechanical and Electrical - The Engine Bay

First carry out all Jobs listed under earlier Service Intervals

- [ ] Job 2. Clutch fluid level
- [ ] Job 3. Brake fluid level
- [ ] Job 4. Battery electrolyte
- [ ] Job 5. Windscreen washer reservoir
- [ ] Job 6. Cooling system
- [ ] Job 27. Remove air trunking to the heater
- [ ] Job 28. Check HT circuit
- [ ] Job 29. Check ignition LT circuits
- [ ] Job 34. Generator/alternator belt
- [ ] Job 36. Check air filters
- [ ] Job 37. Pipes and hoses
- [ ] Job 65. Cooling system
- [ ] Job 66. Check coolant
- [ ] Job 67. Check water pump
- [ ] Job 68. Lubricate heater controls
- [ ] Job 69. Check fuse box
- [ ] Job 70. **EARLY CARS ONLY** Lubricate dynamo
- [ ] Job 71. Fit new sparking plugs
- [ ] Job 72. Renew contact breaker points and capacitor
- [ ] Job 73. Ignition timing
- [ ] Job 74. **948 cc AND 1493 cc ENGINES ONLY** Clean fuel filter and pump
- [ ] Job 75. **1098 cc AND 1275 cc ENGINES ONLY** Clean fuel pump filter
- [ ] Job 76. Fuel connections
- [ ] Job 77. Top up carburettor dashpots
- [ ] Job 78. Set carburettors
- [ ] Job 79. Balancing the carburettors
- [ ] Job 80. Setting the mixture
- [ ] Job 81. Throttle and choke linkage
- [ ] Job 82. **SPECIALIST SERVICE** Exhaust emissions

18,000 miles Mechanical and Electrical - Around the Car

First carry out all jobs listed under earlier Service Intervals.

☐ Job 8. Check horns

☐ Job 9. Windscreen washers

☐ Job 10. Windscreen wipers

☐ Job 11. Tyre pressures

☐ Job 12. Check headlamps

☐ Job 13. Check front sidelamps and indicators

☐ Job 14. Check rear sidelamps

☐ Job 15. Check number plate lamps

☐ Job 16. Check reversing lamps

☐ Job 17. **WIRE WHEELED CARS ONLY** Check wheel spinners

☐ Job 19. Check tyres

☐ Job 20. Check spare tyre

☐ Job 38. Hand brake travel

☐ Job 83. Top-up gearbox oil

☐ Job 84. Adjust headlamps

☐ Job 85. Fuel filler pipe

☐ Job 86. Front wheel alignment (tracking)

☐ Job 87. Rear ride height

☐ Job 88. Front ride height

☐ Job 89. Fuel filler cap

☐ Job 90. Check wheel tightness

18,000 miles Mechanical and Electrical - Under the Car

First carry out all jobs listed under earlier Service Intervals

☐ Job 39. Steering rack

☐ Job 40. Track rod ends

☐ Job 41. Drain engine oil

☐ Job 42. Remove oil filter

☐ Job 43. Fit new oil filter

☐ Job 44. Pour in fresh oil

☐ Job 45. Check front discs

☐ Job 46. Check front brake pads

☐ Job 47. Renew front brake pads

☐ Job 48. **EARLY CARS WITH DRUM BRAKES ONLY** Adjust front brakes

☐ Job 49. Check front brake hoses

☐ Job 50. Lubricate front suspension

☐ Job 51. Refit front wheels

☐ Job 52. Adjust rear brakes

☐ Job 53. Rear check straps and bump stops

☐ Job 54. Lubricate hand brake linkage

☐ Job 91. Front fuel lines

☐ Job 92. Front brake lines

☐ Job 93. **EXPORT MODEL CARS ONLY** Adjust brake pedal travel

☐ Job 94. Exhaust manifold

☐ Job 95. Front dampers

☐ Job 96. Clutch hydraulics

☐ Job 97. Rear brake pipes

☐ Job 98. Exhaust

☐ Job 99. Rear dampers and spring mountings

☐ Job 100. Universal joints

☐ Job 101. Rear axle oil

☐ Job 102. Rear springs

18,000 miles Mechanical and Electrical Road Test

First, carry out all jobs listed under earlier Service Intervals

☐ Job 61. Clean controls

☐ Job 62. Check instruments and controls

☐ Job 63. Throttle pedal

☐ Job 64. Road test of brakes and steering

18,000 miles Bodywork and Interior - Around the Car

First, carry out all jobs listed under earlier Service Intervals

☐ Job 18. Valet bodywork

☐ Job 21. Touch up paintwork

☐ Job 22. Aerial/Antenna

☐ Job 23. Valet interior

☐ Job 24. Improve visibility

☐ Job 55. Wiper blades and arms

☐ Job 56. Check windscreen

☐ Job 57. Rear view mirrors

☐ Job 58. Check floors

☐ Job 59. Chrome trim and badges

☐ Job 103. Bonnet release and stay

☐ Job 104. Body fittings

☐ Job 105. Seats and seat belts

18,000 miles Bodywork - Under the Car

First, carry out all jobs listed under earlier Service Intervals

☐ Job 25. Clean mud traps

☐ Job 60. Inspect underside

☐ Job 106. Rustproofing under the body

Be sure to carry out Job 107 after Job 106

☐ Job 107. Clear drain holes

Date serviced:...

Carried out by: ....
Garage Stamp or signature:

Parts/Accessories purchased (date, parts, source) ....

....

....

....

....

21,000 MILES - OR EVERY 21 MONTHS, whichever comes first

All the Service Jobs at this Service Interval have been carried forward from earlier Service Intervals and are to be repeated at this Service.

21,000 miles Mechanical and Electrical - The Engine Bay

- [ ] Job 1. Engine oil level
- [ ] Job 2. Clutch fluid level
- [ ] Job 3. Brake fluid level
- [ ] Job 4. Battery electrolyte
- [ ] Job 5. Windscreen washer reservoir
- [ ] Job 6. Cooling system
- [ ] Job 7. Inspect pressure cap
- [ ] Job 26. Adjust sparking plugs
- [ ] Job 27. Remove air trunking to the heater
- [ ] Job 28. Check HT circuit
- [ ] Job 29. Check ignition LT circuits
- [ ] Job 30. Distributor vacuum advance and retard pipe
- [ ] Job 31. CONTACT BREAKER POINTS IGNITION ONLY Distributor
- [ ] Job 32. Ignition timing
- [ ] Job 33. Setting ignition dwell
- [ ] Job 34. Generator/alternator belt
- [ ] Job 35. SU carburettors
- [ ] Job 36. Check air filters
- [ ] Job 37. Pipes and hoses

21,000 miles Mechanical and Electrical - Around the Car

First carry out all jobs listed under earlier Service Intervals.

- [ ] Job 8. Check horns
- [ ] Job 9. Windscreen washers
- [ ] Job 10. Windscreen wipers
- [ ] Job 11. Tyre pressures
- [ ] Job 12. Check headlamps
- [ ] Job 13. Check front sidelamps and indicators
- [ ] Job 14. Check rear sidelamps
- [ ] Job 15. Check number plate lamps
- [ ] Job 16. Check reversing lamps
- [ ] Job 17. WIRE WHEELED CARS ONLY Check wheel spinners
- [ ] Job 19. Check tyres
- [ ] Job 20. Check spare tyre
- [ ] Job 38. Hand brake travel

21,000 miles Mechanical and Electrical - Under the Car

- [ ] Job 39. Steering rack
- [ ] Job 40. Track rod ends

  Optional - Carry out Job 1

- [ ] Job 1. Engine oil level

  or

- [ ] Job 41. Drain engine oil
- [ ] Job 42. Remove oil filter
- [ ] Job 43. Fit new oil filter
- [ ] Job 44. Pour in fresh oil
- [ ] Job 45. Check front discs
- [ ] Job 46. Check front brake pads
- [ ] Job 47. Renew front brake pads
- [ ] Job 48. EARLY CARS WITH DRUM BRAKES ONLY Adjust front brakes
- [ ] Job 49. Check front brake hoses
- [ ] Job 50. Lubricate front suspension
- [ ] Job 51. Refit front wheels
- [ ] Job 52. Adjust rear brakes
- [ ] Job 53. Rear check straps and bump stops
- [ ] Job 54. Lubricate hand brake linkage

21,000 miles Bodywork and Interior - Around the Car

First, carry out all jobs listed under earlier Service Intervals

- [ ] Job 18. Valet bodywork
- [ ] Job 21. Touch up paintwork
- [ ] Job 22. Aerial/Antenna
- [ ] Job 23. Valet interior
- [ ] Job 24. Improve visibility
- [ ] Job 55. Wiper blades and arms
- [ ] Job 56. Check windscreen
- [ ] Job 57. Rear view mirrors
- [ ] Job 58. Check floors
- [ ] Job 59. Chrome trim and badges

21,000 miles Bodywork - Under the Car

First, carry out all jobs listed under earlier Service Intervals

- [ ] Job 25. Clean mud traps
- [ ] Job 60. Inspect underside

21,000 miles Mechanical and Electrical - Road Test

First, carry out all jobs listed under earlier Service Intervals

- [ ] Job 61. Clean controls
- [ ] Job 62. Check instruments and controls
- [ ] Job 63. Throttle pedal
- [ ] Job 64. Road test of brakes and steering

Date serviced:...

Carried out by: ....
Garage Stamp or signature:

Parts/Accessories purchased (date, parts, source) ....
....
....
....
....

24,000 MILES - OR EVERY 24 MONTHS, whichever comes first

All the Service Jobs in the tinted areas have been carried forward from earlier service intervals and are to be repeated at this Service.

24,000 miles Mechanical and Electrical - Emission Control Equipment

☐ Job 108. **EARLY CARS ONLY** Crankcase breather

☐ Job 109. Breather hoses and connectors

☐ Job 110. **US MODELS ONLY** Overhaul emission control equipment

24,000 miles Mechanical and Electrical - The Engine Bay

First carry out all Jobs listed under earlier Service Intervals

☐ Job 2. Clutch fluid level

☐ Job 3. Brake fluid level

☐ Job 4. Battery electrolyte

☐ Job 5. Windscreen washer reservoir

☐ Job 6. Cooling system

☐ Job 27. Remove air trunking to the heater

☐ Job 28. Check HT circuit

☐ Job 29. Check ignition LT circuits

☐ Job 34. Generator/alternator belt

☐ Job 36. Check air filters

☐ Job 37. Pipes and hoses

☐ Job 65. Cooling system

☐ Job 66. Check coolant

☐ Job 67. Check water pump

☐ Job 68. Lubricate heater controls

☐ Job 69. Check fuse box

☐ Job 70. **EARLY CARS ONLY** Lubricate dynamo

☐ Job 71. Fit new sparking plugs

☐ Job 72. Renew contact breaker points and capacitor

☐ Job 73. Ignition timing

☐ Job 74. **948 cc AND 1493 cc ENGINES ONLY** Clean fuel filter and pump

☐ Job 75. **1098 cc AND 1275 cc ENGINES ONLY** Clean fuel pump filter

☐ Job 76. Fuel connections

☐ Job 77. Top up carburettor dashpots

☐ Job 78. Set carburettors

☐ Job 79. Balancing the carburettors

☐ Job 80. Setting the mixture

☐ Job 81. Throttle and choke linkage

☐ Job 82. **SPECIALIST SERVICE** Exhaust emissions

☐ Job 111. Oil leaks

☐ Job 112. Clean radiator

☐ Job 113. Water pump

☐ Job 114. Valve clearances

☐ Job 115. Rocker cover

☐ Job 116. Cylinder compressions

☐ Job 131. Engine mountings

☐ Job 132. Drain and refill cooling system

☐ Job 133. Radiator pressure cap

☐ Job 134. Fan belt

24,000 miles Mechanical and Electrical - Around the Car

First, carry out all jobs listed under earlier Service Intervals

☐ Job 19. Check tyres

☐ Job 20. Check spare tyre

☐ Job 38. Hand brake travel

☐ Job 83. Top-up gearbox oil

☐ Job 84. Adjust headlamps

☐ Job 85. Fuel filler pipe

☐ Job 86. Front wheel alignment (tracking)

☐ Job 87. Rear ride height

☐ Job 88. Front ride height

☐ Job 89. Fuel filler cap

☐ Job 90. Check wheel tightness

☐ Job 117. Test dampers

24,000 miles Mechanical and Electrical - Under the Car

First carry out all jobs listed under earlier Service Intervals

☐ Job 39. Steering rack

☐ Job 40. Track rod ends

☐ Job 41. Drain engine oil

☐ Job 42. Remove oil filter

☐ Job 43. Fit new oil filter

☐ Job 44. Pour in fresh oil

☐ Job 45. Check front discs

☐ Job 46. Check front brake pads

☐ Job 47. Renew front brake pads

☐ Job 48. **EARLY CARS WITH DRUM BRAKES ONLY** Adjust front brakes

☐ Job 49. Check front brake hoses

☐ Job 50. Lubricate front suspension

☐ Job 51. Refit front wheels

☐ Job 52. Adjust rear brakes

☐ Job 53. Rear check straps and bump stops

☐ Job 54. Lubricate hand brake linkage

☐ Job 91. Front fuel lines

☐ Job 92. Front brake lines

☐ Job 93. **EXPORT MODEL CARS ONLY** Adjust brake pedal travel

☐ Job 94. Exhaust manifold

☐ Job 95. Front dampers

☐ Job 96. Clutch hydraulics

☐ Job 97. Rear brake pipes

☐ Job 98. Exhaust

☐ Job 99. Rear dampers and spring mountings

☐ Job 100. Universal joints

☐ Job 101. Rear axle oil

☐ Job 102. Rear springs

☐ Job 118. Wishbone bushes

☐ Job 119. Kingpins and hubs

☐ Job 120. Check anti-roll bar mountings

☐ Job 121. Front callipers

☐ Job 122. Lubricate steering rack

☐ Job 123. Check steering free play

☐ Job 124. Check ball joints

☐ Job 125. Rear brake inspection

☐ Job 135. Flushing oil

☐ Job 136. Gearbox oil

☐ Job 137. Suspension mountings

☐ Job 138. Brake discs

☐ Job 139. Renew axle oil

☐ Job 140. Renew brake fluid

☐ Job 141. Brake drums

☐ Job 142. Brake back plates

24,000 miles Mechanical and Electrical Road Test

First, carry out all jobs listed under earlier Service Intervals

☐ Job 61. Clean controls

☐ Job 62. Check instruments and controls

☐ Job 63. Throttle pedal

☐ Job 64. Road test of brakes and steering

24,000 miles Bodywork and Interior - Around the Car

First, carry out all jobs listed under earlier Service Intervals

☐ Job 18. Valet bodywork

☐ Job 21. Touch up paintwork

☐ Job 22. Aerial/Antenna

☐ Job 23. Valet interior

☐ Job 24. Improve visibility

☐ Job 55. Wiper blades and arms

☐ Job 56. Check windscreen

☐ Job 57. Rear view mirrors

☐ Job 58. Check floors

☐ Job 59. Chrome trim and badges

☐ Job 103. Bonnet release and stay

☐ Job 104. Body fittings

☐ Job 105. Seats and seat belts

☐ Job 126. Seat runners

☐ Job 127. Toolkit and jack

☐ Job 128. **WIRE WHEELED CARS ONLY** Wire wheel splines

☐ Job 129. **WIRE WHEELED CARS ONLY** Wire wheel spokes

☐ Job 143. Window regulators

☐ Job 144. Door gear

☐ Job 145. Lamp seals

24,000 miles Bodywork - Under the Car

First, carry out all jobs listed under earlier Service Intervals

☐ Job 25. Clean mud traps

☐ Job 60. Inspect underside

☐ Job 106. Rustproofing under the body

   Be sure to carry out Job 107 after Job 106

☐ Job 107. Clear drain holes

☐ Job 130. Top-up rustproofing

Date serviced:..

Carried out by: ....
Garage Stamp or signature:

Parts/Accessories purchased (date, parts,

source) ....

....

....

....

....

27,000 MILES - OR EVERY 27 MONTHS, whichever comes first

All the Service Jobs in the tinted areas have been carried forward from earlier service intervals and are to be repeated at this Service.

27,000 miles Mechanical and Electrical - The Engine Bay

☐ Job 1. Engine oil level

☐ Job 2. Clutch fluid level

☐ Job 3. Brake fluid level

☐ Job 4. Battery electrolyte

☐ Job 5. Windscreen washer reservoir

☐ Job 6. Cooling system

☐ Job 7. Inspect pressure cap

☐ Job 26. Adjust sparking plugs

☐ Job 27. Remove air trunking to the heater

☐ Job 28. Check HT circuit

☐ Job 29. Check ignition LT circuits

☐ Job 30. Distributor vacuum advance and retard pipe

☐ Job 31. **CONTACT BREAKER POINTS IGNITION ONLY** Distributor

☐ Job 32. Ignition timing

☐ Job 33. Setting ignition dwell

☐ Job 34. Generator/alternator belt

☐ Job 35. SU carburettors

☐ Job 36. Check air filters

☐ Job 37. Pipes and hoses

27,000 miles Mechanical and Electrical - Around the Car

First carry out all jobs listed under earlier Service Intervals.

- [ ] Job 8. Check horns
- [ ] Job 9. Windscreen washers
- [ ] Job 10. Windscreen wipers
- [ ] Job 11. Tyre pressures
- [ ] Job 12. Check headlamps
- [ ] Job 13. Check front sidelamps and indicators
- [ ] Job 14. Check rear sidelamps
- [ ] Job 15. Check number plate lamps
- [ ] Job 16. Check reversing lamps
- [ ] Job 17. **WIRE WHEELED CARS ONLY** Check wheel spinners
- [ ] Job 19. Check tyres
- [ ] Job 20. Check spare tyre
- [ ] Job 38. Hand brake travel

27,000 miles Mechanical and Electrical - Under the Car

- [ ] Job 39. Steering rack
- [ ] Job 40. Track rod ends

    Optional - Carry out Job 1
- [ ] Job 1. Engine oil level

    or
- [ ] Job 41. Drain engine oil
- [ ] Job 42. Remove oil filter
- [ ] Job 43. Fit new oil filter
- [ ] Job 44. Pour in fresh oil
- [ ] Job 45. Check front discs
- [ ] Job 46. Check front brake pads
- [ ] Job 47. Renew front brake pads
- [ ] Job 48. **EARLY CARS WITH DRUM BRAKES ONLY** Adjust front brakes
- [ ] Job 49. Check front brake hoses
- [ ] Job 50. Lubricate front suspension
- [ ] Job 51. Refit front wheels
- [ ] Job 52. Adjust rear brakes
- [ ] Job 53. Rear check straps and bump stops
- [ ] Job 54. Lubricate hand brake linkage

27,000 miles Bodywork and Interior - Around the Car

First, carry out all jobs listed under earlier Service Intervals

- [ ] Job 18. Valet bodywork
- [ ] Job 21. Touch up paintwork
- [ ] Job 22. Aerial/Antenna
- [ ] Job 23. Valet interior
- [ ] Job 24. Improve visibility
- [ ] Job 55. Wiper blades and arms
- [ ] Job 56. Check windscreen
- [ ] Job 57. Rear view mirrors
- [ ] Job 58. Check floors
- [ ] Job 59. Chrome trim and badges

27,000 miles Bodywork - Under the Car

First, carry out all jobs listed under earlier Service Intervals

- [ ] Job 25. Clean mud traps
- [ ] Job 60. Inspect underside

27,000 miles Mechanical and Electrical - Road Test

First, carry out all jobs listed under earlier Service Intervals

- [ ] Job 61. Clean controls
- [ ] Job 62. Check instruments and controls
- [ ] Job 63. Throttle pedal
- [ ] Job 64. Road test of brakes and steering

Date serviced:.......................................

Carried out by: ....
Garage Stamp or signature:

Parts/Accessories purchased (date, parts,

source) ....

....

....

....

....

All the Service Jobs in the tinted areas have been carried forward from earlier service intervals and are to be repeated at this Service.

30,000 miles Mechanical and Electrical - The Engine Bay

First carry out all Jobs listed under earlier Service Intervals

- [ ] Job 2. Clutch fluid level
- [ ] Job 3. Brake fluid level
- [ ] Job 4. Battery electrolyte
- [ ] Job 5. Windscreen washer reservoir
- [ ] Job 6. Cooling system
- [ ] Job 27. Remove air trunking to the heater
- [ ] Job 28. Check HT circuit
- [ ] Job 29. Check ignition LT circuits
- [ ] Job 34. Generator/alternator belt
- [ ] Job 36. Check air filters
- [ ] Job 37. Pipes and hoses
- [ ] Job 65. Cooling system
- [ ] Job 66. Check coolant
- [ ] Job 67. Check water pump
- [ ] Job 68. Lubricate heater controls
- [ ] Job 69. Check fuse box
- [ ] Job 70. **EARLY CARS ONLY** Lubricate dynamo
- [ ] Job 71. Fit new sparking plugs
- [ ] Job 72. Renew contact breaker points and capacitor
- [ ] Job 73. Ignition timing
- [ ] Job 74. **948 cc AND 1493 cc ENGINES ONLY** Clean fuel filter and pump
- [ ] Job 75. **1098 cc AND 1275 cc ENGINES ONLY** Clean fuel pump filter
- [ ] Job 76. Fuel connections
- [ ] Job 77. Top up carburettor dashpots
- [ ] Job 78. Set carburettors
- [ ] Job 79. Balancing the carburettors
- [ ] Job 80. Setting the mixture
- [ ] Job 81. Throttle and choke linkage
- [ ] Job 82. **SPECIALIST SERVICE** Exhaust emissions

30,000 miles Mechanical and Electrical - Around the Car

First carry out all jobs listed under earlier Service Intervals.

- [ ] Job 8. Check horns
- [ ] Job 9. Windscreen washers
- [ ] Job 10. Windscreen wipers
- [ ] Job 11. Tyre pressures
- [ ] Job 12. Check headlamps
- [ ] Job 13. Check front sidelamps and indicators
- [ ] Job 14. Check rear sidelamps
- [ ] Job 15. Check number plate lamps
- [ ] Job 16. Check reversing lamps
- [ ] Job 17. **WIRE WHEELED CARS ONLY** Check wheel spinners
- [ ] Job 19. Check tyres
- [ ] Job 20. Check spare tyre
- [ ] Job 38. Hand brake travel
- [ ] Job 83. Top-up gearbox oil
- [ ] Job 84. Adjust headlamps
- [ ] Job 85. Fuel filler pipe
- [ ] Job 86. Front wheel alignment (tracking)
- [ ] Job 87. Rear ride height
- [ ] Job 88. Front ride height
- [ ] Job 89. Fuel filler cap
- [ ] Job 90. Check wheel tightness

30,000 miles Mechanical and Electrical - Under the Car

First carry out all jobs listed under earlier Service Intervals

- [ ] Job 39. Steering rack
- [ ] Job 40. Track rod ends
- [ ] Job 41. Drain engine oil
- [ ] Job 42. Remove oil filter
- [ ] Job 43. Fit new oil filter
- [ ] Job 44. Pour in fresh oil
- [ ] Job 45. Check front discs
- [ ] Job 46. Check front brake pads
- [ ] Job 47. Renew front brake pads
- [ ] Job 48. **EARLY CARS WITH DRUM BRAKES ONLY** Adjust front brakes
- [ ] Job 49. Check front brake hoses
- [ ] Job 50. Lubricate front suspension
- [ ] Job 51. Refit front wheels
- [ ] Job 52. Adjust rear brakes
- [ ] Job 53. Rear check straps and bump stops
- [ ] Job 54. Lubricate hand brake linkage
- [ ] Job 91. Front fuel lines
- [ ] Job 92. Front brake lines
- [ ] Job 93. **EXPORT MODEL CARS ONLY** Adjust brake pedal travel
- [ ] Job 94. Exhaust manifold
- [ ] Job 95. Front dampers
- [ ] Job 96. Clutch hydraulics
- [ ] Job 97. Rear brake pipes
- [ ] Job 98. Exhaust
- [ ] Job 99. Rear dampers and spring mountings
- [ ] Job 100. Universal joints
- [ ] Job 101. Rear axle oil
- [ ] Job 102. Rear springs

30,000 miles Mechanical and Electrical Road Test

First, carry out all jobs listed under earlier Service Intervals

- [ ] Job 61. Clean controls
- [ ] Job 62. Check instruments and controls
- [ ] Job 63. Throttle pedal
- [ ] Job 64. Road test of brakes and steering

30,000 miles Bodywork and Interior - Around the Car

First, carry out all jobs listed under earlier Service Intervals

- [ ] Job 18. Valet bodywork
- [ ] Job 21. Touch up paintwork
- [ ] Job 22. Aerial/Antenna
- [ ] Job 23. Valet interior
- [ ] Job 24. Improve visibility
- [ ] Job 55. Wiper blades and arms
- [ ] Job 56. Check windscreen
- [ ] Job 57. Rear view mirrors
- [ ] Job 58. Check floors
- [ ] Job 59. Chrome trim and badges
- [ ] Job 103. Bonnet release and stay
- [ ] Job 104. Body fittings
- [ ] Job 105. Seats and seat belts

30,000 miles Bodywork - Under the Car

First, carry out all jobs listed under earlier Service Intervals

- [ ] Job 25. Clean mud traps
- [ ] Job 60. Inspect underside
- [ ] Job 106. Rustproofing under the body
  Be sure to carry out Job 107 after Job 106
- [ ] Job 107. Clear drain holes

Date serviced:..

Carried out by: ....
Garage Stamp or signature:

Parts/Accessories purchased (date, parts, source) ....
....
....
....
....

33,000 MILES - OR EVERY 21 MONTHS, whichever comes first

All the Service Jobs in the tinted areas have been carried forward from earlier service intervals and are to be repeated at this Service.

33,000 miles Mechanical and Electrical - The Engine Bay

- [ ] Job 1. Engine oil level
- [ ] Job 2. Clutch fluid level
- [ ] Job 3. Brake fluid level
- [ ] Job 4. Battery electrolyte
- [ ] Job 5. Windscreen washer reservoir
- [ ] Job 6. Cooling system
- [ ] Job 7. Inspect pressure cap
- [ ] Job 26. Adjust sparking plugs
- [ ] Job 27. Remove air trunking to the heater
- [ ] Job 28. Check HT circuit
- [ ] Job 29. Check ignition LT circuits
- [ ] Job 30. Distributor vacuum advance and retard pipe
- [ ] Job 31. **CONTACT BREAKER POINTS IGNITION ONLY** Distributor
- [ ] Job 32. Ignition timing
- [ ] Job 33. Setting ignition dwell
- [ ] Job 34. Generator/alternator belt
- [ ] Job 35. SU carburettors
- [ ] Job 36. Check air filters
- [ ] Job 37. Pipes and hoses

33,000 miles Mechanical and Electrical - Around the Car

First carry out all jobs listed under earlier Service Intervals.

- [ ] Job 8. Check horns
- [ ] Job 9. Windscreen washers
- [ ] Job 10. Windscreen wipers
- [ ] Job 11. Tyre pressures
- [ ] Job 12. Check headlamps
- [ ] Job 13. Check front sidelamps and indicators
- [ ] Job 14. Check rear sidelamps
- [ ] Job 15. Check number plate lamps
- [ ] Job 16. Check reversing lamps
- [ ] Job 17. **WIRE WHEELED CARS ONLY** Check wheel spinners
- [ ] Job 19. Check tyres
- [ ] Job 20. Check spare tyre
- [ ] Job 38. Hand brake travel

33,000 miles Mechanical and Electrical - Under the Car

- [ ] Job 39. Steering rack
- [ ] Job 40. Track rod ends

  Optional - Carry out Job 1
- [ ] Job 1. Engine oil level

  or
- [ ] Job 41. Drain engine oil
- [ ] Job 42. Remove oil filter
- [ ] Job 43. Fit new oil filter
- [ ] Job 44. Pour in fresh oil
- [ ] Job 45. Check front discs
- [ ] Job 46. Check front brake pads
- [ ] Job 47. Renew front brake pads
- [ ] Job 48. **EARLY CARS WITH DRUM BRAKES ONLY** Adjust front brakes
- [ ] Job 49. Check front brake hoses
- [ ] Job 50. Lubricate front suspension
- [ ] Job 51. Refit front wheels
- [ ] Job 52. Adjust rear brakes
- [ ] Job 53. Rear check straps and bump stops
- [ ] Job 54. Lubricate hand brake linkage

33,000 miles Bodywork and Interior - Around the Car

First, carry out all jobs listed under earlier Service Intervals

- [ ] Job 18. Valet bodywork
- [ ] Job 21. Touch up paintwork
- [ ] Job 22. Aerial/Antenna
- [ ] Job 23. Valet interior
- [ ] Job 24. Improve visibility
- [ ] Job 55. Wiper blades and arms
- [ ] Job 56. Check windscreen
- [ ] Job 57. Rear view mirrors
- [ ] Job 58. Check floors
- [ ] Job 59. Chrome trim and badges

33,000 miles Bodywork - Under the Car

First, carry out all jobs listed under earlier Service Intervals

- [ ] Job 25. Clean mud traps
- [ ] Job 60. Inspect underside

33,000 miles Mechanical and Electrical - Road Test

First, carry out all jobs listed under earlier Service Intervals

- [ ] Job 61. Clean controls
- [ ] Job 62. Check instruments and controls
- [ ] Job 63. Throttle pedal
- [ ] Job 64. Road test of brakes and steering

Date serviced:...

Carried out by:..
Garage Stamp or signature:

Parts/Accessories purchased (date, parts, source)...

....

....

....

....

36,000 MILES - OR EVERY 12 MONTHS, whichever comes first

All the Service Jobs in the tinted areas have been carried forward from earlier service intervals and are to be repeated at this Service.

36,000 miles Mechanical and Electrical - Emission Control Equipment

- [ ] Job 108. **EARLY CARS ONLY** Crankcase breather
- [ ] Job 109. Breather hoses and connectors
- [ ] Job 110. **US MODELS ONLY** Overhaul emission control equipment

36,000 miles Mechanical and Electrical - The Engine Bay

First carry out all Jobs listed under earlier Service Intervals

- [ ] Job 2. Clutch fluid level
- [ ] Job 3. Brake fluid level
- [ ] Job 4. Battery electrolyte
- [ ] Job 5. Windscreen washer reservoir
- [ ] Job 6. Cooling system
- [ ] Job 27. Remove air trunking to the heater
- [ ] Job 28. Check HT circuit
- [ ] Job 29. Check ignition LT circuits
- [ ] Job 34. Generator/alternator belt
- [ ] Job 36. Check air filters
- [ ] Job 37. Pipes and hoses
- [ ] Job 65. Cooling system
- [ ] Job 66. Check coolant
- [ ] Job 67. Check water pump
- [ ] Job 68. Lubricate heater controls
- [ ] Job 69. Check fuse box
- [ ] Job 70. **EARLY CARS ONLY** Lubricate dynamo
- [ ] Job 71. Fit new sparking plugs
- [ ] Job 72. Renew contact breaker points and capacitor
- [ ] Job 73. Ignition timing
- [ ] Job 74. **948 cc AND 1493 cc ENGINES ONLY** Clean fuel filter and pump

- [ ] Job 75. **1098 cc AND 1275 cc ENGINES ONLY** Clean fuel pump filter
- [ ] Job 76. Fuel connections
- [ ] Job 77. Top up carburettor dashpots
- [ ] Job 78. Set carburettors
- [ ] Job 79. Balancing the carburettors
- [ ] Job 80. Setting the mixture
- [ ] Job 81. Throttle and choke linkage
- [ ] Job 82. **SPECIALIST SERVICE** Exhaust emissions
- [ ] Job 111. Oil leaks
- [ ] Job 112. Clean radiator
- [ ] Job 113. Water pump
- [ ] Job 114. Valve clearances
- [ ] Job 115. Rocker cover
- [ ] Job 116. Cylinder compressions

- [ ] Job 146. Overhaul ignition
- [ ] Job 147. Float chambers and heat shields

36,000 miles Mechanical and Electrical - Around the Car

First, carry out all jobs listed under earlier Service Intervals

- [ ] Job 19. Check tyres
- [ ] Job 20. Check spare tyre
- [ ] Job 38. Hand brake travel
- [ ] Job 83. Top-up gearbox oil
- [ ] Job 84. Adjust headlamps
- [ ] Job 85. Fuel filler pipe
- [ ] Job 86. Front wheel alignment (tracking)
- [ ] Job 87. Rear ride height
- [ ] Job 88. Front ride height
- [ ] Job 89. Fuel filler cap
- [ ] Job 90. Check wheel tightness
- [ ] Job 117. Test dampers

36,000 miles Mechanical and Electrical - Under the Car

First carry out all jobs listed under earlier Service Intervals

- [ ] Job 39. Steering rack
- [ ] Job 40. Track rod ends
- [ ] Job 41. Drain engine oil
- [ ] Job 42. Remove oil filter
- [ ] Job 43. Fit new oil filter
- [ ] Job 44. Pour in fresh oil
- [ ] Job 45. Check front discs
- [ ] Job 46. Check front brake pads
- [ ] Job 47. Renew front brake pads
- [ ] Job 48. **EARLY CARS WITH DRUM BRAKES ONLY** Adjust front brakes
- [ ] Job 49. Check front brake hoses
- [ ] Job 50. Lubricate front suspension
- [ ] Job 51. Refit front wheels
- [ ] Job 52. Adjust rear brakes
- [ ] Job 53. Rear check straps and bump stops
- [ ] Job 54. Lubricate hand brake linkage
- [ ] Job 91. Front fuel lines
- [ ] Job 92. Front brake lines
- [ ] Job 93. **EXPORT MODEL CARS ONLY** Adjust brake pedal travel
- [ ] Job 94. Exhaust manifold
- [ ] Job 95. Front dampers
- [ ] Job 96. Clutch hydraulics
- [ ] Job 97. Rear brake pipes
- [ ] Job 98. Exhaust
- [ ] Job 99. Rear dampers and spring mountings
- [ ] Job 100. Universal joints
- [ ] Job 101. Rear axle oil
- [ ] Job 102. Rear springs
- [ ] Job 118. Wishbone bushes
- [ ] Job 119. Kingpins and hubs
- [ ] Job 120. Check anti-roll bar mountings
- [ ] Job 121. Front callipers
- [ ] Job 122. Lubricate steering rack
- [ ] Job 123. Check steering free play
- [ ] Job 124. Check ball joints
- [ ] Job 125. Rear brake inspection

☐ Job 148. Front hubs

36,000 miles Mechanical and Electrical Road Test

First, carry out all jobs listed under earlier Service Intervals

☐ Job 61. Clean controls

☐ Job 62. Check instruments and controls

☐ Job 63. Throttle pedal

☐ Job 64. Road test of brakes and steering

36,000 miles Bodywork and Interior - Around the Car

First, carry out all jobs listed under earlier Service Intervals

☐ Job 18. Valet bodywork

☐ Job 21. Touch up paintwork

☐ Job 22. Aerial/Antenna

☐ Job 23. Valet interior

☐ Job 24. Improve visibility

☐ Job 55. Wiper blades and arms

☐ Job 56. Check windscreen

☐ Job 57. Rear view mirrors

☐ Job 58. Check floors

☐ Job 59. Chrome trim and badges

☐ Job 103. Bonnet release and stay

☐ Job 104. Body fittings

☐ Job 105. Seats and seat belts

☐ Job 126. Seat runners

☐ Job 127. Toolkit and jack

☐ Job 128. **WIRE WHEELED CARS ONLY** Wire wheel splines

☐ Job 129. **WIRE WHEELED CARS ONLY** Wire wheel spokes

36,000 miles Bodywork - Under the Car

First, carry out all jobs listed under earlier Service Intervals

☐ Job 25. Clean mud traps

☐ Job 60. Inspect underside

☐ Job 106. Rustproofing under the body

Be sure to carry out Job 107 after Job 106

☐ Job 107. Clear drain holes

☐ Job 130. Top-up rustproofing

Date serviced:..

Carried out by: ....
Garage Stamp or signature:

Parts/Accessories purchased (date, parts, source) ....

....

....

....

....